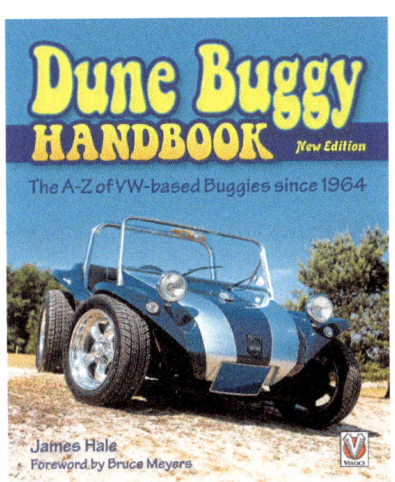

Other great VW/dune buggy books from Veloce –

Speedpro Series
Volkswagen Beetle Suspension, Brakes & Chassis, How to Modify For High Performance (Hale)
Volkswagen Bus Suspension, Brakes & Chassis for High Performance, How to Modify – Updated & Enlarged New Edition (Hale)

Enthusiast's Restoration Manual Series
Volkswagen Beetle, How to Restore (Tyler)
VW Bay Window Bus, How to restore (Paxton)

Essential Buyer's Guide Series
VW Beetle (Cservenka & Copping)
VW Bus (Cservenka & Copping)
VW Golf GTI (Cservenka & Copping)

Those Were The Days ... Series
Dune Buggy Phenomenon, The (Hale)
Dune Buggy Phenomenon Volume 2, The (Hale)

General
Volkswagen Bus Book, The (Bobbitt)
Volkswagen Bus or Van to Camper (T3/T25 & T4), How to Convert (Porter)
Volkswagens of the World (Glen)
VW Beetle Cabriolet – The full story of the convertible Beetle (Bobbitt)
VW Beetle – The Car of the 20th Century (Copping)
VW Bus – 40 Years of Splitties, Bays & Wedges (Copping)
VW Bus Book, The (Bobbitt)
VW Golf: Five Generations of Fun (Copping & Cservenka)
VW – The Air-cooled Era (Copping)
VW T5 Camper Conversion Manual (Porter)
VW Campers (Copping)

Publisher's note: Some of the images in this book are of poor quality, but have been included due to their rarity.

www.veloce.co.uk

First published in 1999. Reprinted in 2000, 2002, 2004, 2006, 2013, May 2016 & February 2017 by Veloce Publishing Limited, Veloce House, Parkway Farm Business Park, Middle Farm Way, Poundbury, Dorchester DT1 3AR, England. Fax 01305 250479 / e-mail info@veloce.co.uk / web www.veloce.co.uk or www.velocebooks.com. ISBN 978-1-787111-34-9 / UPC 6-36847-01134-5

© 1999, 2000, 2002, 2004, 2006, 2013, 2016 & 2017 James Hale and Veloce Publishing. All rights reserved. With the exception of quoting brief passages for the purpose of review, no part of this publication may be recorded, reproduced or transmitted by any means, including photocopying, without the written permission of Veloce Publishing Ltd. Throughout this book logos, model names and designations, etc, have been used for the purposes of identification, illustration and decoration. Such names are the property of the trademark holder as this is not an official publication. Readers with ideas for automotive books, or books on other transport or related hobby subjects, are invited to write to the editorial director of Veloce Publishing at the above address. British Library Cataloguing in Publication Data – A catalogue record for this book is available from the British Library. Typesetting, design and page make-up all by Veloce Publishing Ltd on Apple Mac. Printed and Bound by CPI Group (UK) Ltd, Croydon, CR0 4YY.

Dune Buggy
HANDBOOK
New Edition

The A-Z of VW-based Buggies since 1964

VELOCE PUBLISHING
THE PUBLISHER OF FINE AUTOMOTIVE BOOKS

FOREWORD

by Bruce Meyers

Once upon a time there was a young art student, beach boy, boat builder, car guy who, fun-hog that he was, concocted the 'Meyers Manx' – the world's first fiberglass dune buggy. This sun-dappled lifestyle of 'hanging ten' usually relieved one of worrying about tomorrow's profit. Breaking with tradition came easy to such a beach-bred Californian. Such irreverence was in; convention was out. The scene was set to let the creative juices flow freely, dude.

The Meyers Manx dune buggy became a huge and unprecedented success. The little car had its day in the sun and it was a glorious one. How deeply that saucy little shape has seeped into the culture of humankind. We have assimilated it into our subconscious as casually as the frisbee, hula hoops and skateboards. The Eskimo passes the long arctic night playing with his electric Manx; toddlers ride the merry-go-round's Manx buggies; swimming pool toys and peddle cars look like the Manx – it is the archetypal dune buggy.

James Garner raced Manxes in the Baja 1000, which was first won by a Manx. Chuck Connors chased African elephants in a Manx, whilst Elvis Presley and Steve McQueen cavorted in Manxes on the beach.

In the thirty-odd years since the Manx first appeared, the plastic dune buggy industry at home and abroad has recorded over three hundred different brand names, with total production reaching six figures.

With its look of rebellious audacity and smacking of adventure, it beckoned to the youth of those times, and those still clinging to their youth. Its simplistic design defied all automotive notions, suggesting it shouldn't be taken seriously. However, producing more smiles-per-mile and a higher fun-per-dollar ratio than any other car, before or since, the Manx was and still is the granddaddy of all that excitement, energy, celebrity and those many records, and has left an incredible, indelible skid mark on automotive history.

Bruce Meyers

CONTENTS

FOREWORD 4

ACKNOWLEDGEMENTS 6

AUTHOR'S FOREWORD 7

AUTHOR'S FOREWORD TO THIS REVISED EDITION 8

INTRODUCTION 9

MODELS A-Z
ALBAR 'S' & 'ES' 28
APAL 30
BAJA GT & SAHARA 32
BARRIS 'T' 34
BERRY MINI-T 36
BOSS BUG 38
BOUNTY HUNTER 40
BUGETTA 42
BUGLE & BUGLE 2 44
BUSHMASTER 46
BUSHWHACKER 48
CLAIMJUMPER 50
DESERTER SERIES 1, GS & GT .. 52
DOON 54
DUNE RUNNER 56
EMPI IMP 58
EMPI SPORTSTER 60
FF BUGGY 62

MAGAZINE FRONT COVERS & RECORD SLEEVES 64

MODELS A-Z (continued)
FIBERFAB CLODHOPPER & VAGABOND 66
FIBER JET COBRA & SAND HOPPER 68
FIBER JET ENOS & INDY '500' ... 70
FIBER JET ROUGH TERRAIN 72
FIBER-TECH MANX 74
FUN HUGGER 76
GLITTERBUG 78
GP BEACH BUGGY MK I 80
GP BEACH BUGGY MK II 82
GP SUPER BUGGY 84
GP LDV (LIGHT DELIVERY VAN)..86
GP RANCHERO 88
GT BUGGY 90
HOPPA 92
HUMBUG & BEAUJANGLE CAN-AM 94
HUSTLER 96
HUSTLER GT 98
INVADER 100

GALLERY 102

MODELS A-Z (continued)
JACKSON'S KUSTOM BUGGY 116
JAS 118
KANGO 120
KELLISON SANDPIPER 122
KYOTE (MANTARAY II KYOTE & KYOTE I) 124
KYOTE II (US) 126
KYOTE II (UK) 128
LIMITED EDITION CALIFORNIAN ...130
MANGOSTA 132
MANTA RAY MK I-III 134
MEYERS MANX (MONOCOQUE) ...136
MEYERS MANX (VW FLOORPAN) 138
MEYERS MANX (UK) 140
MEYERS MANX SR 142
MEYERS MANXTER 2+2 & MANXTER DUALSPORT 144
MEYERS TOW'D 146
MINIBUG 148
OCELOT & OCELOT S/S 150
PARABUG 152

ADVERTISING & BROCHURES 154

MODELS A-Z (cont)
POWERBUG 158
PREDATOR 160
PROWLER 162
RAT 164
RENEGADE (US) 166
RENEGADE (UK) 168
RENEGADE 'T' 170
SANDPIPER 172
SCORPION LT 174
SHARK 176
SIDEWINDER 178
STRIPPER 180
SURF BUGGY 182
TRAMP 184
VOLKSROD MK I 186
VOLKSROD MK II-IV 188
VOLKSROD MK V-VIII 190
VULTURE 192

CELEBRITY GALLERY 194

APPENDIX 201

INDEX 205

ACKNOWLEDGEMENTS

> This book is dedicated to Bruce Meyers – my inspiration, and my great friend.

Researching a book about specialist vehicles is never easy, and certainly not the work of just one person. I am deeply indebted to the many dune buggy manufacturers, owners, magazine editors, freelance journalists, photographers and photo libraries that have helped me in my search for information. Many took time out from busy schedules to trace historical articles, provide old photographs, arrange photo-shoots, and generally point me in the direction of others 'in the know.'

All photographs in this book have been credited, where known, to the original photographer or magazine (if this has not been possible, then they are credited to the person from whose collection they came). Whilst I have made every effort to trace copyright holders for photographs featured in this book, I will be glad to make proper acknowledgement in future editions in the event of any omissions at the time of going to press.

I have endeavoured to list everyone who helped in so many ways – thank you all.

To: Mike Key and Paul Knight for all their help with superb photographs.

To: Bob McClurg, Harold Pace, Peter Noad, Brian Coe, Stéphan Szantai, Mark Gredzinski, Bo Bertilsson, Jim Maxwell, John Lazenby, Dan MacMillan, Robin Wager, Richard Cooke, Keith Seume, Mel Hubbard, Giles Chapman, Anthony McKay and Phil Bowen for providing more ace photographs.

To: *Ultra VW* magazine, *Volksworld* magazine, *Custom Car* magazine, *Street Machine* magazine, and *VW Motoring* magazine for looking through their archives for pictures.

To: Bruce & Winnie Meyers, Don Wilcox, Alex Dearborn, Dean Jeffries, George Barris, Tim Figuhr at Fiber-Jet, John Jobber at GP Projects, Dave Fisher at Kingfisher Kustoms, Stuart Hopewell at Volksrod, Martyn Falk at KMR, Barry Warner at Hoppa Street Buggy, Chad Chadwick and Lee Southerton at Doon, John and Sharon Davies at JAS Beach Buggies, and GT Mouldings for researching vehicle details and providing photographs.

To: *Autocar* and *Motor* magazines, the National Motor Museum, Topham Picturepoint, Getty Images, Alamy, the British Film Institute, the Ronald Grant Archive, Kobal Picture Library, Ludvigsen Library, Auto Archive and the Quadrant Picture Library for trawling their archives for historical photographs.

To: Henny Jore, Jan van der Lit, Bob Whyman, Mel Baker, Mike Lewendon and John Jackson for allowing me access to their valuable collections of archive material.

To: Eon Productions, Mentorn Films, Miracle Films, Warner Bros. and United Artists for using buggies in their productions in the first place, thus inspiring a generation of builders.

And a final huge 'thank you' to Peter Rhodes for all the painstaking digital restoration work on classic buggy images that would otherwise have been lost forever.

James Hale

AUTHOR'S FOREWORD

There have been surprisingly few books on dune buggies, despite the huge impact that these fun cars have had on the development of kit-cars as we know them today. Buggies also spawned the huge VW aftermarket parts industry, which began in the 1970s to meet the needs of buggy builders, and has since become today's multi-million dollar business.

The books that do exist cover the construction of the kits, or their preparation for off-road use, rather than on the identification and histories of the many individual marques. A plethora of different buggy designs have been produced since the 1960s in Britain and America, and some continue to be manufactured to this day.

It would be a practical impossibility to catalogue every buggy model, so sketchy is the information on the lesser-known marques. Few of the original manufacturers still exist, and those that do tend to have very limited archives and photographic records. In any case, many of the kits were simply copies or adaptations of the better known, and better made, bodyshells available. Suffice to say, they all contributed to a culture of build-it-yourself vehicles that were as much a part of the youth scene of the 1960s and 1970s as pop music, flower power, and fashion excesses.

The scope of this book has been confined to the US and UK, simply because these countries were (and still are) the most dynamic and original producers of buggy designs. There has also been a great exchange of ideas between the two, and some buggy designs have been produced on both sides of the pond. The kits available have been amongst the most influential in providing inspiration and raw material for would-be car builders, whether for off-road, drag racing or street use. It is easy to forget that the founding father of the glassfiber dune buggy, Bruce Meyers, designed his original Manx buggy purely for off-road use, since many of today's vehicles have been built, or rebuilt, as trophy-winning show cars intended only for boulevard cruising.

Whilst the current trend is for high-tech street buggies, with many being featured in VW and kit-car related magazines, I have attempted to locate original period photographs, wherever possible, to show the cars as they first appeared during the boom period of the late 1960s and early 1970s.

In tracing archive material, I have spent countless hours talking to the people who were involved during the buggy heyday, both American and British. Even after some thirty years, their enthusiasm for the buggies they created, and for the whole era in which the buggy movement evolved, remains undiminished. It has been a great experience, and the results contained in this book should help to document and preserve the era for others to enjoy.

Readers who have any additional archive information, production details or photographs are always welcome to forward them to me, via Veloce, for possible inclusion in any future editions, or perhaps a second volume.

Buggy drivers tend to remain something of an insular group, though certainly no more so than other one-marque motoring enthusiasts. The thought of driving a wildly exhibitionist vehicle with a distinct lack of weather equipment might cause others to doubt their sanity, but all I can say is that on a sunny summer day you can watch silly grins appear on the faces of amazed bystanders, and any niggling worries about impracticality disappear as the doubters become very envious people.

See you on the dunes, friends.

James Hale

AUTHOR'S FOREWORD TO THIS REVISED EDITION

Writing *The Dune Buggy Handbook* in the late 1990s was my attempt to document the history of one of the most flamboyant eras of motoring history the world has ever seen. Up to that point, there had been very little information published on the buggy scene, except in magazines of the 1960s/70s. Although buggies generally fell out of favour in the mid-1970s, by the early 1990s, motoring enthusiasts and journalists were once again ready to embrace the buggy. But knowledge of marques, history and accessory details seemed to be severely lacking. I began to receive more and more questions from builders who were restoring early vehicles, or building them for the first time, who wanted to build 'period perfect' cars, but didn't know where to look for information. The answer was simple: put the knowledge and photographs in a book that everyone could share, and thus *The Dune Buggy Handbook* was born.

The book became a bible for those within the buggy scene. It was written before the advent of the internet, so everything had to be researched the old-fashioned way by talking to the original movers and shakers of the scene, either face-to-face or by telephone. Photographs were still 35mm transparencies, before digital became the new standard in the publishing world. The book was a labour of love, and took me a year – and a lifetime of collecting buggy material – to complete. I always resisted the temptation to go back and change things for subsequent reprints but, after a gap of nearly 15 years since I began work on the original edition, I felt that the time was right to give things a complete overhaul. In the intervening years, I had managed to acquire some significant 'new' photographic archive material from original sources, much of it in color. I had also established many contacts in the US, Australia and Europe as a result of the original edition of the book, and new information had come to light about buggy history worldwide. The result of further work is the book you are now holding – a completely revised and updated *Dune Buggy Handbook*.

As with the original, I have confined the sections on buggy marques to the US and UK, partly because of the sheer volume of material, but also because the wider worldwide buggy scene and its development and influence is already covered in my two *Dune Buggy Phenomenon* books, also published by Veloce. However, *The Dune Buggy Handbook* now includes new sections on celebrities and buggies, the buggy in advertising, and a look at how the buggy has appeared with regularity on magazine and record covers. It's a fascinating insight into the social influence that the little fun car has had on a world that today is ever more worried about environmental issues, global warming, and the future of fossil fuels. How long petrol-powered vehicles – including the buggy – can remain viable remains to be seen. For now, though, enjoy the cars that epitomise sheer unadulterated joy on or off the road. If my book can encourage you to build or restore a buggy, then it will have more than succeeded in its aim.

James Hale

INTRODUCTION

Dune buggies – cult transport for the young generation

Dune buggies, first popularised in California at the beginning of the 1960s, began life as 'backyard,' home-built vehicles, designed initially for exploring the outbacks of the US west coast. It wasn't long, however, before buggies evolved to become the cute, glassfiber-bodied cult cars so beloved of the younger generation. America, and subsequently Britain and most of Europe, was soon in the grip of a new style of motoring as 'Beetlemania' swept through the swinging sixties – a time when 'individuality' and 'fun' were the key watchwords.

However, the earliest buggies were developed in the US much earlier than the 1960s. In the 1920s, motoring enthusiasts were already building lightweight vehicles in which to flit around the California dunes – often just for fun, but sometimes as a way of making money, by taking sightseers across the sands and down to the edge of the surf. These flyweight 'buggies' were little more than stripped-down saloons, which were otherwise almost worthless on the resale market. In the period following WWI and before WWII, the base material for a buggy was often an old family saloon, stripped of body panels to reduce weight, and with the engine set back to place weight toward the rear axle for added traction. Some were just bare chassis, or even

The earliest dune buggies were little more than stripped-down sedans, such as this 1938 'flathead' Ford. (Courtesy Auto Archive)

Photographed in 1959, this pair of 1946-48 Ford and Mercury convertibles with flathead V8 engines were used as stripped-down dune buggies rented from 'Dune Schooners.' (Courtesy Auto Archive)

Buggies built from bare car chassis with seats attached were often the norm, with little regard for safety. Four Wheeler magazine did much to popularise the growing off-road trend. (Courtesy Popular Hot Rodding)

The Dune Buggy Handbook

Advertisers quickly picked up on buggies as a growing leisure trend in motoring. This is a Kodak advertisement from the early 1960s. (Courtesy Kodak)

tubular steel frames, with seats bolted on for the buggy pilot and passengers to strap themselves into as they hurtled across unexplored American trails, and the golden sands of Californian dunes.

However, in the late 1940s, with thousands of servicemen returning to the US from military duty, the sand dunes also became home to another phenomenon – lightweight two-stroke engine motorcycles. The freedom afforded to the young generation by these bikes led to the formation of competitive cross-country and 'enduro' events, which formed the basis of organised off-road events in which the buggy would very soon come to play a huge part. One of the earliest clubs was the Yakima Ridge Runners off-road club, formed by a group of enthusiasts as early as 1947.

With an increasing emphasis in America on going 'off-road,' and using crude, home-built vehicles to explore the expansive back country, buggies began to develop. The buggies generally used home-grown vehicles as the basis for conversion, and it was not unusual to see Chevvies, Chryslers, ex-military vehicles such as Jeeps and stripped 'flathead' engine Fords competing in such events as the New Year's Day races at Buttercup Valley, near Yuma, Arizona, and at regular events on Pismo Beach, California, Afton Canyon, Glamis and Hemet. Decommissioned Jeeps were particularly cheap and plentiful, and builders soon began substituting their basic four-cylinder engines

Buggy drivers took part in organised race meetings on the dunes, and were social events for the whole family. (Courtesy Auto Archive)

Buggies started as crude, ungainly-looking machines, often powered by large V8 engines. Grooved aircraft tyres and a set-back engine provided the traction in the sand. (Courtesy Auto Archive)

Introduction

Left: Much of the work on developing the VW Beetle-based buggy was done by Scott McKenzie of off-road club The Flintstone Scramblers. McKenzie (rear) also pioneered the use of Corvair engines in the buggy. (Courtesy Auto Archive)

with powerful V8 engines. Since it was essential to have the weight at the rear of the vehicle, delivering all the torque through the driving wheels, Corvair-powered, rear-engined vehicles began to achieve notable wins in these organised competitive events in the 1950s. However, with exports of the VW Beetle to the US increasing greatly during this period, it wasn't long before literally thousands of used or damaged examples were sitting around, and their mechanicals soon found their way into these early, and often crude, tube-framed cars; thus, the VW dune buggy was born.

It was Scott McKenzie, of an off-road club called the 'Flintstone Scramblers' in San Fernando, California, who began VW converting in earnest when he came across

Below: Corvair and VW-powered machines were extremely nimble on the sand, with wide Chrysler rims welded on to VW wheel centres and fitted with 'paddle-type' flotation tires.

The fully-independent suspension, rear-mounted and air-cooled engine of the VW Beetle made it an ideal choice as a basis for lightweight buggies. (Courtesy Auto Archive)

The Dune Buggy Handbook

Buggy owners soon formed clubs to hold organised races at Pismo Beach, California, and Yuma, Arizona, where VW-powered buggies out-performed the V8s.

Back-country driving enthusiast Bill Harkey raced this early modified VW Beetle-based buggy in competitive events. (Courtesy Four Wheeler)

The Burro by Tiny Thompson was a commercially available buggy based around a tube chassis with aluminium body panels riveted on. An 80in wheelbase gave the vehicle terrific ground clearance and maneuverability. (Courtesy Burro)

a wrecked Beetle. As a back-country driving enthusiast, Scott figured that the VW could become a good off-trail car if it had low weight and low pressure tires. The Beetle's independent suspension on all four wheels, and transmission ideally suited to rapid shifting, meant that a stripped-down Beetle could be taken across back-country roads at high speeds with relative ease. Ground clearance was considerably improved by shortening the chassis and welding Chrysler rims into the VW rear wheels. Adding large ex-aircraft flotation tires gave the buggy exceptional off-road ability in loose sand. These early buggies, sometimes with angular sheet-metal bodywork resembling the WWII German Kübelwagen, made the Hemet, Indio and Georgetown runs, and won trophies at the Glamis Hill Climbs and Indio obstacle race. McKenzie also successfully ran some of the first Corvair-engined buggies competitively: the commercial value of this was spotted by the Crown Manufacturing Company which subsequently made adaptor plates for the conversion. The success of McKenzie's 'VW dune buggy' meant that it was quickly copied, and laid the foundation for the VW-based buggy craze that was to soon follow.

Bill Chisholm, another early pioneer from southern Californian, can be credited with much of the early development on VW-type cars for off-road use. Chisholm began modifying the VW as a true sand buggy by removing the body and moving all the controls to the rear by some two feet. This relocated the front seats to fit in the stock rear seat area, with pedals moved aft and steering column lengthened. This configuration was good, but later experiments with shortening the chassis by nearly two feet provided the wheelbase for a very nimble buggy, capable of taking him further off-road than any four-wheel drive vehicle. Other early racers such as Bill Harkey also began to re-work the VW platform chassis by shortening it to increase its maneuverability on the sand.

Hilder T Thompson was one of the first to manufacture VW dune buggies commercially – his first car appeared in 1960 under the name of 'Burro' (from the Spanish word for a mule – prized for its hardiness in arid country). The car used a VW engine, gearbox and front suspension, mounted into a specially constructed, triangulated tube framework clad with pop-riveted aluminium body panels. The Burro was much shorter than the original VW (the wheelbase was only 80in), and this, together with its terrific ground clearance, made it a functional and purposeful off-roader, on back roads and in competition. The competitiveness of the Burro, coupled with media exposure in automotive magazines, ensured it began to build a loyal customer base.

Introduction

Following hard on the heels of the Burro was EMPI's 'Sportster,' which used an all-steel welded body accepting bolted-in VW components. EMPI (European Motor Products Inc) had been formed in the US during the 1950s by Joe Vittone to rebuild VW cylinder heads, and supply aftermarket parts and accessories for the VW Beetle. As early as 1958, Vittone, and his friend, Les Prestwood, had modified a severely accident-damaged VW Beetle to make a lightweight dune runner. From this experience, he then developed the Sportster as his attempt to create a more attractive – if angular – production dune buggy. The two-seater Sportster wheelbase was 82.5in (a four-seat model was developed later), and the buggy was sold either as a kit of parts or a set of plans for home construction, to those wishing to build their own cross-country vehicle. Orders soon started flooding in, and such was the level of manufacturing at the EMPI works that the company was even granted State of California licence plates for factory-built cars.

As these off-road and competition vehicles became more commonplace on the dunes, they caught the eye of native Californian Bruce Meyers: surf lover, gifted artist, and skilled glassfiber designer and craftsman. Whilst exploring Pismo Beach with a group of friends, including Ted Mangels, to try out sail yachts, Bruce's attention was drawn to the many unfinished-looking 'water-pumper' dune buggies running on the soft sand. Meyers drove one of the crude and noisy vehicles, and was immediately bitten by the off-road bug. He'd also seen bare Volkswagen chassis being driven around the dunes, and noticed that their light weight and balance, coupled with robust suspensions, made them ideal for skimming over the sand. Knowing he could build something better, in 1962 Bruce began to experiment by cutting out the wheelarches on his daily driver, a VW Kombi bus affectionately named Little Red Riding Bus. By fitting wide Buick wheel rims to the centres of the VW wheels and adding flotation tyres, the bus was now able to reach into outback territory that, previously, Meyers had only been able to dream about. The Kombi was still limited by its weight, however, and so he began to think about ways in which the VW mechanics could be adapted to fit a more maneuverable vehicle.

At around the same time, Roger Smith of VW & Porsche repair shop, Peppertree Automotive in California, had been searching for a WWII German Kubelwagen to use as an off-roader. The search was in vain so Smith designed his own similarly-styled desert car. The result was an angular, aluminium-panelled VW

The EMPI Sportster was a metal buggy built on the floorpan of the VW Beetle in either two- or four-seat versions. Running gear, engine, seats and electrical parts all came from the donor Beetle.

Motor Trend magazine from 1963 featured EMPI Sportsters on the cover. The metal buggy could be bought as a kit, or built from plans.

The Kübelwagen (literally translated as 'bucket car') was simple and effective in design. The stand-up headlight design was to feature in the Manx design.

Roger Smith of Peppertree Automotive built a lightweight, metal-bodied, VW-based off-roader called 'Rivets' to cruise to Pismo beach. The vehicle was one of the inspirations for the Manx buggy, as evidenced by the fender line. (Courtesy Road Test Dune Buggy)

The Dune Buggy Handbook

This all-wood dune buggy was created by boat builder Ted Mangels in just 30 days, and was powered and suspended using VW parts like the monocoque-designed Manx.

The wartime German Schwimmwagen and Kübelwagen military vehicles provided inspiration for the styling of the first glassfiber dune buggy, the Meyers Manx. (Courtesy Volksworld)

Ted Mangels' wooden buggy was appropriately named 'Splinters,' and used marine grade mahogany plywood for strength and lightness.

The high fender line, short-wheelbase and balloon-like tires of the amphibious Schwimmwagen would heavily influence the development of the world's first glassfiber buggy. (Courtesy BBT)

off-road vehicle he called 'Rivets.' The basis was a square tube space frame to which was added the front and rear VW Beetle suspensions and drive assemblies, giving an 80-inch wheelbase. Smith, and his son, Steve Rieman, created quite a stir amongst Pismo beach onlookers: so much so that Ted Mangels was inspired to build his own lightweight buggy, called 'Splinters,' in marine grade plywood on a metal frame, with VW suspensions attached. Taking just 30 days to build, this monocoque high-sided buggy resembled the German military Schwimmwagen with its high fender line and 'stand-up headlights,' and it was fitted with the suspensions and drivetrain of the VW Beetle. Rivets was a nimble dune runner, if somewhat ungainly in styling, but it also grabbed a lot of attention on the California dunes with its off-road ability.

It was witnessing the development of such vehicles that fuelled Bruce Meyers' desire to build a light, open-topped vehicle that could be used to cross previously-impassable terrain, play tag with the surf on the beach, and be driven on the street. The result was the Meyers Manx.

A graduate of the Los Angeles Art Centre School, Meyers had a natural eye for line and form. Drawing inspiration

Introduction

The Italian Ghia-designed Fiat 500 'Jolly' was styled as a fun car and beach buggy, and came with cutaway sides, wicker seats, and optional fringed sunshade top. (Courtesy Auto Archive)

Surfer and glassfiber specialist Bruce Meyers styled his own monocoque buggy in his one-stall garage in 1963. The first buggy pulled from the moulds in 1964 was dubbed 'Old Red.'

from the German Schwimmwagen and Kübelwagen military vehicles, Italian Fiat 'Jolly cars' of the 1950s, as well as from 'cartoon-type' vehicles, and his own artistic ideas of 'form through function,' the first true glassfiber-bodied dune buggy took shape in Meyers' one stall garage at Newport Beach, California. Working from his own rough drawings, and using a small-scale model to get the proportions correct, Meyers developed a stylish pattern of a short, stubby vehicle that looked like a cross between a foreign sportscar and a small boat. This was perhaps not surprising, since Meyers had previously been employed building a 42ft glassfiber catamaran, and many of the skills required for the complex features of the boat were used during construction of the initial buggy shape. Inspired by repair work he had undertaken on a Porsche 356 Coupé, Meyers used a similar principle of building a unitised body/chassis with lateral stiffeners for his off-road car. Since the mechanical underpinnings of the Porsche were so similar to the VW Beetle running gear, he was able to take many of his design pointers from the legendary German sports car. Even so, working on his own was a slow, painstaking process, and he

The Meyers Manx buggy was never intended for production, but created such interest that Bruce Meyers made 12 of the monocoque buggies before re-tooling the design for the shortened VW floorpan to lower costs. (Courtesy Bo Bertilsson)

The Meyers Manx was a masterpiece of automotive design, with its 'form through function' approach, and off-road capability. (Courtesy Meyers Manx Inc)

The Dune Buggy Handbook

Right: An airborne Manx shows the strength of Meyers' glassfiber fun car design.

Far right: Monocoque Manx at an off-road rally at Mammoth Wash, California, in 1966 uses paddle tires to kick sand in the face of competitors. (Courtesy Scott Malcolm)

Buggy convoys like these two Manxes and Splinters were regulars in the US mountains, deserts, forests and lake areas for camping, fishing or exploring trips.

The short-wheelbase buggy proved the ideal form of transport for back-country travel through terrain that even FWD vehicles would find impassable.

could only put in the hours at night once his day job as a glassfiber pattern-maker and marine fabricator for Newport Beach boat builder, Jensen Marine, was over.

With financial support from his wife, Shirley, the buggy pattern was eventually finished, and the first 'Manx' bodyshell was prised from the mould in May 1964. Christened 'Old Red,' the body was a semi-monocoque design, to which Beetle suspension components, and other mechanicals, were bolted. The cute-looking body was a masterpiece of glassfiber design, carrying in-built steel tubing to spread stress and load over a major portion of the panelling. It also had a Porsche-style hoop at the rear to locate the Beetle engine and transmission. Using the lessons learned in the boat-building industry for cost-effective production, the Manx kit was a simple design in which form followed function. It had the high fender line of the VW Schwimmwagen to keep spray from being thrown up; the short-wheelbase of Splinters for maneuverability; the stand-up headlights and sheer construction simplicity of the VW Kubelwagen, and the open and fun design of the 'jolly cars,' blended together into one cute package.

Meyers' red demonstrator quickly attracted media attention, and he made just 11 more of these fun car kits before a major problem came to light – the price! Meyers was losing money fast, even with the kit priced at $995, and it was obvious that a redesign was needed if he was ever

Introduction

The Meyers Manx was redesigned to use the shortened VW floorpan, running gear and engine, and quickly became an affordable convertible fun car for American teenagers.

going to make a business of his idea. Taking inspiration from the early off-road racers that had utilised the complete VW Beetle rolling chassis, albeit with a 14.5in section cut out to improve ground clearance and maneuverability, the Manx was quickly re-tooled and re-launched on this platform. At a stroke, the production problems of the Manx seemed to be resolved, and the kit could be made quicker and cheaper, without any loss of quality. The simplicity and style of the design, as well as the relative cheapness of the new glassfiber kit, ensured its success, with customer demand outstripping the rate at which Meyers' workshop could meet orders. Looking similar to the original design, the new buggy had a fixed front hood housing the stock fuel tank beneath, a separate dashboard, and a main bodyshell that bolted down on the VW chassis shortened to an 80in wheelbase. The Manx kit 'A' cost only $498, but left builders to provide metalwork parts, lights and windscreen. The more comprehensive 'B' kit included these parts and cost $635, but still found far more customers.

Promotional shot of a pair of Manxes for a 1965 B F Meyers & Co. buggy brochure.

Below: As demand for the Manx increased, B F Meyers & Co fell prey to copyists. A Manx II version of the kit was introduced to reduce the kit price, and make the bodies stackable for easy transportation.

Left: The strength and agility of the Manx was demonstrated by off-road antics such as this.

Buggies became stars of big and small screens very quickly. The original 1968 United Artists film *The Thomas Crown Affair* starred Steve McQueen and Faye Dunaway, and an awesome 180bhp Chevrolet Corvair-powered Manx. (Courtesy Kobal Collection)

The Thomas Crown Affair Manx was specially built for United Artists in just eight weeks by Pete Condos and Eckley Tur at Con-Ferr Manufacturing in Burbank, California. Features of the buggy included sunken headlights, a boat windscreen, and lowered sides. (Courtesy UA/Mirisch/Simkoe/Solar/Pictorial Press Ltd)

The newly-formed BF Meyers & Co factory began turning out more and more kits a day, but production still couldn't keep up with demand. Motoring journalists loved the buggy, and wanted it on the front cover of their magazines; young people loved it because it was cheap to build and looked great, and TV producers and film makers scrambled to get it into shows and films. Chuck Connors used a Manx in the 1960s show *Cowboy in Africa*, whilst big screen stars Paul Newman (*Winning*) and Elvis Presley (*Live a Little, Love a Little*) drove them in their movies. However, it was the modified, Corvair-powered Manx driven by Steve McQueen in *The Thomas Crown Affair* that really fired the imagination of the buggy-buying public and further increased demand.

Many of these newly-built Manxes were destined for use purely on the street, with no pretention to serious off-roading. However, the kit soon proved its competition worthiness at Baja, winning the first organised 'Mexican 1000' off-road race. The Manx also set a new speed record for the gruelling Tijuana to La Paz run, showing its durability and manufactured-in quality. The Manx went on to dominate US west coast slalom racing, and, in the capable hands of Ted Trevor, won the under 3-litre class at the 1966 Pikes Peak Hill Climb with a 140bhp Corvair engine and Crown-adapted VW transaxle fitted.

The Manx proved a serious off-road competitor, with drivers Ted Mangels and Vic Wilson beating every type of vehicle to win the first organised Mexican 1000 race at Baja in 1967.

The Manx helped open up the American backcountry to thousands of enthusiasts and explorers. Here, Bruce Meyers and fellow off-roader Ted Mangels plot a race route through Baja, California. (Courtesy Meyers Manx Inc)

Don Wilcox puts in an unmatched qualifying time at practice for the Pikes Peak Hillclimb in 1966, in a blue Manx with turbocharged Corvair engine, built by Ted Trevor of Crown Manufacturing. (Courtesy Don Wilcox)

Introduction

Advertising for Gates Tires used the image of Ted Trevor's Manx buggy being driven in earnest to publicise the company's Commando and Wide Trac off-road tires.

The Manx was a true fun car on the dunes, but also got close to the water's edge, too.

So maneuverable was the 'Volksvair' Manx that Ted Trevor, and co-driver Don Wilcox in a similarly race-prepared Manx, out-performed other sportscars, stockcars and most other open-wheeled vehicles in the USAC racing championships. Such humiliation for factory teams, like Shelby Cobra entrants, soon saw the buggies eliminated from the Pikes Peak programme.

Popularity of the buggy soon extended all along the Californian coastline, and new designs followed the Manx. Unable to keep up with customer orders, and with Meyers insisting on the highest levels of quality on all his kits, unscrupulous dealers and 'knock-off' manufacturers sensed an opportunity to make a fast buck by copying the basic design. In the late 1960s it was estimated that over 50 manufacturers were producing buggy kits in the California area alone. Sometimes their products were simply 'me-too' copies, poorly made and infringing the Manx design, and Meyers tried to stop the spiralling number of copies by developing a cheaper Manx II kit, and through direct legal action. Even with a patent, however, Meyers lost a landmark court case over the design of his glassfiber buggy, and this opened the floodgates for copyists to cash in on his original idea. Despite the infringement of the Manx design, there were some excellent new buggies being developed, too, including the EMPI Imp, the Kyote (designed by Hollywood car builder Dean Jeffries), and the neat Berry Mini-T. All identified and carved a particular niche in what was very quickly becoming a crowded and cutthroat marketplace. Buggy accessory shops, buggy tire shops, buggy building and paint shops, buggy magazines and books: all followed the wildfire success of the buggy concept. The

The first meeting of the Manx Buggy Club proved how popular the little fun car had become, starting a revolution in motoring for the younger generation. (Courtesy Meyers Manx Inc)

The EMPI Imp was the company's glassfiber entry into the buggy market, following its successful Sportster kit. The well-marketed Imp became a serious competitor to the Manx.

Citation buggy bodies were amongst those that bridged the gap between the traditional Manx and Model-T inspired kits.

19

The Dune Buggy Handbook

Highly customised buggies began appearing at auto shows and car customising shows on the US west coast. (Courtesy Tribune photo archives)

Fun motoring – buggy style! (Courtesy Classic Stock/Alamy)

As the buggy concept grew, a whole new industry developed around it to provide accessories, go-faster parts, magazines and books. Building your VW based Dunebuggy by Peter Ezzell and John Quan was an early publication catering for those building their own cars.

Dune Buggies and Hot VWs was the first of several magazines to be launched in the US on the strength of the buggy scene. The first issue featured the Meyers Manx. Many other magazines have since made buggies cover stars.

Buggies featured on many LP record covers of the era. The LP Wild Wheels on the RCA label is the soundtrack to the film of the same name starring Don Epperson.

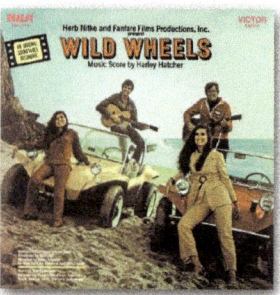

motoring scene quickly accepted that the word 'buggy' encompassed an entire sub-culture.

It was the younger generation that adopted the buggy as a form of transport, uniquely its own. With teenagers the catalyst for a 1960s revolution in society, buggies satisfied the postwar generation's desire for a fun car that could be used on the road, was visually very different and unconventional, and within its price range. For a country starved of cheap native sportscars (except for the Corvette, the only two-seater worthy of the name), the buggy was the perfect answer. A used or crashed Beetle could be picked up from the scrapyard for as little as $50, and, even with a standard 1200 Beetle engine, the buggy's light weight gave it exhilarating performance.

Manufacturers quickly catered to the exclusive needs of this new and fashionable market by producing buggy kits in iridescent metalflake finishes, complete with a myriad of highly chromed, colored and polished accessories. Meyers Manx flowered vinyl tops even appeared during the late 1960s and early 1970s at a time when hippy flower power ruled.

Buggies were soon the main features at auto shows and US west coast top car customising shows, which also provided the springboard for sales of specially-

Sears, Roebuck & Co offered glassfiber buggy kits in a range of ten colors from its mail order catalogue in the late 1960s. (Courtesy Auto Archive)

Proving the lifestyle attraction of the buggy, Playboy magazine featured a major dune buggy article in its July 1969 issue. Buggies featured included the Meyers Tow'd, Jeffries Manta Ray II Kyote, Berry Mini-T, and an EMPI Imp. (Courtesy Dean Jeffries)

engineered buggy parts, including seats, exhaust systems, and go-faster engine parts. The supply of parts and accessories developed into a specialist area for Beetles and other VW-based kit-cars generally, and is a huge industry in its own right today. So great was the demand for kits and accessories that buggy kits could even be ordered right out of the pages of the famous Sears mail order catalogue! Further proving the mass-market acceptability of the buggy concept, men's lifestyle magazine Playboy also jumped on the bandwagon, in 1969, with a major buggy feature that aimed to show a more complete 'sand safari' approach to the phenomenon, the magazine reviewing picnic equipment and printing camping food recipes as well as trying out a Meyers Tow'd, EMPI Imp and Manta Ray II Kyote, amongst others, on the dunes.

The buggy craze soon spread to other countries around the world, although it was better suited to those with warmer climates and plenty of open space. South Africa became a natural home for the buggy, and was responsible for the introduction of off-road racing on specially-created tracks. The most significant buggy from this country was the Lolette, which is actually still in production. Australia established a licensed production for the Meyers Manx, before stringent motoring laws made buggy building 'down under' very difficult.

Whilst mainland Europe gave some early media exposure to the US buggy scene, continental countries initially seemed less than enthusiastic about the buggy ethos. The Dutch magazine De VW ran a feature on the American buggy scene in 1966, yet it would be a full three years before Holland, Germany and France began production of any home-grown designs. Some manufacturers opted to license US design production, and thus the German AHS Imp (similar to the EMPI original), the Dutch BAC Woestijnrat (Desert Rat, a copy of the US Deserter), and the Dutch Sandman (taken from a US kit, and still produced today as the Hot Rod Sports Car buggy) started the ball rolling. Other original designs, such as the German Karmann GF buggy, the Belgian Apal buggy range, the Dutch Vogels 'Birds Buggy,' the

The Deserter buggy by Dearborn Automobile Co was continually developed and became a serious racing vehicle. It was followed by the equally performance-based Deserter GT.

The British Volksrod Mk I buggy had a simple and stark design and was produced purely for off-road use. The design was developed when similar buggies were seen in American magazines. (Courtesy Volksrod)

The Dune Buggy Handbook

Designed by Warren Monks during 1967, the Volksrod Mk I pioneered the buggy scene in the north of England when it was launched in 1968. (Courtesy Robin Wager)

GP established its name for strength and quality through success in regular competitive events, including autocross. Like the Meyers Manx, the design was copied by less scrupulous companies. (Courtesy Auto Archive)

The GP Beach Buggy was the south of England's answer to the alternative car craze. It quickly became the definitive British buggy design, and drew the attention of London's media, television and celebrities. (Courtesy Paul Skilleter)

Italian ATL Explorer, and the Austrian Custoca 'Amigo' buggies all subsequently began to emerge, and offered European builders a real choice of styles.

It was Britain, perhaps surprisingly, that greeted the buggy in a way unmatched by any other non-Stateside country. Considering the nature of the British climate, and the fact that some of the earliest buggy designs fell foul of the law, no-one could have foreseen that buggies would become as popular as they did.

Who was first to produce a buggy kit in Britain is open to debate, though the entirely home-grown Volksrod Mk I, produced by Warren Monks at Doncaster-based firm Volksrod, almost certainly pipped the more publicised GP buggy to the post. London-based GP Speed Shop, run by Pierre du Plessis and John Jobber, was ideally positioned to capitalise on the requirements of the Kings Road trendsetters, who needed a new, head-turning vehicle to replace the short-lived Mini-Moke at the coffee bar concours on sunny afternoons. The buggy was ideal for the young and fashionable set because it looked so different, and could easily win the Kings Road traffic lights Grands Prix.

Very quickly, buggy fever overtook Britain. Spurred on by buggy front cover appearances in leading automotive magazines such as *Custom Car*, *Motor* and *Autocar*, builders reached for their spanners and the price of used VWs rocketed. Not all the finished buggies were built to a quality standard, but these were heady days, and, once caught up in the fun and excitement of it all, the idea was to build and keep on moving. Overnight thousands of people became car builders and a club fraternity grew as the once-cottage industry became big business. Buggy shells were soon churned out from various manufacturers' garages and workshops the length and breadth of the country in order to meet the unrelenting demand. Some were imitations of the GP shape, whilst others were new shapes styled after Stateside designs such as the Manta-Ray and Bugle. A couple of true American buggies, the Renegade and Kyote, were even made in Britain under licence (and both are still in production today).

Introduction

The GP Super Buggy looked like a stretched short-wheelbase vehicle. At the rear the engine was completely covered, making it suitable for export markets. (Courtesy Autocar)

The GP design was also produced as a long-wheelbase version called the Super Buggy. Here, one of the cars rears up at an off-road event. (Courtesy Autocar)

This Manta Ray buggy appeared on the front cover of the first issue of Custom Car magazine in 1970, and set the British buggy scene alight. The Manta Ray design is still in production in the UK. (Courtesy Custom Car)

The British buggies of the 1960s and 1970s were hardly sophisticated (banded steel wheels and motorcycle-type exhausts were among the few concessions to aesthetic customising), but still drew admiring glances from other road users. For the younger generation, such exhibitionism was usually reward enough for their labours in building the car. Serious off-road work was usually left to those involved in autocross, where the buggy became a force to be reckoned with. The maneuverability and light weight of the buggy made it ideal for the sport, and several major off-road successes were scored in the special buggy classes created by event organisers. Buggies quickly developed to make them more habitable in the British climate, and designs such as the much-refined Volksrod Mk II and Bugle Buggy began to appear to the delight of customers who often wanted to drive the cars as fashion statements, rather than having any serious pretentions to driving off-road.

The British press realised there was good copy in buggies, and they regularly featured as competition prizes or courtesy vehicles for personalities. Upper crust magazines *Motor* and *Car* gave the buggy movement its moment of fame in their pages, with the latter even running a regular buggy column by Carol Brown entitled 'Buggy Off.' British TV also saw its fair share of buggy appearances, including the popular *Cliff Richard Show*, as well as *Anita in Jumbleland* and *Ace of Wands*.

One of the most popular British buggy kits of the 1970s was the Bugle, designed purely as a two-seater and aimed at the rich and famous as complete road-going fun cars. (Courtesy Bob Whyman)

23

The Dune Buggy Handbook

Volksrod redesigned its buggy into a more road-going and legalised version called the Mk II. With faired-in headlamps and large folded-over box section sides, the buggy was exceptionally strong. It was also developed into a long-wheelbase version called the Mk II FL. (Courtesy Volksrod)

Motor magazine carried a special buggy feature in 1970, putting the Bugle, GP Beach Buggy, Hustler and Powerbug through their paces. (Courtesy Motor)

Promotional shots from an early Volksrod brochure, the Mk II design was created with the British climate in mind. It also featured a removable rear cover for easy access to the VW engine. (Courtesy Auto Archive)

1971 was the year of the buggy in Britain. Manufacturers, encouraged by buggies appearing in *The Thomas Crown Affair* and the Walt Disney feature film *The Computer Wore Tennis Shoes*, starring Kurt Russell, built them in huge numbers. An American buggy, the Scorpion, was imported specially for the *Daily Telegraph* stand at the 1971 London Motor Show, and Brands Hatch hosted a unique buggy race just after Christmas of that year. The Scorpion design re-surfaced as the Invader in the UK, and demonstrated that the basic Meyers Manx design was gradually moving toward more refined sports-type buggies.

In 1972, however, interest in glassfiber-bodied buggies began to wane on both sides of the Atlantic. Stateside builders had moved on to other types of vehicle (for off-roading, the lighter, stronger, and more powerful rail-type buggies had become the accepted vehicle in which to compete successfully and win the long, arduous desert races). Road buggies had been replaced by increasingly stylised and sophisticated kit-cars, such as the Beaujangle Can-Am in the UK, and the Shalako in the US, or high performance VW Beetles. Britain's climate had finally proved a distinct turn-off to buggy builders and motoring journalists alike.

Introduction

Realising there were more rainy days than sunny ones, and being more acclimatised to 'proper' cars, the British press did much to hasten the demise of the buggy through negative road tests. Many manufacturers, who had initially launched their products in a rush of enthusiasm, now tasted bitter economic reality and went out of business. The boom was over.

Buggy clubs and conventions kept the faithful together through a decade in which the fledgling kit-car industry blossomed, until the early 1980s, when interest in all-things buggy was rekindled. A whole new generation of builders rediscovered the fun that could be had with this wind-in-the-hair, distinctly different form of motoring. Buggies began to reappear at VW-related motoring shows in increasing number, and the extremely high quality of the builds (or rebuilds) proved that buggy owners and their vehicles could not be easily dismissed. Whilst the trend for today's buggies seems to be focused predominantly on 'strictly street,' in both California and Britain buggies have also become formidable drag-strip competitors, with flyweight bodyshells and space frame chassis.

The name 'Manx' has become used to describe the generic style of all buggies that resemble Bruce Meyers' design, and original Manx kits and complete cars now command high prices. Their stark simplicity, the quality of construction that became an industry yardstick, and ability to deliver more smiles per hour than any other fun car, have ensured them a place in automotive history. Indeed, the very first Manx buggy – 'Old Red,' built in 1964, having been on display at the Balboa Park Automotive Museum in San Diego for many years – is now back with Bruce Meyers himself.

Bruce Meyers has once again become very active with dune buggies, forming and running his own Manx Dune Buggy Club. By organising events in the Californian outback, the club has brought together enthusiasts who want to do what the

The US-designed Renegade buggy by Glassco (foreground) was made in the UK under license by PABC from a set of imported moulds. The lady sitting on the rollbar is Carol Brown, who wrote a regular column in *Car* magazine called 'Buggy Off.'

The Invader buggy was directly sired from an imported American Scorpion LT buggy made by Desert Fox Sand Buggies in Arizona. The buggy kit was imported especially for the *Daily Telegraph* stand at the 1970 London Motor Show. (Courtesy Mike Key)

Glassfiber buggies, such as this Sandwinder, continued to be used in the US for back-country exploration, though there was a shift toward lighter and stronger 'rail' buggies for serious competition. (Courtesy Burly Burlile)

The Dune Buggy Handbook

The American and British kit car scene moved toward more stylised VW-based vehicles such as this Humbug (produced in Britain as the Beaujangle Can-Am) during the 1970s. (Courtesy *Custom Car*)

The Shalako by Dick Dean took the basic VW-based buggy concept to an altogether different level in the US with its futuristic sports car shape.

The development of lighter and faster competition racing rails sounded the death knell for the early Stateside glassfiber-bodied buggies. The growing trend was covered by magazines such as *Dune Buggies & Hot VWs* in the US, and *Custom Car* in the UK.

buggy does best – going off-road and making many new friends. After all, the buggy was made to get people talking, and owners certainly find themselves talking to many new people – some asking if they built it themselves, others talk about the fact that they owned one, way back when, and finally, those who want to know where they can buy one! Proving that he has been able to put issues due to the copying of his revolutionary design behind him, Meyers has returned to the limelight with a range of new buggy designs. The long-wheelbase Manxter 2+2 and DualSport have been designed for the modern world, being easy to build and with safety in mind. For those still looking for a more classic shape, Meyers has now introduced a new Manx kit in both 'Traditional' or 'Kick-Out' variants to satisfy buggistas.

It may be nearly 50 years since the first glassfiber buggies hit the roads and off-road trails, but the concept – and, to a large extent, the designs – have remained relatively unchanged in the years since. The buggy does not pretend to be anything other than what it is on the surface: a cute, honest, go-anywhere fun car that can take to the dunes or the street in style, and which can be built by anyone who has a few tools, some common sense, and a lot of enthusiasm.

26

Introduction

Events such as regular buggy conventions in Britain, and the formation of clubs around the world, kept the dune buggy spirit alive and well after the initial 1960s/70s buggy boom.

Above, left: Bruce Meyers established a Manx dune buggy club that organises events for buggy owners in the US, and also regularly attends large VW shows, such as this one in France.

Bruce Meyers has taken centre stage once again with the production of classic Manx kits and development of all-new designs, including the Manxter 2+2 and 'Kick-Out' Manx buggy. (Courtesy Meyers Manx Inc)

Modern buggies are often built in a 'retro' style, emulating a period look from the 1960s. Others, such as this Manta Ray, are built as dual-purpose vehicles for road and race use. (Courtesy Bob Cook)

ALBAR 'S' & 'ES'

DATA PANEL

Production dates
Albar 'S': 1971-1994
Albar 'ES': 1983-1986

Numbers built
Albar 'S': 400 (approx)
Albar 'ES': 10

Export markets
Switzerland, Austria

Wheelbase
94.5in

Identification tips
Albar 'S': Traditional buggy shape pushed to the extreme: rear periscope air intake, front air dam, twin fillers on front hood, boxy side panels
Albar 'ES': Unitised bodyshell with low sides, front air dam, alloy windshield frame, optional rear racing-style wing

As one of the UK's leading buggy manufacturers in the 1970s, GP was keen to distribute vehicles further afield. It came as no surprise, therefore, that licensed production was set up in other countries, such as Spain and Germany, with buggy bodyshells also exported worldwide.

One of the main markets was Switzerland, where importer Alois Barmettler began distributing the original GP Super Buggy (based on the full-length VW Beetle chassis in order to comply with strict European motoring laws governing construction and use of kit vehicles). When GP introduced an updated model with interchangeable hardtops (known as the Buggy-LS-Hardtop), it, too, found its way to Switzerland. This new buggy, with integral glassfiber windshield frame, wider back fenders, hardtop and opening doors, soon found many new customers in Swiss and Austrian markets.

The Albar Company (as the distribution concern became known) then asked GP to produce an even more outlandish version for display at the Geneva Motor Show. The resulting Albar 'S' buggy took the original GP shape to the extreme, featuring a low front spoiler, wide side panels with dummy air intakes, and a racing-style periscope on the rear deck for added engine cooling. Large, round tail lights were fitted into special mouldings in pairs on each side of the bodyshell rear, and the interior had an ergonomically-shaped dashboard for maximum instrument visibility. It even included a locking glove compartment.

The front hood sported twin fuel tank fillers near the windshield, which was tall and distinctly angular. A detachable hardtop with gull-wing doors was sold as an optional extra (it fitted to the lip running around the top edge of the bodyshell and a groove around the windshield frame). This outrageous-looking buggy began to achieve healthy sales, although Albar started to turn attention to developing and manufacturing a second design – the Albar 'ES.'

Sharing some features with the 'S' design, such as front air dam and dashboard, the 'ES' was, however, very different in construction. Manufactured as a one-piece bodyshell to fit an unmodified Beetle chassis, the new buggy was laminated in fire-retardant resin to meet European TÜV vehicle regulations. Cheaper and simpler to build than its upmarket brother, the new 'ES' buggy featured a more conventional alloy windshield frame, central fuel filler set into the single front hood styling ridge, and a much deeper flange to the body waistline. This gave the body more of a curved appearance around the wheelarches as it rose to follow the line of the massive tyres beneath.

Confirming its status as a buggy for road use only, the Albar 'S' could be fitted with luxurious interior trim and seating options available from the accessory catalog.

Models A-Z

The tall periscope could be used to increase the flow of cooling air to the VW engine, or the base could be adapted to mount a Formula 1-style rear wing.

Today's version of the Albar buggy pushes the design still further, with heavily raked screen and Ferrari Testarossa-style side panels.

As with all Albar buggies, a vast range of accessories was available. The 'ES' could be fitted with side panels featuring deep air scoops, and a racing-style rear wing that attached to the rear deck. A proper heating system and demister, driven by a small electric blower unit, was also available for the range. Such production car refinements confirmed the designs as primarily road cars, with little pretence of off-roading.

Both buggies were imported to the UK, and then manufactured under licence from Albar (a move that didn't find favour with original designer GP). One Six Two Engineering of Bethnal Green, London, run by vehicle distributor Ted Kellerman, made the entire range of Albar vehicles available to UK buyers. Few were sold, however, during the three years that the company traded. Albar itself has continued to develop and sell variants of the long-wheelbase kits in mainland Europe.

The Albar 'ES,' with unitary bodyshell and traditional alloy windshield frame, was a cheaper kit option. The design had noticeably lower sides, but still fitted the stock VW floorpan.

A pair of Albar buggies at an international convention in Holland.

The Albar 'S' was developed from the design of the long-wheelbase GP buggy, but featured a low front spoiler, wide side panels, and periscope on the rear deck.

DATA PANEL

Production dates
1971-1992 (in UK)

Numbers built
60 (approx in UK)

Export markets
France, Spain, Germany, Norway

Wheelbase
94.5in

Identification tips
Low, utilitarian bodyshell, with 'sit up and beg' front fenders. Bulge on front hood, enclosed engine bay and hinged engine cover. UK-built models had smooth side panels

Buggy designer Apal in Belgium also produced the kit in a short-wheelbase form.

When the influence of the growing buggy scene began to create an impact in mainland Europe during 1970, some enthusiasts bought UK vehicles, such as the GP and Volksrod buggies, that were made under license, whilst others designed their own. One of the first home-grown builders to make a significant impact was Apal in Belgium, with short- and long-wheelbase buggies aimed very much at the utility market. The design was to become one of the biggest sellers in Europe during the height of the buggy boom.

The new Apal buggy subsequently made its presence felt in the UK when leading VW tuning firm Cartune began licensed production of the long-wheelbase variant from its works in Middlesborough, north Yorkshire. Apal had already achieved a measure of official VW acceptance, so the move seemed a logical step for the UK VW specialist.

The bodyshell itself was very strong and well conceived, if somewhat unconventional in styling. The low sides emphasised its utility nature, with narrow, boxy fenders featuring small flares to the outer wheelarch. At the front the fenders took on a 'sit up and beg' appearance, whilst conventional headlamps were mounted on posts each side of the front hood.

The hood – a neat design – featured a recessed front licence plate mounting which also helped lock the unit in place. A bulge in the hood provided cover for the rather utilitarian VW fuel tank neck. The dashboard – which was rather plush for a utility vehicle – was produced in either left- or right-hand drive with mock vinyl effect finish. A proper mount ensured a secure location for the VW steering column, whilst the floor-mounted central binnacle provided support for the whole unit. For those requiring a more 'finished' look to the interior of their buggy, the Apal dashboard even had a glovebox recess to take a standard VW liner.

At the rear, the bodyshell had a properly boxed-in compartment to prevent mud and water getting onto the engine, whilst a full-width, hinged rear body panel covered the entire exposed back of the car in the interest of legality. Once raised, engine access was superb. The stock VW tail lights remained on the main bodyshell beneath the panel, and were visible through oval openings in the rear hatch when lowered.

The buggy was sold as a complete conversion kit with the glassfiber parts, a set of wheels, a John Aley rollbar, and a host of minor extras such as mirrors and wipers. Seats, including the rear bench seat, could be ordered at extra cost, or those from the VW sedan could be utilised. Other available accessories included a set of four glassfiber mud spats, though these were later changed for a pair of proper full-length, smooth side panels. These differed significantly from the more curved units sold by the Apal company in Belgium.

With Cartune's branch in Middlesex offering to tune customers' VW engines to any degree of power, the company looked set to take the buggy world by storm, but the combination of utilitarian looks and high initial price limited the number sold.

By 1972 production had moved to another Yorkshire manufacturer, Lightspeed Panels, but only a few buggies were made. The moulds were left untouched until the mid-1980s when they were rescued and refurbished by GT Mouldings. With a new kit-car explosion in full swing, and the original alloy windshield frame changed for a glassfiber one, the buggy was looking as good as its basic design allowed, and many kits were laminated for eager customers. However, as GT Mouldings moved on to produce its own designs, the Apal moulds were sold twice more to would-be car manufacturers, before eventually arriving at the door of Country Volks. Ultimately, they were broken up when the company ceased trading in 1992.

Cartune sold the Apal buggy in the UK as a complete kit with a set of wheels, rollbar, and other fittings to ensure easy construction by the customer.

The Apal buggy was best known as a long-wheelbase design, with styling that was extremely utilitarian, and re-used the donor VW beetle seating.

UK-built Apals used flatter side panels than the curved originals. This example also features a non-standard tinted windscreen.

In mainland Europe, the Apal is one of the most successful buggies ever to be produced, and some graced magazine front covers of the day.

BAJA GT & SAHARA

DATA PANEL

Production dates
1970-1987

Numbers built
Baja GT: 55 (approx)
Sahara: 8

Export markets
None

Wheelbase
Baja GT: 78.5in
Sahara: 94.5in

Identification tips
Rectangular headlights set into a pseudo grille at the front of a smooth front hood. Pointed tail fins swept up from rear bodywork with a glassfiber Targa rear screen assembly and roof panel. Sahara was long-wheelbase, with a more flared rear section and kamm-tail back

Designed and made in 1970 by Roger Penfold and Patrick Sumner (operating in Chichester under the very apt trade name of Speed Buggies), the Baja GT was a step away from the traditional buggy shape: an attractive marriage of buggy and sportscar styling. From the somewhat angular front and faired-in rectangular headlamps, to the raised wing sections and flat back panel, the Baja GT was certainly a distinctive and eye-catching buggy at a time when most manufacturers were content to merely borrow designs and ideas from others.

Like the Manta-Ray buggy, the Baja GT body was moulded in one piece, complete with front hood, dashboard and inner tub, and was released from a complex set of bolt-together sectional moulds. This was a bonus for the builder in that several panels did not have to be aligned during construction, though it made lamination more difficult and therefore time-consuming. It also caused some problems with fitting the VW Beetle petrol tank into the special metal frame beneath the front section of the buggy, and meant that access to the tank was possible only with the bodyshell removed.

If the body styling itself wasn't original enough, then the glassfiber bolt-on windshield frame, the neat Targa-style rollbar cum rear screen, and the lift-off Targa roof certainly were. This made the buggy even more individual at a time when individuality was the name of the game.

With the installation of a 2.3-litre Corvair engine in the tail boosting power by 120bhp, the Baja GT demonstrator's performance was as stunning as its looks. Such performance, coupled with the 16in shortened VW floorpan on which the car was based, gave the buggy mind-numbing acceleration, if decidedly 'interesting' handling.

Speed Buggies was unusual amongst British manufacturers in offering the Corvair engine package; a development the company had perfected previously as agent for the Manta-Ray buggy. However, the company's engineering excellence was never capitalised on, and lack of promotion of the buggy led to falling sales, and the owners pursuing business interests elsewhere. Even with the UK buggy boom in full swing, the project was passed on to Richard Park, who ran his own specialist engineering business from the same 'Rodding Scene' premises as legendary British hotrodder Geoff Jago.

The Baja GT fared little better second time around, and the project was abandoned and the moulds mothballed when the buggy bubble burst in late 1972. In 1977 the Baja GT got another chance when the project was bought by Alan Warren of Hayling Island-based boat builder Audy Marine (which already produced a futuristic, VW-based kit called the Zeta), in an attempt to capitalise on the growing interest in kit-cars during this period.

The unique styling of the kit, together with an added promotional push by marketing agent Special Car Consultants, ensured new sales. The buggies were never the mainstay of the company's business, however, and as marine glassfiber work increased, the Baja GT was again neglected. Perhaps the buggy's greatest triumph is

The body styling featured sharply-finned tops to each fender at the rear, and a long hood with recessed headlights at the front.

Models A-Z

Designed by Speed Buggies of Chichester, the Baja GT shape was a radical departure from classic buggy styling, with a glassfiber rear Targa roof panel and a lift-off roof section (Courtesy *Hot Car*)

Audy Marine continued production of the Baja GT design, with its white demonstrator being built in the late 1970s.

This show-winning Baja GT had widened rear fenders, flush-fitting Jaguar fuel filler cap, a fully chromed engine, and hand-crafted tubular bumpers. (Courtesy Richard Cooke)

that fledgling manufacturer GT Mouldings (which took its name from the GT of the buggy) was set up in 1981 specifically to produce this kit, later going on to develop it into a similarly styled long-wheelbase variant called the Sahara.

Both buggy designs were dropped from GT's range of kits in the late 1980s as the company moved on to produce other buggy kits, and eventually its own very successful GT Buggy design. The Baja GT moulds were sold to a company called Budges Buggies in Chatteris, Cambridgeshire, and the Sahara moulds went to a Greek VW enthusiast, though stayed in the UK. Neither kit has subsequently resurfaced, but the legacy lives on with the few buggies that have survived since the buggy's heyday.

The short-wheelbase Baja GT design was lengthened by GT Mouldings to become the Sahara buggy in the mid-1980s.

Baja GT brochure from GT Mouldings.

33

BARRIS 'T'

DATA PANEL

Production dates
1969-1971

Numbers built
Unknown

Export markets
None

Wheelbase
80in

Identification tips
'T' Roadster or Panel Truck with vintage look, simulated carbide lamps and radiator shell for VW or tube chassis, and a choice of VW running gear or a Corvair engine

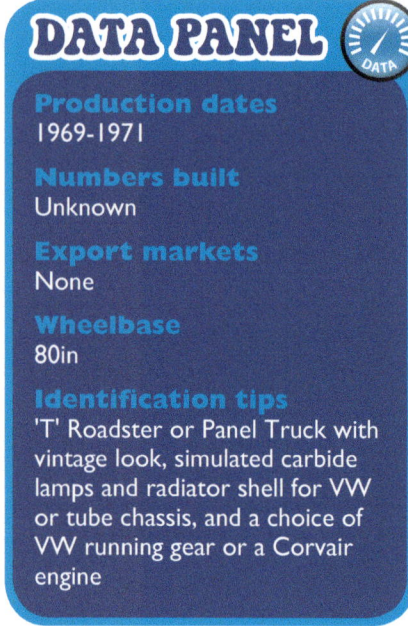

Hollywood customiser George Barris began producing his own 'T' design after building a special buggy for a celebrity customer. (Courtesy Sports Buggies).

George Barris, designer and customiser of vehicles for Hollywood productions, was no stranger to the world of unusual cars. It was no big surprise, therefore, when he was asked to build a buggy for a celebrity customer. Barris soon realised that designing and producing a uniquely-styled buggy would be a shrewd business move, and so the Barris Manufacturing Company of Anaheim, California, soon became involved in the buggy business, beginning production in 1969.

Noting that one of the problems manufacturers faced was distribution of kits, Barris set about establishing a network of franchised distributors to cover most US states. The distributors became an extension of the main factory, and could produce complete kits from moulds duplicated at the Barris company, thereby saving substantially on shipping costs and time. Investment by the franchised distributor was substantial, but included the production moulds and staff training for production and assembly of Barris bodyshells, chassis shortening, and building of customers' vehicles.

Besides manufacturing out-stations, Barris also had ambitious plans to set up a network of 500 retailers. These were franchised under the Barris Sports Center banner, and carried stocks of parts for both his and other dune buggies, as well as having examples of fully-finished cars on display. These retail centers were also equipped to shorten the VW chassis, wire-up dune buggies, or build a vehicle to a customer's specification. The complete retail and distribution program was supported by a heavyweight advertising campaign in automotive and consumer publications, and was a well planned, if ambitious, move into a somewhat volatile marketplace.

Barris and his staff decided to steer away from the traditional-looking buggy style, attempting instead to capture the look of a pseudo-vintage Model T, but brought right up to date with a glitzy makeover. With the option of VW or Corvair powerplants fitted to the standard shortened VW floorpan, or a special lightweight tubular steel chassis, the new Barris 'T' buggy scored a direct hit in the identity stakes. With period-style flat fenders, dropped sides, and a long, sloping front hood capped with a radiator shell, the buggy was a total departure from the usual. Carriage-type front headlights and side lamps adorned the front, and leather straps were added as mock hold-downs for the hood. Similar buckle straps located the trunk lid, which was situated over the engine.

The Roadster body sported a pair of quilted bucket seats, a full-width rear seat, and a well-fitting soft-top that could be folded flat or removed to give open-top motoring. At the rear, a bumper mount provided for a spare tire, which itself was protected by a double bar rear

Models A-Z

bumper. The unique styling was taken a stage further when Barris, encouraged by businesses wanting a sign-written promotional vehicle, developed a full C-Cab hardtop to make the buggy into a panel van. Fully enclosing the buggy, the practical van had two opening side panels and large doors to the box-shaped back, and thus resembled a 'pie-wagon.'

As a development to the basic open-topped buggy theme, the Panel Truck was a very successful styling modification. Barris went on to produce another two-seater design called the 'Fun Buggy,' but it never had the same impact as the audacious 'T' designs. The expectations of the Barris Sport Centers were never fully met, and, with the buggy scene beginning to show signs of faltering, the Barris operation moved back to its Hollywood customising roots, none the worse for its venture into the world of dune buggies.

The Barris 'T' roadster had a pseudo-vintage look with carriage-type lamps, period flat fenders, and a mock radiator shell. (Courtesy Sports Buggies)

To ensure extensive distribution of his kits, Barris sold dealerships and manufacturing rights to other companies under the 'Sports Center' banner, in an ambitious expansion program.

Period photo of Barris employees working on the buggies.

The C-Cab hardtop turned the design into a neat advertising vehicle, or spacious light panel van. The bodyshell fitted a shortened VW floorpan, or a specially built tubular frame chassis developed by Autodynamics.

BERRY MINI-T

DATA PANEL

Production dates
1969-1971

Numbers built
Unknown

Export markets
Belgium

Wheelbase
Mini-T: 80in
Mini-T IV: 94.5in

Identification tips
Roadster-look, with bobbed fenders and flat rear deck area. Four-seater fitted the full-length chassis and featured a hinged engine cover

Drawing inspiration from Henry Ford's 'Tin Lizzy,' the Mini-T was a dune buggy that appealed not only to buggistas, but also hot rodders, classic car enthusiasts, and those who thought the roadster look was just plain cute. Dick Berry Senior, and his son, Dick Junior, first produced the buggy in 1969 at their Berry Plasti-Glass works at Pismo Beach, California, after years of experience acquired constructing specialist glassfiber bodies for the automotive world.

Designed for an 80in wheelbase VW chassis, but with re-sited emergency brake, gearlever and footpedals, and a lengthened steering column, the Mini-T had a flawless glassfiber outer bodyshell of one-piece construction, with an inner cockpit shell bonded in. The method of registering and bonding the two parts for a unitised finish, with continuous color impregnation at the seam, emphasised the quality workmanship that went into the bodyshell. With rich gelcoat colors, a hand lay-up to the first glassfiber layer, plus substantial chopper-gun application to subsequent laminations, the bodies were strong and ripple-free.

The design of the body, with its clamshell 'T' front fenders and bobbed rear fenders, gave the buggy a certain character – if minimal tire coverage. The rear end styling featured a pickup bed which housed the fuel tank and provided a flat area on which to fit a small luggage rack, or lash down a limited amount of luggage. The engine was largely uncovered under the pickup bed, but rear bumpers and fan pulley guards were available to help legalise the exposed back end. The pickup bed came painted in a flat black material to give the illusion of a vinyl tonneau cover over a recessed bed. A flat, chromed, fuel cap sat on the cargo area and gave access to the VW filler neck beneath.

The interior was compact, with a single bench providing seating for three, and matching black Naugahyde quilt-effect side panels. Snap-in carpets were an option, and completed the overall effect of a well-finished car. The dashboard had a basic rectangular instrument panel as part of the one-piece construction, housing the VW speedometer and switches, and

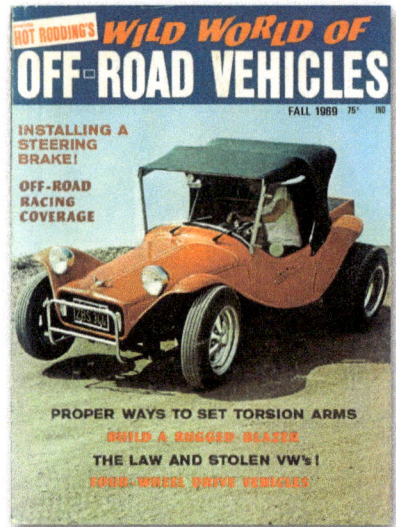

The model's styling crossed the boundaries between hot rod, classic car, and traditional dune buggy design, and it appeared on many magazine covers.

After years of experience in the glassfiber business, Berry Plasti-Glass entered the expanding dune buggy marketplace with the Mini-T.

Models A-Z

Berry advertising emphasised the fun element of the buggy. A four-seater version was added to the range for those whose friends and families didn't want to be left out.

Above: Berry 'T' C-Cab optional hardtop gave more space at the rear of the vehicle, and provided an area for advertising for the enterprising small business. (Courtesy Ed Radlauer)

was finished in the same black, non-reflective paint material as on the rear deck. Ahead of the dashboard sat the vintage-looking windshield in its polished aluminium frame. The outward slant of the frame emphasised the vintage look, and a thin dark stripe running horizontally across the glass (about 4in from the top edge), gave the appearance of a two-piece windshield.

The optional soft-top, in black heavy-duty vinyl, also added to the vintage 'T' appearance, with its single oval rear window and pram-effect top bows. Wind-wings attached to the windshield frame helped keep rain from the vehicle interior if side screens were not used, and the period look was completed by a winged hood ornament that gave the impression of an old Motometer.

Berry introduced a slalom/gymkhana version of the buggy, with a custom-made, wrap-around windshield and a single bucket seat for racers.

By 1970, a removable C-Cab hardtop was added to the range for those requiring more interior space. For families, the Berry Mini-T IV four-seater (a version designed for the full-length VW chassis), also appeared that year. The added length allowed for a proper back seat, separate front seats, and a small ledge for luggage.

The fenders were more all-enclosing for street legality, and the added body length put the fuel tank behind the back seat (with an easy-to-reach filler cap under the new hinged engine cover with its non-functional spare tyre feature).

Although both buggies ceased production in the States, the four-seater found its way to Britain as the Renegade T. A modern-day version called the Roadster-T is still produced by Berrien Buggy in the US.

Berrien Buggy in the US still makes a close copy called the 'Roadster-T.' This eye-catching example was built in the UK.

The period look of the Mini-T was enhanced by the addition of a Motometer, wind-wings, and quilted interior trimming. The buggy was, however, a capable off-roader, and a slalom version of the design was also produced.

BOSS BUG

DATA PANEL

Production dates
1971-1991

Numbers built
Unknown

Export markets
None

Wheelbase
80in

Identification tips
Recessed scoops on front hood; Boss Bug emblems; sculpted side panels and wood-grain effect dashboard insert on vinyl glassfiber dashboard

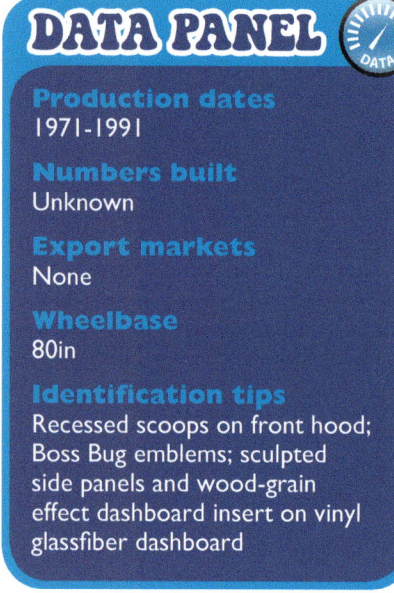

Boss Bug advert from 1971. The design remained in production for 20 years, over which time most other traditional dune buggy manufacturers disappeared.

With many pirate manufacturers climbing on the 1960s buggy bandwagon, and producing sub-standard glassfiber kits, the Boss Bug from Perfect Plastics Industries of New Kensington, Philadelphia, made a pleasant change. Introduced to the Stateside scene somewhat later in the day than most other manufacturers' offerings (during early 1971), the Boss Bug was designed for ease of assembly, and to a standard that was unusually high within the kit-car industry.

Although traditionally styled, the new buggy did, however, have many individual points of its own. One immediately noticeable feature was the front hood design, which comprised a pair of recessed scoops situated toward the windshield end. These allowed the windshield wiper mounts to sit lower on the front hood than was possible on most buggies, and the central ridge between the scoops provided a useful location for the washer nozzle. A Boss Bug emblem and the fuel filler were positioned at the very front of the hood.

The leather-grain moulded dashboard, in black or white, was pre-bonded to the hood to prevent annoying rattles, and a wood-grained instrument panel – which fitted neatly onto the dashboard fascia – gave the buggy a production car look. The heavy-duty glassfiber bodyshell was designed for the shortened VW chassis, and came in either plain or metalflake gelcoat finish. The bodyshell was completely finished with a black body undercoat to prevent stone-chip damage and give a quality finish.

Available as a complete 'A' kit, the package included the bodyshell and front hood, headlight shells and parking lights, windshield, and a complete hardware kit. The value-for-money package also included a pair of heavy-duty glassfiber, low-back bucket seat shells, Boss Bug emblems, and the requisite frame shortening and assembly instructions. A 'B' kit was also available for those working to a limited budget, and this comprised the body and front hood only.

So that buggy builders could put together an economical fun car that was well finished and fully 'streetable,' the manufacturer also offered a long list of optional extras. Top of the list of things needed to meet the strict requirements for road registration and state inspections was a pair of sculpted side panels. These perfectly complemented the overall style of the buggy, and sat below the fenders and body waistline, creating proper front and rear wheelarches.

Another thoughtful addition was a glassfiber engine cover that sat on the rear deck of the body to allow clearance on tall carburettors, such as Holleys. Options

Models A-Z

for completing the interior included front seat covers, and a rear seat finished in either a custom stitched design, or a deep-buttoned, deluxe Naugahyde leather-grain finish. Custom-fit carpets with a sewn-in vinyl gearshift trunk were also available, and a scuff pad could be snapped into the interior for extra comfort.

A convertible top in black or white material could also be had, together with zippered side curtains made of sewn-in clear vinyl material, and a large rear window with zippers. Alternatively, a smart hardtop could be fitted, the deluxe version of which had mounting hardware and chrome gutter trim already fitted.

Perfect Plastics put great emphasis on the quality of its products, factory inspection of all kits, and materials used in construction. Billed as the "kit that fits," the Boss Bug (and the long-wheelbase Renegade 'T'-inspired Tuff Tub kits) were certainly well thought out. Brochures even included a reprinted Gene Booth article from the spring 1968 edition of *Dune Buggies and Hot VWs* on "Good glass and how to get it" – an ethos that PPI adhered to during the Boss Bug's long production life.

The Boss Bug by Perfect Plastics was designed to be easy to build, and manufactured to a very high standard.

Brochure cover showing the distinctive front hood design of the buggy with its recessed scoops, forward-mounted fuel filler cap and Boss Bug emblem. The company also manufactured the Tuff Tub kit for the full-length VW chassis.

The basic kit came with the option of a convertible top or a glassfiber hardtop. The range of available optional extras included interior panels, custom-fit carpets, and deep-buttoned seats.

BOUNTY HUNTER

DATA PANEL

Production dates
1969-1971

Numbers built
Unknown

Export markets
France, England

Wheelbase
80in

Identification tips
Ultra-low, sleek sports buggy, with sharply angled front hood and Renault Dauphine windshield. Inbuilt front headlights mounted into fenders. Optional low hardtop and wide side panels.

At a time when most buggy designs were uninspired copies, the only solution to the quest for individuality was to design and build your own. Brian Dries, a buggy enthusiast whose love of these vehicles began whilst watching many of the early dune buggies racing at Pismo beach, initially built himself a traditional-looking, Corvair-powered buggy on a 1965 VW chassis. Parked outside a muffler shop in Burbank, California, a chance meeting with automotive designer and industrial prototype maker Mel Keys led to conversations about building their own design. The two got on well, and they decided to go into partnership to build an all-new design of buggy, just to have one each.

Starting with another Manx clone kit as a base, Keys produced a mock-up in wood and plaster in the backyard of his home. Taking about six months in their spare time, Key's and Dries' dramatic new design was finished in early 1969. The sleek new design was visually well-balanced and less buggy than sports car. Using a curved and very raked windshield taken from a late 1950s Renault Dauphine car mounted in cast aluminium posts, the buggy was christened the Bounty Hunter.

The sleek and low bodyshell was longer than most designs and had an angled, almost pointed, front hood, and a curvaceous fenderline throughout. Unusually for a buggy, the front headlamps were built into pods, which formed part of the sweeping front fender mouldings. These enhanced the racecar look, and gave the appearance of a low front end. The rear of the bodyshell featured the traditional-looking fender cut-ins, which also gave a neat styling touch to the ultra-low glassfibre hardtop, which was a later addition to the design. To provide adequate occupant headroom with the hardtop fitted, the front seats were mounted low in a reclined position, and the rollbar set in a tilted-back configuration towards the rear.

With a mould made, and quickly realising the potential of their creation, Keys and Dries set up in business to meet the orders of those who had persuaded them to reproduce their design. Rather

Problems for the blue metalflake Bounty Hunter used in the 1968 film *The Big Bounce*, directed by Alex March and starring Ryan O'Neal and Leigh Taylor-Young. (Courtesy BFI/Copyright Warner Bros)

Models A-Z

The aerodynamic lines of the Bounty Hunter, with inbuilt headlamps and smooth side panels, gave the impression of motion even whilst stationary. (Courtesy Mike Key)

A French Bounty Hunter buggy finished in a faultless metallic red paint and powered by the powerful VW Type 4 engine – a favourite conversion in Europe.

than laminating kits themselves, production was subcontracted to Glassco in Van Nuys, a company better known for producing Catalina fibreglass boats. Metalflake kits were made for $195 apiece. By retailing them at $295 and turning a $100 profit, Keys and Dries received $50 each for little work. Just five Bounty Hunter bodies were produced by Glassco before Dries decided he wanted to further improve the design and produce the bodies himself. Keys didn't want to go into the dune buggy business, and was busy with full time work at Production Models (where he sculpted the 11-foot long model of the USS Enterprise used in the *Star Trek* TV show), and so the partnership was dissolved. Dries went on to establish Glass Enterprises of Burbank to market the revised kit until 1971.

The buggy soon attracted the attention of film producers, too, and a glistening blue Metalflake Bounty Hunter became a star in the 1968 Warner Bros movie *The Big Bounce*, starring Ryan O'Neal and Leigh Taylor-Young.

The Bounty Hunter has continued to make its presence felt in the Volkswagen scene, even to the present day. Enthusiasts in both France and the UK have reproduced the buggy, some 40 years after the original appeared, and the Bounty Hunter design also became the basis for two other buggies, the Deserter GT and the Renegade, which have their own sections in this book.

Under the name of Glass Enterprises of Burbank, Brian Dries began production of his neat buggy design with a low hardtop, inbuilt headlamps, and smooth side panels.

British-built Bounty Hunter in the sun at a buggy convention.

BUGETTA

DATA PANEL

Production dates
1968-1970

Numbers built
150 (approx)

Export markets
UK

Wheelbase
82in

Identification tips
Low-slung body covering wide racing wheels and tyres, with pod-mounted headlamps on front hood. Lightweight monocoque chassis with aluminum panels, and VW or Corvair suspension, transaxle and engine

The glassfiber buggy was originally conceived as a dual-purpose vehicle, suitable for either highway or off-road use, although, from the outset, many of the buggies were intended only for use on the road. Immediately, Corvair-powered vehicles began to make an impact on the buggy scene, as the Chevrolet six-cylinder, air-cooled powerplant had greater power and reliability than the VW engine, and parts were readily available in the US.

Builders rapidly began to find ways of utilising not only the Corvair engine, but the drivetrain and suspension components, too. Two early platform-type frames for Corvair buggies were the Con-vair, from Con-Ferr, and the Manx-vair from Meyers. Designed to take a complete Corvair rear end, including engine, transaxle and suspension, the frames could also be fitted with either a Corvair or the more familiar VW front suspension. Both had 80in wheelbases and could accept most of the glassfiber bodies designed for the shortened VW chassis. Some body modifications were usually necessary to accommodate the Corvair rear suspension, and Meyers made a special version of the Manx buggy to fit its 'Vair frame.

Other buggy designs, such as the Sand Shark and the Otto Kross I by Auto Craft, also used Manx-styled bodies on special frames. The Otto Kross even mounted the Corvair engine ahead of the transaxle, similar to the design of a contemporary sportscar. Recognising the trend toward powerful road-going buggies, Jerry Eisert, a veteran Indianapolis racecar builder and Group 7 vehicle designer, decided to build his own buggy in 1968, in his Eisert Racing Enterprises workshop in Costa Mesa, California. Putting his

Period advertising for the Bugetta, with the emphasis on the buggy being available as a turn-key car and not just a kit. This approach highlighted the growing trend for more sophisticated vehicles that was to pave the way for the modern kit-car scene.

Models A-Z

meticulous craftsmanship to work, he built the Bugetta, a rear-engined, Corvair-powered buggy with a special monocoque chassis designed to give stable high speed handling characteristics on the road. Built up from formed aluminum panels riveted together into a lightweight, but extremely strong, structure, around the steel monocoque, the 82in wheelbase Bugetta was sleek and good-looking. The low lines and wide fenders, covering low-profile tyres, gave the buggy a sportscar appearance.

Initially, the Bugetta was only available as a complete vehicle, using new Chevrolet components and carrying a factory warranty. The front suspension was fully independent and adjustable, using Eisert-designed A-arms connected to Corvair spindles. Early coil shock units were soon replaced by double transverse torsion bars, and steering was courtesy of an Eisert-manufactured rack and pinion. Late model, fully independent Corvair rear suspension components were used at the rear, whilst brakes were stock '69 Corvair drums. The engine was any standard Corvair unit with 4-speed, all-synchro or Powerglide, automatic transmission.

The bodyshell could accommodate four passengers in comfort, and the interior was well finished. The rear seat could also be removed to give additional storage space. The low windshield and special aluminum wheels emphasised the race look, and the 25-gallon front fuel tank gave long-range driving ability.

Other versions of the Bugetta were also made for those who already had VW running gear, or wished to mix and match the suspension units and engine. These kits used the same monocoque chassis and glassfiber bodyshell, but could run either VW front and Corvair rear, or VW suspension all round, plus the VW transaxle, engine, steering and brakes.

Whatever the make-up, most Bugettas stayed as street machines, although some were off-roaded, most notably in the 1968 Mexican 1000 race.

With an optional soft-top, or glassfiber hardtop and full bumpers, the Bugetta was an eye-catching design; one that paved the way for other vehicles, and also inspired the British-made Bugle buggy.

The Bugetta could accommodate four in comfort. The interior was fully quilted in black Naugahyde, and, with a fully-fitted carpet, the general impression was of a luxury sportscar. (Courtesy Road Test/Dune Buggy)

The Bugetta had all the engineering hallmarks of a Group 7 racecar, together with an aerodynamic bodyshell that covered the ultra-wide wheels and tyres.

Designed by Jerry Eisert as a road-going sportscar, the Bugetta buggy used Chevrolet Corvair running gear and the Corvair flat-6, air-cooled engine. (Courtesy Bob McClurg)

43

BUGLE & BUGLE 2

DATA PANEL

Production dates
1970-1972/1980-2009

Numbers built
850 Bugles
20 Bugle Plus2s
15 Bugle2s

Export markets
America, Saudi Arabia, Malta, Portugal, Cyprus, Jordan, Sardinia, Switzerland

Wheelbase
78.5in Bugle
94.5in Bugle Plus2
82.5in Bugle2

Identification tips
One-piece body with inset sloping Beetle headlights, wide wheelarches and a rear trunk area in a squared-off back end. Often fitted with a fixed rear screen in fiberglass housing

With London in the grip of a youth revolution in the late 1960s, there was a large and expanding market for a trendsetting vehicle that could take the place of the late-lamented Kings Road cruiser, the Mini-Moke.

Sensing an opportunity, entrepreneur Roland Sharman set up a company to build luxury buggies for the rich and famous using GP buggy kits. The Sharman Drag Co Ltd produced complete cars with full trim, carpets and soft-tops, and sold them under the name of Bugle Buggies. Following the demise of this original company, Sharman's newly-formed Bugle Automotive Traction and Manufacturing Company of London Ltd continued to sell road-going fun cars from premises in the crypt under St Jude's Church in West London.

Despite a second financial embarrassment, Sharman managed by early 1970 to obtain financial backing, and had researched the needs of the British buggy-buying public. As a result, his own buggy design, the Bugle, came into being (bearing more than a passing resemblance to the American Bugetta buggy produced by Jerry Eisert). The name 'Bugle' came from Sharman's wife, who thought that the American-made Andeck Brute exhaust pipes looked like bugles at the rear. The new design was moulded at Sheerness by a sub-contractor, and was a distinguished and different style to the all-too-familiar shape of the traditional buggy.

Moulded in a range of metalflake colors, the Bugle had a well-made unitised bodyshell, with a fuel tank ready-moulded into it between the rear bulkhead and the small trunk area. This was soon changed, for reasons of safety and legality, for a proper metal tank with a racing-style filler cap. The body was a pure two-seater, fitted with an alloy-framed windshield and a neat, Targa-style, glassfiber rollbar surround, into which was fitted a smoked plexiglass rear screen.

This unusual screen arrangement allowed the soft-top and sidescreens to fit between the two, whilst keeping out the elements. The Bugle also allowed

The Bugle buggy was designed by Roland Sharman as his first step toward becoming a 'proper' car manufacturer. This is one of the later Bugle 2s.

Models A-Z

wide wheels to be fitted without the problems of tire coverage associated with most British buggies. The rear wheelarches could legally accommodate up to 14in wheels, and Bugle Automotive was an agent for the very desirable chromed slot wheels from Rocket Wheel Industries of California. Headlights for the Bugle were standard sloping VW Beetle units, which looked right at home in the pods on the sweeping front hood.

Working under the new name of Lotusmere, and with production switched to a large factory in Reading, Roland Sharman attempted his most ambitious sales plan yet by signing up a string of 115 dealers across the country. With sales fired by the front cover appearance of a Bugle buggy on Motor magazine in 1970, the kit was developed into a long-wheelbase version called the Bugle Plus 2, to maximise its potential. Featuring proper seating for four people, and a new lockable glassfiber trunk lid instead of the previous tonneau cover, the Bugle seemed to have a bright future.

Despite coming close to a deal with Volkswagen to sell complete Bugle buggies on brand new chassis, the project faltered in 1971 when financial backing was withdrawn. After one last attempt to relaunch the buggy in late 1971, trading as Bugle Marketing and Development, Sharman finally called it a day, and the Bugle was left in the wilderness until production was restarted in the 1980s by Chris Watson's Yorkshire-based garage, C W Autos.

Produced for many years by buggy stalwart GT Mouldings, and called the Bugle 2 in a revised format for a 12in shortened chassis, the project was taken on by Bugle enthusiasts Tony and Rob Armstrong in the mid-noughties, but has slipped out of production again in recent years.

In its true element, a Bugle takes to the beach during a British buggy convention. The design used stock VW Beetle headlights, and a rear-mounted, metal fuel tank sited between the back bulkhead and trunk area.

Above, left: Full-page advert from the Bugle Automotive Traction & Manufacturing Company of London Ltd. At the height of the buggy boom, Bugle adverts were icons of the British buggy scene, and have never been bettered.

Above: The October 1970 issue of Motor magazine did much to promote the Bugle, and the whole British buggy scene generally.

Promotional photo of The Bugle – a distinctive two-seater buggy, with metalflake finish, a fixed rear glassfiber screen frame, plexiglass screen, and a small trunk area.

BUSHMASTER

DATA PANEL

Production dates
1968-1970

Numbers built
200 (approx)

Export markets
None

Wheelbase
80in

Identification tips
Flat-sided bodyshell with interchangeable front hoods taking either inbuilt VW headlights or grille-mounted units. Variety of side panels and optional gull-wing hardtop

The body styling of the Bushmaster was flatter than most, but wide cutaway fenders allowed maximum wheel travel on rough terrain (Courtesy Chan Bush)

Following in the footsteps of Texan Carroll Shelby, who named his sportscar Cobra after the snake, Rob Robertson of Austin, Texas, decided to call his new design of dune buggy the Bushmaster after a similarly deadly reptile. With the aid of a professional designer, Robertson's buggy was built to be a functional off-roader, constructed from the best quality materials, and available to customers at an affordable price.

The Bushmaster Company developed the buggy in late 1968 for the typical 80in wheelbase VW chassis. Using a hand lay-up method of glassfiber construction, the bodies were of excellent quality, and even used light-resistant gelcoat colors to prevent fading. The design was totally original, with wide, cutaway fenders and a flatter body section than most buggies. One of the neat features of the Bushmaster range was the interchangeable front hood designs. On the standard body, the headlights were stock VW units mounted in the leading edge of the hood. A sports version changed the hood to one with the headlights mounted low in a recessed grille.

The appearance of the buggy sides could also be altered using a variety of different side panel mouldings available from the company. This mix-and-match approach gave the builder a vast choice of options, from something totally utilitarian to a sleek sports buggy. Interior-wise, a flat instrument housing sat in the centre of the dashboard behind the alloy windshield, and seating was provided for two adults in the front, with room for two medium-sized children in the rear on the flat seat area.

A range of soft-tops or hardtops was available for the same basic body. The soft-top was a folding affair, with side curtains made to fit over the rollbar, and was fully removable in good weather. For those living in colder states, the much more exciting hardtop fully enclosed the buggy, and gave it something of a Grand Touring appearance. With swing-up gull-wing doors, the stylish hardtop captured the classic design of the Mercedes 300-SL coupé, making entry into the buggy surprisingly easy. Made of strong, low-weight, woven glassfiber cloth, the pre-colored top could also be fitted with sliding plexiglass windows, mounted in the forward-hinging side screen frames. At the rear, a full-width plexiglass window opened upward, in a similar fashion to that on a stationwagon. Hinged at the top, the screen fastened at the bottom corners with two push-button-type fasteners when not in use.

The whole ensemble could be removed from the bodyshell when not needed. The top made the Bushmaster a more acceptable design to the wide range of customers looking for weather protection in the not-so-sunny states, especially when used in conjunction with the original VW heating system.

Models A-Z

The Bushmaster was available as a complete kit, together with a pre-shortened chassis, and a range of accessories which included the top options, a rollbar and a steel skidpan for serious off-roading. Alternatively, the basic body kit could be supplied on its own for those who wished to fabricate items themselves, and could also shorten the floorpan.

With clean and simple lines, and a plethora of options which included a full tube frame chassis built to take VW components, the Bushmaster was all things to all men. However, as the world moved on, this buggy got left behind (as so many did), and few examples seem to have survived.

Bushmaster's option and accessory catalog was so extensive you could practically design your own bespoke buggy: anything from a utilitarian pickup truck, to a highly desirable, sleek, gull-wing GT coupé. (Courtesy Chan Bush)

The Bushmaster buggy appearance could be altered by changing the front hood and adding side panels. The design was fully road legal, and was equally at home off-road. (Courtesy Chan Bush)

Driver Rob Robertson gets all four Bushmaster wheels off the ground in a 1969 off-road race. (Courtesy Eric Rickman)

Period advertising for the Bushmaster, showing the many options available. The basic bodyshell remained the same, with hoods, hardtops and side panels all changeable.

BUSHWHACKER

DATA PANEL

Production dates
1968-1970

Numbers built
800 (approx)

Export markets
Hawaii, Miami, Puerto Rico and Jamaica

Wheelbase
80in

Identification tips
Curved body style with sweeping shovel-nose front hood. Stand-up headlights, and centrally-mounted driving light at front. Kicked-up back with flat panel for rear lights and licence plate. Curved side panels

During the early days of the dune buggy, one of the biggest problems for designers of original buggy styles was piracy. Bruce Meyers, with his Meyers Manx, was not alone in experiencing such problems: two other such 'victims' were architect Don Haskin and business manager Max Becker, who were partners in various car businesses in America in the late 1960s. Their first venture, between 1966 and 67 under the name of Phoenix Automotive, was the production of a kit car called the Shrike, based on the full-size VW 1600 Squareback/Fastback chassis. Only four were made before a failed business deal ended the car's production.

Undeterred, between 1967 and 68 Haskin and Becker established 'The Bug House' in Studio City, California, where they produced and sold aftermarket VW products under the Intac Inc name. These included some of the first glassfiber panels for the VW Beetle, and flip-fronts that were later copied for the booming Baja Bug industry of the day. By 1968, the pair had begun developing their own dune buggy. Under the new name of KDM Enterprises, and based in North Holywood, Haskin chose to craft a streamlined sports buggy rather than a Manx clone. Styled with 'Coke bottle' curves like a Ferrari 330 P4, the design capitalised on the vogue in automotive design for curved body shapes. Haskin's love of period hot rods ensured the new design ended up as an odd mix of sports car looks with a higher-at-the-back hot rod roof. Designed to fit a shortened chassis, and featuring a sweeping and dramatically long front hood, the new Bushwhacker buggy was styled more for street than with any pretention to off-road driving. At the very front of the hood was a small indentation designed to accept a VW Squareback reversing light, which was wired as an additional driving light. The design was also the first to use integrated side pods.

Haskin started selling kits but, with US President Johnson relaxing the patent laws to promote business at the time, another supplier named Sand Chariots in Fullerton, California, was quick to copy the design. Dubbed the Ocelot, the most noticeable difference was a shorter front hood. The move was so swift that both the Bushwhacker and the Ocelot made

The first Bushwhacker promotional theme shot for car rental at Hilton hotels ultimately didn't get approval, but was an interesting concept, nevertheless. (Courtesy David Haskin)

Models A-Z

The Bushwhacker buggy was designed from scratch, rather than being a Manx clone, and was one of the first buggies to use side panels. (Courtesy David Haskin)

The design was quickly copied as the 'Ocelot' buggy, and both vehicles appeared in the very same issue of Dune Buggies and Hot VWs magazine. (Courtesy David Haskin)

their debut in the same August 1968 issue of *Dune Buggies and Hot VWs* magazine. An even closer copy of the Bushwhacker named the Ocelot S/S (for Super/Sport) subsequently appeared, with the curves of the original perfectly replicated, apart from removal of the front-mounted central light, and reshaping of the bottom of the dashboard to a more squared-off design.

The deception annoyed designer Haskin so much that he immediately pulled his Bushwhacker kit from the market and, instead, moved into the production of turn-key street-legal cars for rental in resort areas such as Hawaii, Miami, Puerto Rico and Jamaica. In 1969, the company supplied no fewer than 500 units, making it the seventh largest car maker in the US, and requiring the buggy to pass basic legal safety tests. The rental car theme was metalflake colors with pinstriping, Hawaiian print tops and sand-colored interiors. The Bushwhacker logo was a kangaroo wearing goggles and holding a flower, hand-painted on the buggy front hood.

The Hilton hotel chain was one of the first major customers to use the Bushwhacker rental buggies in Hawaii, and about 50 were covered in big rainbow stickers – the Hilton Hotel logo at the time – with a big 'H' on the front hood. It was hardly surprising that the makers of Jimi Hendrix's movie *Rainbow Bridge* decided to rent and use one of the buggies in the guitarist's film being shot in Hawaii.

The Bushwhacker story is one of many whereby US patent laws that were once designed to protect innovative new businesses were ultimately to stack the odds against the entrepreneur. The Haskin and Becker creation may have long since gone, but the designers survived the cutthroat days of the 1970s unscathed.

Flower power tops, metalflake paint and custom pinstriping were all part of the color scheme for rental car buggies. (Courtesy David Haskin)

Bushwhacker manufacturer KDM Enterprises became the 7th largest auto maker in the US after it entered the car rental market in Hawaii, Miami, Puerto Rico and Jamaica. (Courtesy Mel Baker)

49

CLAIMJUMPER

DATA PANEL

Production dates
1968-1971

Numbers built
500 (approx)

Export markets
None

Wheelbase
80in-85in

Identification tips
One-piece bodyshell with inset front headlights, wide, tall fenders and low flyscreen. Later version had full windshield, fitted side panels, and headlights mounted from behind the bodywork

One of the pioneers of dune running in the US was Scott McKenzie, a sportscar racer in the mid-1950s, and lifelong driver of off-road desert Jeeps. By 1959 he had designed a VW-powered, jeep-type off-roader called the Chimp, and eventually built a total of ten of these vehicles for other 'trail rodders.' In 1961, McKenzie built a VW-based, Corvair-powered off-roader which was a successful competition vehicle. Realising the potential of building such vehicles for others, he founded his Sandmaster Company in 1966 in North Hollywood, California, just as the market for glassfiber buggies blossomed.

Meanwhile, seasoned racer Don Arnett wanted to enter the gruelling Stardust 7-11 race, and had specific design ideas for a buggy that could withstand the punishing cross-country enduro. Arnett and McKenzie joined forces to produce the glassfiber-bodied Claimjumper purely for racing. The body was 23in longer than that of the usual sports-type buggy, designed so that the rear spoiler would cover the Corvair engine, which was fitted with six Weber carburettors with modified air cleaners. Corvair rear suspension could also be fitted, and the wheelarches were higher than on most vehicles (to cater for the tall tyres and suspension travel during punishing off-roading).

With the body moulded in one piece in a combination of hand lay-up and chopper-gun techniques, the glassfiber was very strong. Up front, the headlights were recessed, not only for a cleaner look, but also for their protection. The slanting front hood gave the driver a clear view forward, and a small flyscreen gave minimal protection against dust and dirt entering the interior. A double competition rollbar and Nevada canvas top provided safety, and protection from the sun. Proving the quality of the vehicle's design and construction, the Don Arnett-driven Claimjumper took second place in its class on its first outing, and paved the way for a production version.

Sporting even taller fenders, and a rear area set up to carry cargo or small seats for two extra people, the Claimjumper entered production in 1968, becoming part of the huge off-road inventory of parts and accessories offered by the Sandmaster company. Much of the company's promotion budget was spent on racing cars, rather than placing advertisements, but the buggy was so successful that it was never short of customers. Sandmaster also sponsored several drivers in off-road events, such as hill climbing, desert racing and sand dragging. The production Claimjumpers fitted a variety of wheelbases from 80in to 85in, to allow greater flexibility for individual chassis set-ups in racing or engine

As well as the Claimjumper, Sandmaster also produced the Hustler, with even greater success than its predecessor. The neat and purposeful aluminum-skinned body made for a lightweight racer in off-road competition. (Courtesy Charles E Nerpel)

Models A-Z

requirements. The shortened 80in VW floorpan was the standard road choice.

By late 1970, modifications to the design brought an all-new Claimjumper bodyshell, designed principally for road use. With an 84in wheelbase, the new body had more room for rear seat passengers, and faired-in side panels to finish the previously exposed sides. Headlights were changed to fully enclosed (and legal) sealed beam pod-mounted units. These were fixed to the front shock absorber mounts and appeared through cast-in openings in the front of the fenders. A full windshield and VW windshield wiper assemblies were other concessions to road use. Tail lights were taken from the 1963 Pontiac Tempest and fitted the bodies perfectly.

As the company became more involved in racing buggies, its other design, the Hustler, overtook the Claimjumper in importance, particularly as rail-type buggy designs were more in vogue. Although the Claimjumper eventually disappeared, it did prove itself a worthy racer in its short lifetime.

With its emphasis on racing, Sandmaster's advertising also promoted the success of the Claimjumper in serious competition. The company also stocked a huge range of off-road parts for all types of VW-based racing buggies.

Scott McKenzie was one of the founding fathers of the off-road movement in the US. He built numerous trail cars before combining forces with Don Arnett to produce the Claimjumper buggy purely to race in the Stardust 7-11 enduro. (Courtesy Charles E Nerpel)

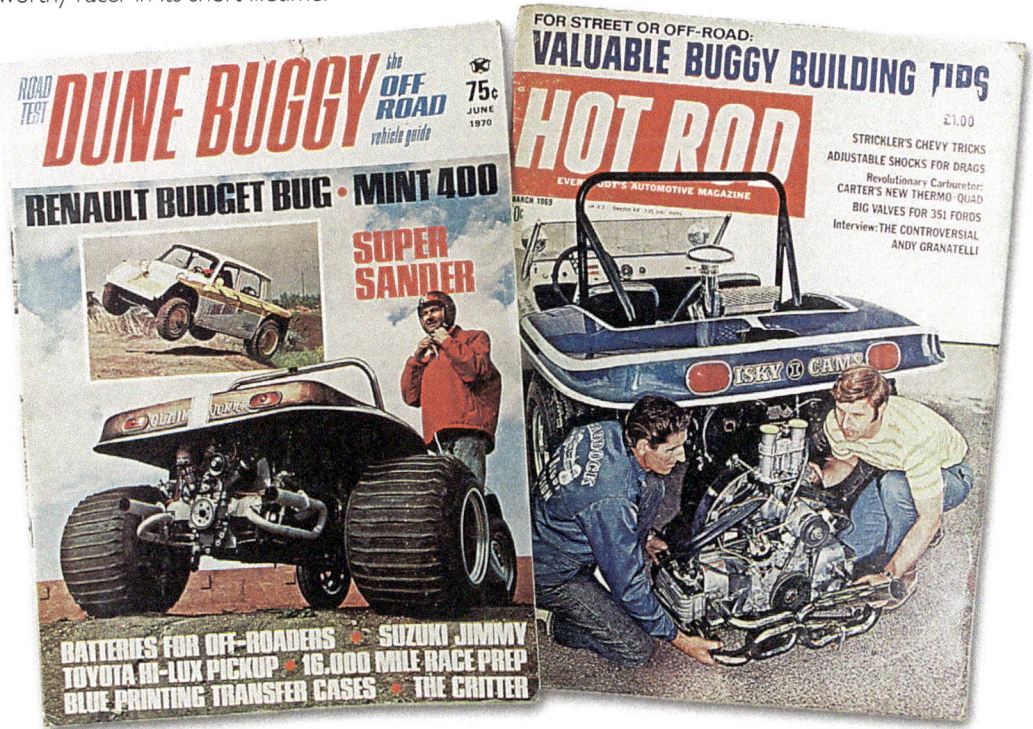

As a competition vehicle, the Claimjumper made several appearances on the front covers of contemporary magazines, including Hot Rod and Road Test Dune Buggy.

51

DESERTER SERIES 1, GS & GT

DATA PANEL

Production dates
US: 1967-1971
Germany: 1975-1983

Numbers built
1250 (approx)

Export markets
Worldwide

Wheelbase
GS: 85in GT: 84in

Identification tips
Originally a Manx-inspired body (Series 1) with greater engine and tire coverage. The GS added a mid-engine configuration and full space frame. The GT was an updated Bounty Hunter design with VW or space frame chassis.

Having been refused a Manx dealership on the grounds that a VW agent had already been given the licence in Massachusetts, skilled engineer and sportscar enthusiast Alex Dearborn decided instead to manufacture his own buggy. Called the Deserter, the design was developed in 1967 for racing at SCCA (Sports Car Club of America) events in 1968. Similar to the ubiquitous Meyers Manx, but with a longer 84in wheelbase to the VW chassis, and a certain amount of road legalisation to meet strict eastern US vehicle codes, the Series 1 car began to sell well.

Based at Marblehead, Massachusetts, the Dearborn Automobile Co quickly developed a line of accessories for other Deserter owners who wanted to run their buggies in road races. The glassfiber bodies for the Deserter buggies were supplied by next-door neighbour Autodynamics Inc, the largest racecar manufacturer in the US at the time, owned and run by friends Ray Caldwell and Fred Jackson. This allowed Dearborn access to full manufacturing facilities for the Deserter, so its chassis tuning – rather than sheer horsepower – could be developed to outpace not only other lookalike buggies from California, but other sportscars, too. For race events, such as one held at Lime Rock in 1968, the Deserter tore into the competition of bigger machinery – Lolas and Sting-Rays – and enjoyed considerable success.

In 1970, Autodynamics acquired Dearborn's company and continued with development and production of the VW-based Deserter. plus a new offering, the Deserter GS (the initials standing for 'Grand Slalom.') The GS used an Autodynamics-built tubular space frame, instead of the VW chassis, and had a wheelbase of 85in. The chassis was designed to carry a stock Corvair or Porsche 911/912 engine, giving it a power-to-weight ratio better than any sportscar, yet the bodyshell was virtually identical to the original Deserter. Autodynamics' experience in Group 7 racing, combined with development of the original car, had produced a buggy which

With the addition of an Autodynamics tubular chassis, the Deserter became a serious racing vehicle with mid-mounted Corvair or Porsche 911/912 engine, and was re-named the Deserter GS. (Courtesy Alex Dearborn)

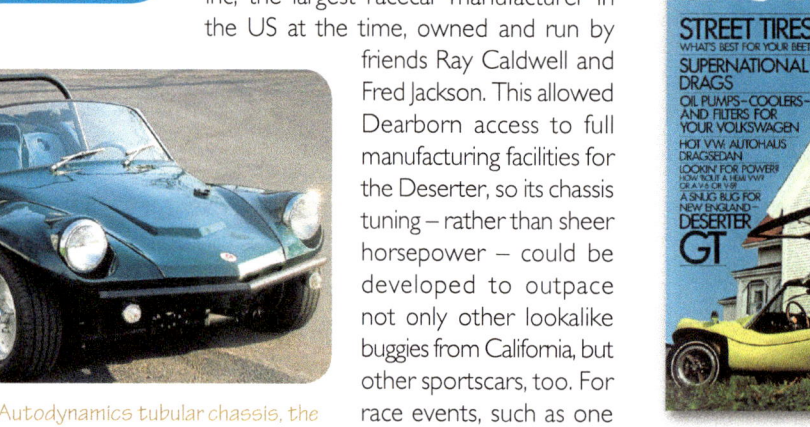

The Deserter GT was a cover star of many magazines, including *Dune Buggies and Hot VWs*.

was more rigid than other contemporary buggies, offered better weight distribution, and could successfully compete in autocross. The Deserter GS came as individual parts (a comprehensive kit with no welding necessary), or race-ready as required. All the kit builder needed to do was add the engine, VW transaxle and front end. With a top speed of well over 120mph, the new buggy could out-accelerate, out-corner and out-brake practically anything on the road, and at a fraction of the cost.

Dearborn became Caldwell's marketing director during the same year. When the Autodynamics organisation became involved in a contract to run the Dodge factory-sponsored Trans-Am vehicles, Dearborn contacted Brian Dries, designer of the Bounty Hunter buggy, and made arrangements to build the car in a modified format for East Coast distribution. This legitimate deal was a sign of the integrity of the Autodynamics corporation, and a tribute to the originality of the Dries design.

Relaunched as the Deserter GT with an 84in wheelbase, and mounted to the VW chassis, the buggy was 6in longer overall than the Bounty Hunter and, with a gull-wing hardtop also developed from the original design, sported a low, mean look. The doors were hinged at the centre and used support struts to hold them up for easy entry and exit. They could also be fully removed for a 'T'-top appearance.

With the sliding windows closed, the Deserter was a fully-enclosed sportscar with high-speed handling qualities. The GS space frame could also be added for those looking for the ultimate performance buggy that could go as fast as it looked like it should.

With the loss of the Dodge racing contract, Autodynamics underwent an extensive reorganisation and moved into other, non-racecar markets. Although the Deserter GT disappeared suddenly from the Stateside buggy scene, it did have a second life in Europe and was produced in Basle by Autodynamics Europe, but the rights to produce the VW-based kit were eventually bought by Autohaus Kuhn in Germany as an addition to its other buggy kit, the Hazard, during the 1980s. The Dearborn Automobile Company Inc still exists to this day, however, with Alex Dearborn at the helm working on classic car restoration.

The Deserter was a traditional-looking buggy, but with an 84in wheelbase and greater tire and engine body coverage to meet eastern US legislation. (Courtesy Alex Dearborn)

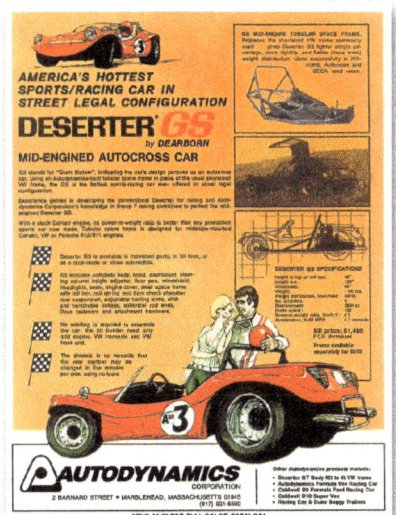

Left: This 1970s Deserter GT advertisement shows the ultimate development of the buggy when Dearborn licensed the Bounty Hunter design for US east coast production.

The Deserter GT continued in production in Europe long after it disappeared from the Stateside buggy scene, and was shown at 'Autosalon' at the Geneva Motor Show in 1969. (Courtesy *Custom Car*)

Left: Deserter brochure, showing the wide range of kit options and parts available.

DOON

DATA PANEL

Production dates
2001-date

Numbers built
SWB: 18 LWB: 32

Export markets
Morocco, Belgium, Holland

Wheelbase
79.2in

Identification tips
Very modern design with return lip to body edges, opening front hood, dashboard panel integrated to panel beneath hood, headlamps fixed to recess mouldings in front fenders, wiring ducts along both sides and across the rear body tub

A trio of Doon buggies at the British Volkswagen Festival at Malvern. (Courtesy Chad Chadwick)

First introduced to the UK in 2001, the Doon buggy was the brainchild of Simon 'Chad' Chadwick and Richard Crees. The two work colleagues, who worked in the Traffic and Road Safety section of a local council in the West Midlands, had both owned buggies and had experienced first-hand the deficiencies of the designs. Intent on making their own buggy, they had firstly been tempted by the chance to buy the moulds of the GP buggy in May 1999. The moulds, however, were in poor condition so instead, the pair opted to design their own kit from scratch. The Doon name came from the Black Country pronunciation of the word 'dune,' and allowed for the design of a distinctive two-wheeled logo of the new buggy.

During the summer of 1999, the pair bought a couple of old buggy shells, intending to create a hybrid glassfiber shape from which to take a mould. This idea was soon shelved, and instead an all-new pattern was created from MDF board. The intention was to produce a fresh, modern take on the traditional buggy, and eliminate some of the poor design elements of other designs. Styled for a shortened chassis, the new buggy was to have an opening front hood, with the battery positioned beneath it to improve weight distribution and security. The body was also to have wide rear fenders to legally cover wide wheels and take twin carburettors. By August 2000, the basic shape of the new buggy was complete. With return lips to the body edges, the new buggy was designed with strength and safety in mind, but required a complex set of bolt-together moulds to produce it. The final pattern was produced with the help of ex-Westfield laminator John Spratt, before a splash mould was taken and a glassfiber pattern produced for further refinement.

With the plug completed and sprayed in early 2001, production moulds were taken and the first new body formed. This made its debut at the Beach Buggy Bonanza 3 and West of England Kit Car Show event at Malvern in August of that year. Initial sales were slow, and after the first three kits were produced in 2001, no orders came in 2002. Sales started slowly in 2003 after Doon was commissioned to produce a featured build car for *Volksworld* magazine during 2003 to be given away at the April show in

Models A-Z

Short-wheelbase Doon shows off the clean modern lines of the design, introduced to the UK in 2001. (Courtesy Chad Chadwick)

The Doon was able to accommodate a full roll-cage fitted right up to the front windscreen due to the neat design of the dashboard. (Courtesy Chad Chadwick)

2004. Around this time, the company's sales agents, Volksmagic, received a request to build a long-wheelbase version of the buggy. Doon dutifully re-patterned the buggy and made new moulds for the longer design. Essentially the same at the back, the buggy had a revised design from the rear fenders forward to avoid it looking 'stretched,' and has gone on to outsell the SWB kit by approximately two to one.

In 2007, Chad Chadwick took over full control of the Doon Buggy business, but subsequently ceased trading as Doon in September 2009 due to other commitments. However, not wanting to see Doon disappear from the buggy world, Lee Southerton of local build agent Volksmagic in Oldbury, West Midlands, agreed to take on the provision of Doon kits under licence. The Doon has made its presence felt on the UK buggy scene, and a number have also been exported. In Morocco, where two kits were shipped via Belgium, the buggy was re-named the Fennec, as Doon was apparently a rude word in Moroccan. The Doon has also appeared on TV in episode 5 of the first series of ITV's *Kingdom*, starring Stephen Fry, where the buggy was run into the sea whilst chasing a racehorse on the beach. Different and distinctive, the Doon has proved to be a survivor on the UK buggy scene.

A long-wheelbase version of the Doon was introduced in 2003. This car was built with a 'Herbie' color scheme. (Courtesy Chad Chadwick)

The very first Doon to hit the road was used extensively in promotional material. The buggy features Porsche Boxster wheels, Porsche IRS suspension, and a 2-litre engine (Courtesy Chad Chadwick)

One of the first LWB Doon buggies. With no need to shorten the chassis, this version of the buggy has out-sold the original SWB design. (Courtesy Chad Chadwick)

DUNE RUNNER

DATA PANEL

Production dates
1967-1971

Numbers built
Unknown

Export markets
None

Wheelbase
80in and 94.5in

Identification tips
Generally available with low step-in sides, a squared-off rear licence plate area, and a variety of front hoods, including a Mercedes style 'T-Bird' and Shelbyette GT, plus a pickup option. Short- and long-wheelbase bodyshells were also available

Although a plethora of new designs and names hit the US buggy world in the latter part of the 1960s, the Road Runner was launched in 1967 to prove that the buggy format could work as well on the street as it did on the dunes. Designer Jim Taylor of Dune Buggy Enterprises in Westminster, California, produced his buggy with low, step-in sides that swooped back behind the windshield, thus allowing easy entry and exit. However, the innovation that uniquely identified the marque was the interchangeable front hood designs.

The first was a 'Mini-Mercedes' style, also somewhat reminiscent of an old Packard, which could be augmented with a metal grille at the front to complete the effect. A more conventional hood was also available for the traditional look, and could be added to either the Road Runner bodyshell or the company's other bodyshell, a more traditional, Manx-inspired shape. The Mercedes hood was also supplied in color-matched glassfiber so that owners of other buggy kits could instantly change the look of their vehicles. The square-rigged snout had another benefit: because of its raised stance, the buggy could accommodate another 5-gallon fuel tank beneath it, thereby increasing operating range and making it a popular choice with off-road dune racers.

The buggy interior also allowed for a proper rear seat because of the slightly longer bodyshell, and provided better engine coverage. The extremely well-made, hand-laid glassfiber bodies were just one of the huge inventory of accessories and aftermarket parts the company supplied to buggy enthusiasts. Its large, illustrated catalogue listed everything from wheels, bumpers, tuned headers and skidplates to tow bars and soft-tops. The huge showroom ensured fast and efficient delivery of most parts.

Bodies were available in either an 80in or full 94.5in wheelbase, and in solid or metalflake colors. Kits were supplied in three stages, the most basic providing just the body, hood and dash, in either a heavy-duty (road) lay-up, or a lightweight racing option. The more comprehensive

The buggy had the option of matching side panels, a neat interior trim package with matching rear seat, and chromed items such as bumpers and rollbar.

Launched originally as the Road Runner, the Dune Runner was aimed at street as well as off-road use. Low, step-in sides were a unique feature of the design, as was the wide variety of different front hood options.

kit added the windshield, lights and rollbar, whilst the top-of-the-range package included bumpers, hard or softtop, and a skidplate. By 1969, the buggy had been renamed the Dune Runner to capitalise on its off-road potential, and more front hoods added to the growing list of parts available to buggy customisers.

A 'T-Bird' bubble front hood, and a Shelbyette GT style option, gave the Dune Runner distinctive character, whilst increasing the choice to no fewer than fifteen different variations available to customers. With the short-wheelbase, full-length, high and low side, and wide fender models, the Dune Runner catered for every taste.

A final addition in mid-1969 was a neat pickup body style, which extended the rear deck above the engine and added a large capacity carrying area that could be fully enclosed. The pickup capitalised on the growing interest in utility-type buggy designs beginning to appear at the time, and ensured the company stayed in business longer than many of the Manx-type copyists. By offering kits that were competitively priced, exquisitely laminated, and available through a large network of authorised dealers, Dune Buggy Enterprises was a major influence on the US dune buggy scene.

Even when the market moved on, the company achieved follow-up successes with another buggy-style vehicle called the Concept One, and a kit-car called the Avenger, before becoming a distributor of all-terrain vehicles.

Most kits were sold in short-wheelbase form, but few were built as well as this promotional vehicle for the Mooneyes performance equipment supplier in Santa Fe Springs, California.

Who wouldn't want to go cruising down to the surf in this Dune Runner buggy?

Gold paintwork, polished chrome, and a neat interior featuring many Mooneyes accessories make this Dune Runner real eye candy.

EMPI IMP

DATA PANEL

Production dates
1969-1970

Numbers built
Unknown

Export markets
UK

Wheelbase
82.5in

Identification tips
Low, curving sides and clamshell front fenders; rear fender recesses; 1970 Imp also had sculpted side panels and full engine panel, plus a tachometer recessed into the front hood

EMPI (Engineered Motor Products Inc) was already a successful VW aftermarket parts supplier when it entered the glassfiber dune buggy market with the EMPI Imp.

Already owner of the highly successful VW aftermarket parts manufacturer EMPI (Engineered Motor Products, Inc), Joe Vittone took a long, hard look at the changing trends within the fiberglass buggy market in the US, and decided to launch his own.

Although familiar with the off-road market through the production of the somewhat slab-sided, metal 'Sportster' buggy kit, Vittone saw that a new generation of buyers were looking for street cars with smoother lines and lighter weight. This presented him with a new opportunity, and so the EMPI Imp dune buggy was born.

EMPI tried to ensure that the new kit was delivered to customers in a professional way: the quality of the fiberglass bodyshell was controlled by manufacturing it in the company's own workshops; warehousing and distribution of kits was also handled in-house; and a comprehensive support system, coupled with superb sales literature, ensured demand was generated and orders handled efficiently through EMPI's existing dealer network.

Design of the Imp body was also carefully researched, and featured downswept sides for ease of entry and exit, and wide rear fenders with distinctive indents for additional body strength and styling. The rear deck covered the top part of the engine for legality, and provided a squared-off licence plate mount. The rear lights were VW units, mounted vertically on the outermost part of the fender.

Styling at the front was different from the traditional designs, with sweeping clamshell fenders giving the vehicle a more rounded appearance. The front hood carried an EMPI Imp badge beneath the central styling ridge, upon which sat the flip-up fuel filler. The Imp windshield frame was made of extruded aluminum, ready for a glass installer to cut and fit approved safety glass (for the vehicle to be street legal). The dashboard and headlights were supported and strengthened by proper metal brackets, and the hood and dash supplied pre-bonded for ease of assembly.

Following the example of its Sportster, EMPI designed the Imp to fit a VW chassis shortened by 12in, claiming that this gave rear wheel traction every bit as good as the shorter chassis; had little effect on ground clearance over abrupt drop-offs, and provided more legroom, making the Imp a true four-passenger buggy. The slightly longer wheelbase also helped rid the vehicle of the worst of the bump-steer characteristics normally associated with lightweight dune buggies.

Introduced in 1969, the Imp was constantly updated to ensure compliance with changing motor laws and to make it street legal in all 50 states. By 1970 a new Imp had side panels, providing the wheel covering required in most states for street use. A full-length engine cover was also added, with a removable opening for easy access to the engine. The body featured moulded-in rear seat contours, which required the upholstered seat panel to be snapped on for full comfort, but prevented the rear seat moving forward in

Models A-Z

Classic design of the Imp was made fully road legal with the addition of a full engine cover and side panels. This ensured its success throughout the US. (Courtesy Mike Key)

an accident. The ensemble was completed with a better-fitting front hood design, with a recess for an outside tachometer, and a dashboard that would accept either old or new model VW Beetle steering columns. The quality and design of the Imp was further improved by the addition of quality EMPI accessories, such as Sprintstar wheels and 'Dyno-tuned' exhaust systems.

The Imp buggy sold well, and an Imp on display at the 1969 Frankfurt Auto Show led to the licensed production of the buggy in Europe by a company called AHS (Autohaus Süd-Hannover), and later Karmann in Germany.

The Imp remains a testament to good design, professional marketing and excellent manufacture. Few have survived to the present day, though reproductions of this classic design have been produced by Unique Supply of Redlands, California, and Kobus Cantraine in Belgium.

EMPI advertising was as good as the products themselves.

The neat Imp buggy, with clamshell fenders and swept-down sides, was a milestone in original US buggy design.

The company's brochures were amongst the most professional produced during the US buggy boom, and show off the neat Imp buggy and the company's wide range of accessories.

59

EMPI SPORTSTER

DATA PANEL

Production dates
1963-1970

Numbers built
Unknown

Export markets
Unknown

Wheelbase
SWB: 82.5in LWB: 94.5in

Identification tips
Very angular sheet-steel bodyshell for shortened or stock VW Beetle chassis. Two-seater had small pickup-style cargo bed at back. Spare tyre mounted to front hood. Fold-flat windshield

Following the dune buggy's commercial introduction by Hilder T Thompson with his 'Burro' Buggy in 1960, a young entrepreneur by the name of Joe Vittone saw an opportunity waiting to be exploited. Since the 1950s, Vittone had run a VW dealership called Economotors in Riverside, California, and was in the right place at the right time. Having developed a valve-guide tool to enable the rebuilding of Beetle cylinder heads, he set up a new business called EMPI (European Motor Products Incorporated, later re-named Engineered Motor Products Incorporated) which quickly flourished. The company established a reputation across the US for many high performance and after-market parts.

Located in California, Vittone was exposed to the growing off-road movement and development of VW-based buggies. His friend, Les Prestwood, had a crashed Beetle in his yard, and asked Vittone how to turn it into a usable car again. The front and rear accident-damaged sheetmetal was cut away, and the vehicle fitted with wide wheels and tyres, and a souped-up EMPI engine to make a passable off-road vehicle. This was in 1956 – early days for the VW buggy – but the car's angular look helped shape the development of a productionised version in the early 1960s. Built on the floorpan of a VW Beetle, the company's 'Sportster' buggy had a body made of 20, 18 and 12-gauge sheet metal, which the company chose for economy of manufacture. The basic kits were sold at $895 from the factory (deluxe and super-deluxe kits were also available) or, alternatively, customers could buy a set of plans for $9.95 and fashion their own kit. Kits came in a two-seat version with a small pick-up bed for the shortened VW chassis, or a four-seat family version for a stock chassis. Deluxe kits with lighting and electrics were also available. The only major modifications involved shortening the cables and gearshift rod (for the short-wheelbase model), cutting and shortening the seat frames, modifying the neck of the requisite Transporter petrol tank, and sourcing a swept-up exhaust system for off-road use. The front windshield was typically Jeep-like, folding flat on to the spare tyre mounted to the front hood of the car. Besides selling kits, the EMPI company soon began selling complete turn-key Sportsters to the growing number of customers keen to try the buggy experience. Such was the level of activity that the company was even granted State of California licence plates for its factory-built cars, thus becoming an automotive manufacturer.

The EMPI Sportster had its beginnings in 1956 when the company modified a VW Beetle by cutting away damaged sheetmetal. (Courtesy Beaulieu Motoring Library)

Boxy, utilitarian, basic ... The Sportster design was all about low-cost fun in the sand and off-road. (Courtesy Auto Archive)

60

Models A-Z

EMPI also sold a vast array of performance and off-road parts, and was one of the first companies to realize that it could increase sales of its wares through sophisticated marketing, and by creating a nationwide of dealerships. EMPI's promotional brochures, packaging and advertising strongly positioned the company for the future when the buggy market would suffer a downturn in sales. EMPI was also quick to realize the potential of adapting the six-cylinder air-cooled Chevrolet Corvair engine to the VW gearbox, having seen them used in the earliest dune buggies built by Scott McKenzie, who was one of the true pioneers of the buggy scene in the US. Vittone's own Sportster demonstrator was powered by a Corvair unit, giving it an incredible power-to-weight ratio and exhilarating off-road performance.

In the early 1960s, the success of the Sportster, both on the dunes and in the motoring media, was one of the many inspirations for Bruce Meyers' glassfiber Manx buggy. As Meyers struggled to meet demand for his products, build a distribution network to sell his kits, and fend off copyright pirates, EMPI approached Meyers to offer a distribution network for the Manx through its nationwide agents.

When Meyers refused to avoid losing control of his brainchild, EMPI responded by developing the EMPI Imp, and became one of the true challengers to the Manx buggy.

Customers could build their own buggies from a set of plans sold by EMPI, thus making the Sportster a cheap-to-build fun car. (Courtesy Foreign Car Guide)

The four-seat version of the Sportster bodyshell fitted straight on to the stock VW Beetle chassis, and could be built with basic hand tools. (Courtesy Mike Key)

Ghosted view of the Sportster from the cover of the EMPI catalogue from 1964.

FF BUGGY

DATA PANEL

Production dates
1983-1993

Numbers built
Unknown

Export markets
South Africa, Sweden, Portugal, Spain, Kuwait and Holland

Wheelbase
SWB: 79.5in LWB: 94.5in

Identification tips
Stand-up headlights; integral dashboard and front hood, neat side panels fitting under noticeably curved side lip of bodyshell; small mounting area for rear lights on a chopped-off back

Two long-wheelbase FF buggies were used in the UK TV series *Challenge Anneka*, and were built by Sussex-based company Stevespeed. (Courtesy Volksworld)

From the ashes of former buggy manufacturer and glassfiber producer Fibre-Fab came a new company: FF Kit Cars and Conversions Ltd. Run by industrial model maker Tim Cooksey, the company gave the whole UK buggy scene a much needed shot in the arm with the introduction of the FF Buggy in 1983.

Beginning life in Britain, courtesy of a set of imported American Balboa buggy moulds, the FF buggy was enhanced by the addition of a new 'snub-nosed' front hood and sculpted side panels. The new hood was a neat one-piece unit with integral dashboard, to which the flat alloy windshield frame directly bolted. This unitary design made construction simpler for the customer and speeded manufacture.

Based on a Beetle floorpan shortened by 15in, the FF kit looked much more like a traditional-style buggy than did the Rat, the company's previous offering. Distinctive features of the kit included the neatly recessed petrol tank filler cap in the front hood, and the central instrument housing on the dashboard. At the rear, a soft-top rain lip ran around the top edge of the bodyshell and down the rear wing section, before blending into the body. The flat rear light sections, each side of the engine access opening, allowed the VW Polo's rear light units to fit perfectly (when turned upside down and swapped left to right).

The buggy's side panels were an optional styling accessory that complemented the sweeping sides and high rear end, and emphasised the angled stance of the car. By filling the cavernous gap between the wheels and also forming wheelarches, the side elevation of the buggy was greatly improved. As a result, the short-wheelbase FF kit was perfectly proportioned and looked attractive, even with the soft-top up in typical British weather. Side screens did a fair job of preventing water getting inside the car.

The buggy was also noteworthy for the excellent quality of the glassfiber work, courtesy of Formula 1 race car body laminators near Littlehampton, West Sussex. This was further enhanced by the option of metalflake finishes, popular during the first buggy boom and the early days of customising in the 1960s. Despite the practical problems, around 75 per cent of all FF buggies had this type of finish (which said something for owner priority). The buggy's good looks and ease of construction ensured it was well received by an attentive British motoring press, and road test articles duly appeared in magazines such as *Kit Car*, *Kit Cars and Specials* and *Auto Express*.

The popularity of the FF reached its peak when it was developed into a long-wheelbase model, which was now even easier to build. Two such cars, in eye-catching blue and yellow paintwork, were built by UK company Stevespeed, and used for the British prime-time TV show *Challenge Anneka*, where TV presenter Anneka Rice travelled around the country in the long-wheelbase FF, hurling cameramen off the back and trying to talk over the rorty exhaust.

Support for the buggy waned, however, following a change of company ownership

Models A-Z

in 1986 and the new company, Country Volks, ultimately disappeared in 1993.

Despite the moulds finding new owners when the contract laminators cleared out their storage facilities in around 2006, the FF went out of production. The design did make a great impact on the British buggy scene at a time when there were few other new buggies. With the design looking fresh, in the minimalist way traditional buggies do, it had no pretension to be anything other than a fun car for the young at heart.

Anneka Rice poses with one of the two buggies from her TV series. Blue gelcoat finishes and painted yellow star graphics made them instantly recognisable.

The stubby rear end of the bodyshell allowed rear lights to be fitted to the flat panels on each side of the engine access opening. (Courtesy Mike Key)

The FF buggy was directly sired from US Balboa company's Lido design, and arrived in Britain courtesy of an imported set of moulds.

With few other buggies still available in the 1980s, the FF prospered. It was subsequently stretched to fit the full-length VW Beetle floorpan and became even easier to build.

The Dune Buggy Handbook

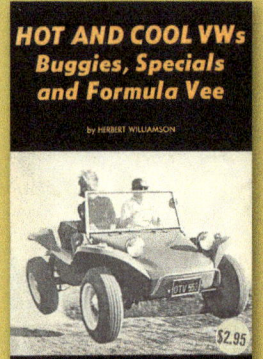
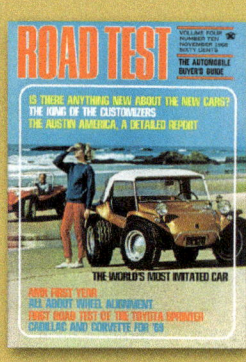

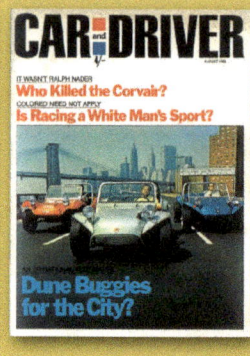
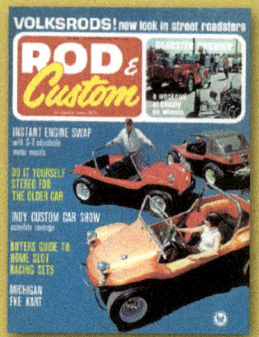

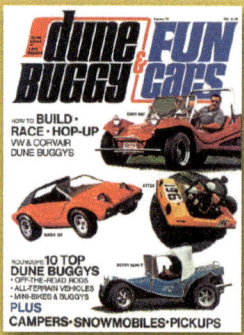

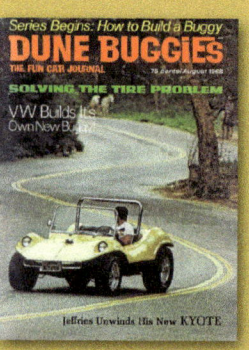

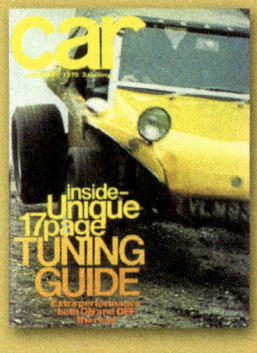

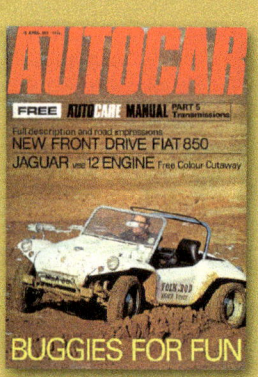

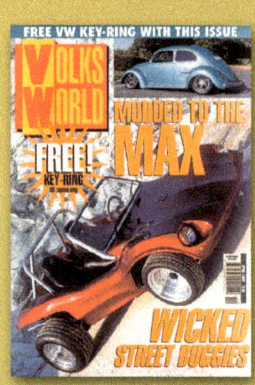

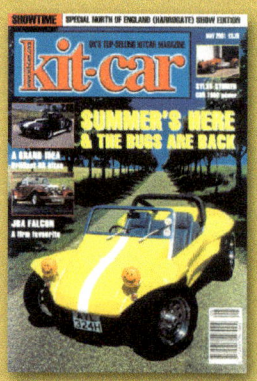
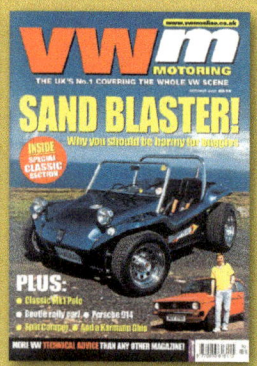
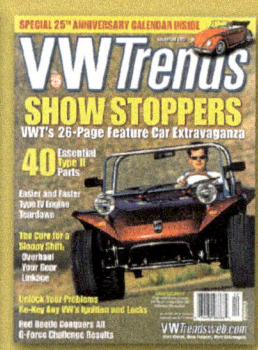

Magazine front covers & record sleeves

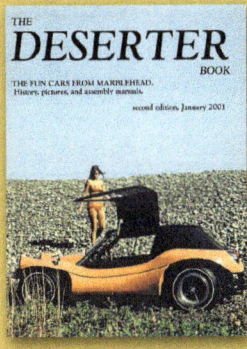

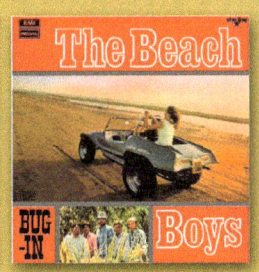
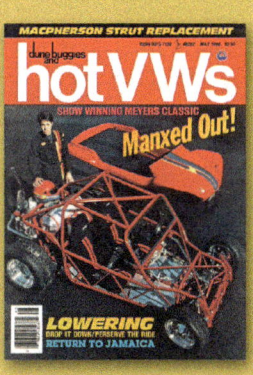

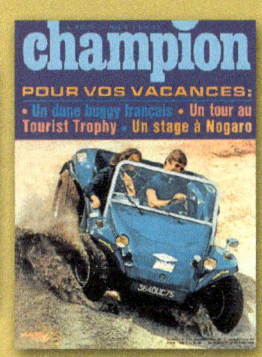

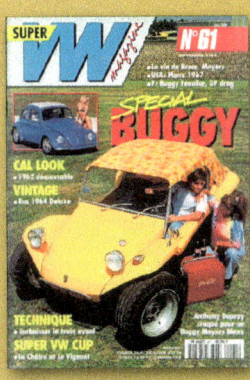

65

FIBERFAB CLODHOPPER & VAGABOND

DATA PANEL

Production dates
1968-1970

Numbers built
Unknown

Export markets
None

Wheelbase
Clodhopper: 80in
Vagabond: 94.5in

Identification tips
The Clodhopper was a traditional dune buggy with very rounded fenders and textured interior. The Vagabond was a more utility-style, full-length buggy, with stock VW fittings, rear engine hatch and a luggage well behind the rear seats

Fiberfab advert from the late 1960s detailing the company's range of kits.

Having produced replacement glassfiber automotive panels and race car bodies for many years, the Fiberfab division of Velocidad Inc, of Santa Clara, California, decided to capitalise on the interest in VW-based cars. Its first cars were inspired by Grand Tourers reminiscent of the Ford GT-40 racing car, and were called the Aztec Avenger GT-12 and Azteca 1. Both were designed for the full-length VW floorpan, but with the option of a Crown Corvair engine conversion.

In 1968 Bud Goodwin, Fiberfab company president, decided to enter the fun car market with an easy-to-build vehicle called the Vagabond Sportster. The utility-styled buggy was intended primarily for road use, and was a straightforward swap for the old VW Beetle steel bodyshell. Building the Vagabond was simplicity itself, eliminating the additional effort and cost of shortening the stock floorpan.

Due to its one-piece fabrication, the body was extremely rigid, with the only opening panel being the deck lid for access to the engine. The fuel tank had to be relocated, and sat in a fabricated metal cradle attached to the shock absorber mounting towers. A flip-up fuel tank filler cap sat atop the sloping front hood area of the buggy, which also provided mountings for the stock VW headlights in the shaped fenders. A windshield and frame, and two frame-stiffening rails, were provided in the kit, whilst virtually all of the other components came from the donor VW. These included the seats, tail lights, electrical switches and wiring harness.

A flat moulding at the rear of the interior allowed for a back seat, and additional storage space was provided by a well between the seat and the engine compartment. Optional extras,

Models A-Z

though few, included a chromed rollbar for occupant safety, and a folding cloth top. At the side of the buggy, a chrome trim strip from a Camero covered the necessary mould split-line, and provided some body protection. Unusually, the bodyshells were only supplied in a black primer for spray painting, which allowed builders to use their imagination when choosing a final color. Mag-wheels, supplied by American Racing Equipment and marketed by Fiberfab, completed this high quality, distinctive buggy.

Fiberfab's second buggy, a more conventional design, was introduced just as the buggy scene mushroomed in the US in 1968. Christened with the somewhat unfortunate name of Clodhopper, the buggy was, nevertheless, a worthy contender in the ever-expanding array of bodies for the shortened VW chassis. Manufactured in the same high quality glassfiber as the rest of the Fiberfab range, the bodyshell came in a finished gelcoat color with the option of metalflake or two-tone solid color. The interior of the bodyshell had a permanently textured surface and integral, heavily reinforced battery well. The noticeably curved, and uniquely-styled, front and rear fenders offered good clearance and coverage for large tyres.

Clodhopper options included a chromed rollbar, full hardtop or convertible vinyl top, and a range of accessories such as the chrome fanbelt guard, skid plate, bumpers and bucket seats. Pacer chrome wheels – 8in front and 10in rear, fitted with Firestone tyres – were also available and completed the ensemble.

As the buggy scene faded away, Fiberfab simply returned to commercial work, and more exotic body styles for both the VW and English 92in wheelbase chassis, such as the Triumph TR 3-4, MGA, and Austin Healey.

Fibrefab's buggies were promoted to the surfing crowd in a more traditional short-wheelbase design called the Clodhopper and a more utility Vagabond model, designed for the full-length VW chassis (Courtesy Auto Archive)

Fiberfab advert shows the Vagabond and the 'new' Clodhopper buggy. Despite the uninspiring name, the conventionally-designed buggy was well made, and came in a wide range of solid or metalflake colors.

The Vagabond was intended to be used purely on the street, and was a well-made and distinctive design. (Courtesy Alex Dearborn)

A Clodhopper doing what the buggy does best – having fun on the beach. (Courtesy Car & Driver)

FIBER JET COBRA & SAND HOPPER

DATA PANEL

Production dates
Cobra: 1970-2007
Sand Hopper: 1970-1998

Numbers built
Unknown

Export markets
None

Wheelbase
80in

Identification tips
The Cobra style is sharply raked with wide fenders, and an opening engine cover with mock air scoops on the hood. The Sand Hopper was an updated Tow'd design

Billing itself as "the world's largest dune buggy manufacturer," the company of Fiber Jet of Roseville, California, can rightfully claim to have kept the Stateside dune buggy industry alive and well for many years. Set up in 1970 by Tim Figuhr, Fiber Jet produced several different dune buggy designs until production faltered in 2007. One of the earliest of its designs was the Cobra, which remained the most popular in the range.

The Cobra was originally produced to fill the void in availability of glassfiber-bodied, VW Beetle-based buggies, following the demise of many manufacturers and their products. Developed from a traditional buggy kit, the Cobra soon took on an identity uniquely its own. The bodyshell had a 'raked forward' stance that gave the buggy a look of motion even when standing still, and the wide fenders front and rear ensured that all but the widest tyres could be accommodated.

At the front the hood ended abruptly in a blunt nose with a twin metal grille arrangement. A wide styling ridge provided the mount for the fuel tank filler, finished in a pointed 'V' at the front of the hood, whilst mock air scoops adorned each side. A somewhat incongruous front spoiler was also available as an optional extra. Although the choice of pod-mounted headlights was left to the builder, most Cobra buggies were fitted with small, chromed, rectangular units which complemented the ground-hugging stance at the front.

For a small additional charge the factory could also make the engine cover a removable item, which enabled easy access to the VW engine. On each side of the panel, stock VW tail lights were mounted to the rear deck. For the sides of the buggy, a pair of 'running board'- style side panels were available as an optional extra, and helped form proper wheelarches around the tires for street legality. A soft-top or hardtop option was also offered. The latter was available in a vinyl finish, had the luxury of a glass rear window, and could be ordered in solid or metalflake colors.

The design of the Cobra front hood also appeared as part of another Fiber Jet buggy design called the Beachcomber. Available only for the full-length chassis, the design added a deep curved front spoiler and inbuilt, twin round headlight units. With a wide back, and stationwagon-type hardtop with lifting tailgate, the Beachcomber was a practical design for those requiring more interior space. The Beachcomber, though, was never as popular as the tough-looking Cobra and was eventually dropped.

Fiber Jet also recreated several 1970s

Many Cobra buggies were built with small rectangular headlights to give the vehicle a modern look. This company demonstrator also included a fully-quilted interior for the gold metalflake body. (Courtesy Fiber Jet)

Models A-Z

designs, including the 'Mini-T' and the Sand Hopper. The Mini-T closely resembled the designs of the original Berry-styled vehicle and the later Kellison Super 'T' pickup, but added a hardtop and wooden pickup bed to create an attractive two-seater buggy. The Sand Hopper had its roots in the design of the Meyers Tow'dster, featuring the same tube chassis to which the VW suspension bolted, and was clothed in a set of minimalist, lightweight, glassfiber body panels and fenders. The buggy eventually received a face-lift in the form of redesigned rear fenders with wide running board side panels, whilst the fenders at the front were dropped.

Engine cooling was aided by a racing scoop on the rear deck, and a Formula 1-style rear wing was also offered, but seemed out of place with the overall off-road design.

Both designs have fallen by the wayside now, and Fiber Jet has since concentrated its efforts on replacement panels for Porsches and other sports cars.

The Sand Hopper was a recreation of the original Meyers Tow'd, but brought up to date with full running boards, wide rear fenders, and an engine-cooling air scoop on the rear deck (Courtesy Fiber Jet)

The aggressively-styled Cobra buggy had an angled front hood and raked-forward bodyshell for a pleasing modern look and stance. (Courtesy Fiber Jet)

Metal grille arrangement to the front, and mock air scoops flanking the central hood styling ridge were unique features of the Cobra design. (Courtesy Fiber Jet)

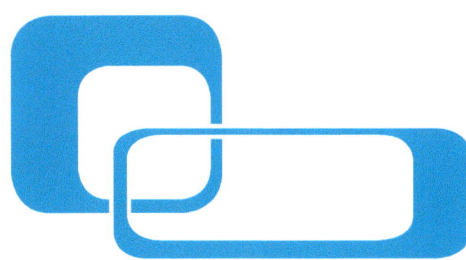

Front cover of the Fiber Jet brochure, which included the full range of the company's buggies, such as the Super 'T' Pickup, the Beachcomber, and the Enos '500.'

69

FIBER JET ENOS & INDY '500'

DATA PANEL

Production dates
Enos '500': 1976-2007
Indy: 1989-2007

Numbers built
1500 (approx)

Export markets
None

Wheelbase
80in

Identification tips
Enos '500' had classic Balboa Lldo buggy looks, with sloped front hood, abruptly truncated for the licence plate mount. The Indy version added wide, racing-style side panels with dummy filler caps, and a Porsche-style rear wing

Amongst buggy designs that have appeared under different names and been produced by different manufacturers is one that originated as the Lido by Balboa Buggies in California. It soon reappeared as the El Lobo, then the La Tigre, and also in Britain as the FF Buggy. A similar design, called the Enos '500,' also appeared in the Fiber Jet catalog over many years. The main reasons for the enduring popularity of the buggy are ease of construction, good looks, and the fact that its styling has never dated.

The Enos '500' was designed for the traditional shortened VW floorpan, and took the classic Manx style a stage further toward the round fender line of the equally desirable EMPI Imp. At the front, the clamshell-type fenders swept back and down to form a wide sill, over which the driver and passenger could easily slide into their seats. Rising up again, the body formed a wider rear wheelarch that ended in a flattened area at the back for the rear light clusters and the centrally mounted licence plate (with twin licence plate lamps on each side). The rear lights were often the compact units from a Ford Mustang.

The front hood was not dissimilar to that of the company's other buggy, the Cobra. Raked forward, and with a central 'V'-shaped styling ridge, the nose ended in a recessed flat area that conveniently housed the licence plate. Round or small rectangular headlamp units could be fitted, and frontal appearance could also be changed by the addition of a small front spoiler, mounted below the lower edge of the front hood. The all-in-one front hood and dashboard unit had mounts at each side to fit the polished alloy windscreen frame, and windshield wiper mountings in front of the glass. The dashboard was a shaped affair, with room for full instrumentation on the driver's side, and a recessed area and grab-handle for the passenger.

As a mounting point for those wishing to fit a soft-top, or the optional vinyl-finish glassfiber hardtop, there was a raised lip around the top edge of the rear part of the bodyshell, which also helped to keep water out of the vehicle. Builders had the option of fitting the Fiber Jet running board-styled side panels, or the more enclosing pod-type panels.

To keep the design alive and fresh, an update of the kit was offered in 1989. Named the Indy Enos '500,' the new buggy added features to the original design to give an Indianapolis race look, belying its less exotic VW Beetle base. Although the bodyshell and front hood were the same mouldings, the look of the buggy was changed by the addition of extra wide

Chromed 5-lug wide wheels and wide tyres were a neat addition, and gave the Indy Enos '500' buggy its classic look. (Courtesy Fiber Jet)

Models A-Z

The modern Indy Enos '500' by Fiber Jet owed its curvaceous lines to the Lido buggy, and was a cute, go-anywhere fun car that was inexpensive to build and great fun to drive. (Courtesy Fiber Jet)

An original Lido buggy at Bug-In #11, with flamed pearl paint, BRM wheels on the back, and wire wheels at the front. Flyweight buggies like this Jim Dutchers Speed Shop car were formidable drag race competitors. (Courtesy John Lazenby)

side pods, and a Porsche-style rear wing similar to that on the turbo 911s. The pods themselves could be fitted with dummy filler caps on the top edge for the Indy look, but could house large capacity fuel tanks behind the fascias to give extended driving range. The company demonstrator also had a set of louvres added to the pods, though these were strictly non-functional.

Available in solid or metalflake colors, the Indy Enos '500' brought one of the longest surviving US buggy designs up to date. Whilst company concentration on the production of glassfiber panels for sports cars has halted buggy production, the Enos design has helped ensure that the classic lines of the Lido has not disappeared from the buggy world.

Bringing the design into the 1990s called for some wide, racing-style side panels, mock filler caps, and a rear wing. The Indy Enos '500' brought a traditional design bang up to date. (Courtesy Harold Pace)

The Enos '500' shared the classical and timeless Lido design, but with more rounded fenders and an abruptly truncated front hood. (Courtesy Fiber Jet)

71

FIBER JET ROUGH TERRAIN

DATA PANEL

Production dates
1976-1996/1996-2007

Numbers built
1500 (approx)

Export markets
None

Wheelbase
SWB: 80in LWB: 94.5in

Identification tips
Traditional-style buggy in short- or long-wheelbase form. Optional hardtop and running board-styled side panels. Revised buggy had dropped sides and full side pods

Since Fiber Jet offered one of the largest range of dune buggy bodyshells available from a single manufacturer, it should come as no surprise, then, that this would include a traditional-looking, short-wheelbase buggy. The Rough Terrain was classically styled, and featured wide rear fenders and all-enclosing rear bodywork covering much of the VW engine beneath (it also included a licence plate mount). At the front, stand-up headlights flanked an interchangeable front hood, the options for which were either a recessed centre section with a diamond shape embossed on the front, or a wide and pointed area that gave a flat mounting site for the fuel tank filler.

Interchangeable front hoods was an idea that had been tried on buggies before, and the Rough Terrain hood could also be used on another of the company's models, the 'Super Pickup' buggy. The latter had a Model T-type front and pickup bed back, with an opening deck lid, the design closely following the style of the ubiquitous 1970s Sand Rover 'T' pickup produced by Poty Enterprises. The Super Pickup did not survive, however, but the Rough Terrain certainly did, and a long-wheelbase version was soon added to the range to cater for the market in easy-to-build, road-going buggies. Hardtops and running board-styled side panels were available for both long and short variants of the buggy.

Successful as the Rough Terrain was, company president Tim Figuhr decided in November 1996 to update the design and maintain the competitiveness of the low-cost buggy in the expanding US kit-car market. The revised body was available in long-wheelbase form only, and had noticeably lower sides to the bodyshell. Front and rear fenders were wider than before, and the rear of the body now featured an opening engine access panel. Tail lights were twin, round, commercial-vehicle types sunk into the rear deck.

The full-length, glassfiber hardtop made the Rough Terrain a very practical design. Full-length side panels offered some tire coverage, and also made the buggy street-legal.

Models A-Z

Fiber Jet's original Rough Terrain bodyshell was lengthened to fit an unmodified VW Beetle floorpan, making for a quick and straightforward conversion. (Courtesy Fiber Jet)

This highly chromed engine is typical of modern buggies, and runs as good as it looks. Rear lights are Chevrolet Vega units fitted to the green and gold metalflake-sprayed bodyshell. (Courtesy Mike Key)

The front hood still had different options available, but the pod-mounted headlights were changed in favour of rectangular units mounted to metal brackets, run off the front suspension rather than being located on the inner part of the front fenders. The body was available with a moulded-in gelcoat color of the customer's choice, or metalflake at a small extra charge. A grey primer finish could also be ordered if the kit was to be spray painted.

The Rough Terrain was available in either a basic body kit, consisting of just the bodyshell, front hood and dashboard mouldings, or a deluxe package which included two padded buggy bucket seats, a wiring loom, a windshield, a hardtop, a rollbar and lights, which represented exceptional value for money. A rear bench seat and carpet set were the only other parts listed to complete the somewhat spartan buggy interior.

A pair of optional side panels were offered for a more stylish look, dramatically curved to fit under the buggy sides. The hardtop option available for the original Rough Terrain design was now either all-enclosing or a touring top to keep occupants cool in the hot sun (essentially just a roof section with back supports).

The revised Rough Terrain, one of the newer buggy designs available in the US, won many new customers who prefered the advantages of a longer wheelbase (more interior room and a smoother ride on the street). The Rough Terrain has, however, also become a casualty of the company's move toward sports car panel production, and – including the Manx-styled model introduced in 2001, and other models – took a back seat from 2007.

The newer design of the revamped Rough Terrain bodyshell had much lower sides for easy entry and exit, whilst the curved side panels sat between the body waistline and edge of the floorpan. (Courtesy Fiber Jet)

This show-winning, long-wheelbase buggy follows the Rough Terrain design, though with a lower front hood. The stock Mustang seats are velour-covered to match the color of the paintwork. (Courtesy Mike Key)

FIBER-TECH MANX

DATA PANEL

Production dates
1968-circa1998

Numbers built
3000 (all designs)

Export markets
None

Wheelbase
Manx/Coestoga: 80in
Touring/Manx LWB: 94.5in

Identification tips
Traditional Manx shape with restyled hood and squared-off licence plate mount. Conestoga had elongated rear and stationwagon hardtop. Touring was a Mini-T inspired long-wheelbase design

Few early buggy manufacturers continued production for more than a few years; blossoming in the heyday of the 1960s buggy boom, then fading quickly as the craze gave way to other forms of automotive expression (particularly the street rod scene which still flourishes today). One notable survivor, however, was Fiber-Tech of Santee, California, which continued to fly the flag for the Manx buggy name long after the original Meyers Manx disappeared, despite the fact that there was no official connection between the original B F Meyers company and Fiber-Tech's revised Manx design.

Formed in 1968 on the outskirts of San Diego, Fiber-Tech offered three different dune buggy styles. The first, and most recognisable, was a kit for the 80in wheelbase VW floorpan. Closely resembling the original Manx, the new 'Manx body' buggy did have some distinguishing features which identified it as a new moulding. At the front, the hood had a central styling ridge, forcing the fuel tank neck to be repositioned to one side. This was achieved by turning around the VW tank and mounting a flush filler cap.

At the rear, the somewhat abbreviated Meyers Manx body design was changed

The recreated Manx design by Fiber-Tech had a small styling ridge to the centre of the front hood, and a squared-off engine cover. Many owners cut this away to show off their show standard full-dress engines. (Courtesy Keith Seume)

Models A-Z

Lowered and color-matched suspension, drag race-style wheels, and a full roll-cage are the hallmarks of a modern buggy. (Courtesy Keith Seume)

The brochure listed the basic parts needed to start a buggy project. Full-length and short-wheelbase models were available, with the option of side panels and a glassfiber hardtop.

to feature a larger engine cover with a flat licence plate mounted centrally on the bodyshell. This cover not only provided greater weatherproofing for the VW engine, but made the design more acceptable in different states. Nevertheless, the cover was often cut away to show off full-dress engines in areas where such a thing was possible. The kit was supplied as just a basic body and hood in white glassfiber, though the dashboard came in a black gelcoat finish. Other colors were available, though at extra cost.

Optional (but entirely necessary) components such as a windshield frame, headlights and a soft-top, were also available. For all-weather practicality, a glassfiber hardtop with fixed rear screen was available, whilst side panels and a central console were options that could be fitted to the buggy for a neater appearance.

Another bodyshell, the Conestoga, was also available for the shortened floorpan – it seated four and gave the vehicle more of a stationwagon look. By using an elongated rear fender section ending in a flatter back panel over the engine bay, the bodyshell allowed for an extra large storage space behind the rear seats. A set of quilted interior panels and seats, front and rear, completed the very neat appearance of the buggy.

The inside of the vehicle was kept dry by a full hardtop, which rose just ahead of the rear seats and provided ample headroom for tall, rear seat passengers, and maximised load carrying capacity for bulky items. Fixed rear windows were fitted to the hardtop for a very production car image. A final neat touch were wind wings, which could be fitted to the windshield frame posts to prevent buffeting.

The third kit was a Touring Body, designed for a standard length VW floorpan. Not dissimilar to the long-wheelbase Berry Mini-T, the buggy bodyshell had the open sides and flowing running boards of its predecessor, though, unfortunately, did not continue long in production.

Over a 30 year period, Fiber-Tech kept the legend of the Manx alive and well, and Tom Stout's RTS Enterprises – the actual manufacturer of the kits for the last 15 years or so, and owner of the project – continued to produce two kits around this basic design for many years. The original short-wheelbase car was subsequently joined by a stretched version. Recognising the need for more street-usable buggies, the long-wheelbase Fiber-Tech buggy was a neat update on traditional buggy lines.

The Fiber-Tech Manx buggy captured the spirit of the original Meyers design – brought up to date here with flawless sky blue paintwork on the body and roll-cage of this strictly street machine. (Courtesy Keith Seume)

75

FUN HUGGER

DATA PANEL

Production dates
1968-1970

Numbers built
200 (approx)

Export markets
None

Wheelbase
94.5in

Identification tips
Monoshell construction of modern-styled full-length bodyshell; integral front windshield and rollbar; stock VW headlamps and rear tail lights

Long-wheelbase buggies were unusual, even in the halcyon days of the buggy boom, when most new manufacturers seemed content to pirate a copy of a traditional-looking, short-wheelbase design. The Fun Hugger was, therefore, something of a first, designed from the outset to be a modern and stylish sports buggy for the unmodified VW chassis, without looking anything like a Meyers Manx.

Leo Lyons began his company, Lyons Equipment Co, in San Bernardino, California, when a friend asked him why he wasn't making dune buggy kits. Launched in 1968, the Fun Hugger was an original and very different-looking design. Produced in hand-laid glassfiber for a stronger bodyshell with more uniform thickness, the construction was also very different to anything that had gone before. Rather than a single unit bodyshell and separate front hood, the new buggy was actually constructed from several entirely separate sub-structures, which were moulded individually and then bonded together into a unitised body.

The individual pieces consisted of an inner and outer shell, a forward bulkhead, dashboard, headlight mounts, engine area, and all splash panels. Although longer than a Manx-type body, the Fun Hugger was both lighter and stronger, thanks to this multi-piece construction which minimised body flexing under all on- and off-road conditions. The body also took stock VW headlamps and tail lights, fuel tank and steering.

One of the innovative design features of the somewhat futuristic-looking buggy was that the stock VW seats, front and

The Fun Hugger body, whilst being longer than that of a Manx, was both lighter and stronger due to its multi-piece construction. However, it was not a cheap kit, and this limited its appeal in a price-conscious youth market. (Courtesy Petersens)

Models A-Z

rear, fitted into the narrow interior, and, as with a stock Beetle, the rear seat even folded forward to allow plenty of room at the back for additional storage. Also something of a first was a proper spare tire well behind the rear seat.

Offered in four levels of kit, the cheapest 'A' kit provided just the body without the outer side panels and back panel over the engine. The lay-up thickness of the bodyshell was increased to compensate for the loss of strength due to these panels being absent. A more expensive 'B' kit added the necessary mounting hardware, plus the sturdy front windshield with ready-fitted glass, mounted as part of an integral front rollbar. A built-in mount under the front also allowed for the use of the stock VW windshield wiper mechanism. 'C' and 'D' kits were similar to the first two, respectively, but included the additional side and rear panels.

Lyons also offered a vast range of optional extras for the buggy, including glassfiber 'fastback' and 'Surrey' tops, a neat chromed rear rollbar, and a chromed exhaust system. The header unit sat high under the raised rear back of the buggy, which extended far enough back to give a fair amount of coverage to the VW engine, preventing problems in wet weather.

The basis of the buggy was its simplicity to build, being a true bolt-on body, which recommended its construction to the absolute amateur. Able to carry up to five people in comfort, it was also aimed at the family man who wanted more than just a two-seater runaround. Whilst not cheap at over $500, and with metalflake color options and other accessories driving the price higher still, the Fun Hugger was a distinctive and well-made buggy that stood out from the crowd.

The Fun Hugger was very much a product of its time. Rapidly changing fashions left it without a market, and it soon disappeared as buggies made way for more sophisticated VW kit-cars and off-road racers.

The Fun Hugger design was a radical departure from the norm, and was produced as a modern and stylish sports buggy. Changing fashions meant that the design soon passed its sell-by date, however. (Courtesy *Road Test/Dune Buggy*)

The dramatically-shaped back of the Fun Hugger left the VW engine somewhat exposed, but did provide some cover in the wet. (Courtesy *Road Test/ Dune Buggy*)

Late 1960s advertisement for the Fun Hugger. The buggy was aimed at those looking for an easy-to-build convertible capable of carrying five adults in comfort.

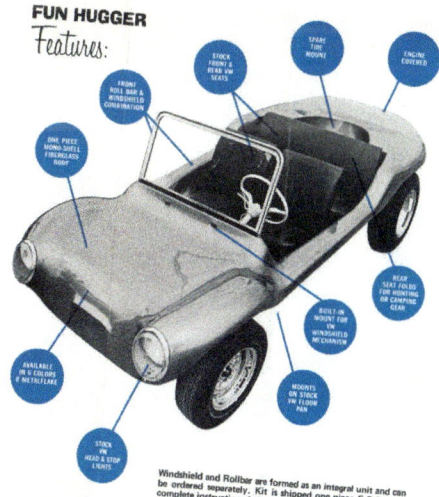

GLITTERBUG

DATA PANEL

Production dates
1966-1970

Numbers built
1500 (approx)

Export markets
None

Wheelbase
80in (except LWB variant)

Identification tips
Traditional-looking buggy with a styling ridge on the front hood. The Pickup had long, wide, rear fenders, full-length hardtop, and an opening tailgate

Whilst today the words 'dune buggy' can mean anything from a lightweight racing rail to a competitive sand dragster, in 1964 they described a glassfiber body on a shortened Beetle chassis. The Manx created a huge demand for such kits, and boosted the concept of fun cars and off-road racing. The small backyard dune buggy operation became a whole new industry, with manufacturers in the US and abroad rushing to produce different variations on the basic buggy theme.

One of the designs that followed the Manx by just a few seasons was the Glitterbug, produced by Glitterbug Inc of San Fernando, California. Whilst continuing the traditional dune buggy lines, the Glitterbug had wider and deeper fenders which prevented water from the front tyres spraying into the interior. Another noticeably different feature was the front hood, which had a styling ridge running down the centre and, with the VW fuel tank turned around, the filler cap was further back for safety.

The filler cap was a Corvette unit, which gave the buggy a clean and up-market appearance, and, at the front, a neat, chromed bumper further enhanced looks. Interior-wise, the dashboard was shaped to fit the stock VW speedometer, but also allowed a separate tachometer to be mounted. A moulded plastic tray sat over the VW tunnel, forward of the gearshift, to hold small items and drinks cups.

With a range of options, including side panels and a hardtop in color-matched glassfiber, the Glitterbug was a neat and eye-catching vehicle. Supplied in a range of metalflake finishes, it also lived up to its flamboyant name. The kit was soon developed into a long-wheelbase version for those who didn't want to shorten the VW floorpan, and a further variant was also in the pipeline. Anticipating the needs of those who wished to go camping, or who needed a stationwagon derivative, Bill Harkey, owner of Glitterbug Inc, developed a short-wheelbase car into a pickup that could also be fitted with a hardtop arrangement.

Launched in late 1969 as the Sportsman Pickup, the new buggy had an elongated back with a flat top section to accommodate the separate hardtop. The buggy also featured extremely wide rear fenders to cover tall and wide off-road tires, making it a true go-anywhere vehicle. An opening tailgate in the rear of the body gave access to the flat cargo bay, if a flat VW Squareback or Corvair engine was used. For those preferring to

Sensing a move toward a market requiring a stationwagon-type buggy, Glitterbug Inc developed its short-wheelbase design into the Sportsman Pickup. The new kit became a favourite with both outdoors enthusiasts and off-road racers.

Models A-Z

This Glitterbug Sportsman buggy was owned by racer Bill Harkey, and won first in class at the IDRA Phoenix Tri-State Championships of 1969.

The Glitterbug was a serious contender, in both quality and style, to the Manx which preceded it by only a few seasons. (Courtesy Road Test/Dune Buggy)

stay with the upright Beetle engine, a special engine cover box was provided, at the rear of the pickup bed, though this reduced usable space in the rear.

The stationwagon/camper top could be mounted permanently or left removable, and could be converted to any number of different styles, simply by changing the window arrangements. Side curtains made the buggy a fully enclosed and true all-weather vehicle. The hardtop was designed to fit over a standard rollbar so no safety features were lost, and the interior was large enough for a proper rear seat set-up, plus the large carrying space.

Filling a gap in the buggy market for those looking for a vehicle that could explore the country with total practicality, or for those requiring a family estate, the Glitterbug was eminently successful. In off-road competition, too, the buggy achieved many race wins, often in the hands of company employee Don Guth.

Whilst the original manufacturer has long since gone, the Glitterbug moulds were rediscovered in the 1990s by an English VW restorer, and passed to GT Mouldings, which used the front hood on its GT Buggy design.

The Glitterbug Pickup was a serious off-road competitor, especially in the hands of Don Guth. The massive rear tires were easily accommodated under the cavernous rear arches. (Courtesy Auto Archive)

The Glitterbug Sportsman buggy was driven by Californians Jim Tabor and Roy McIntyre in the 1969 Las Vegas Nevada race, but they failed to finish. (Courtesy Auto Archive)

GP BEACH BUGGY MK I

DATA PANEL

Production dates
1968-1977

Numbers built
1750

Export markets
France, Switzerland & other agent exports

Wheelbase
78.75in

Identification tips
Narrow fenders, central recessed circular badge on the front hood, and aluminium windshield surround. Flat licence plate mounting on engine cover

Given the unreliability of the British weather, it was, perhaps, not surprising that it took someone from a sunnier climate (South Africa) to introduce the buggy to the UK. Pierre du Plessis, proprietor of the GP Speed Shop, and a racing car mechanic on Grand Prix Lolas, Ferraris, and the like, spotted a Lolette buggy in Johannesburg whilst working for David Piper during the Kyalami Nine Hour Race. Inspired, in 1966 he imported an American Manx buggy bodyshell above the sleeping compartment of a Formula III support vehicle, following a race in the USA.

Working from small premises in Brentford, Essex, with his partner, John Jobber, the pair modified the bodyshell during 1967 to produce the GP Beach Buggy; the 'GP' standing for 'Grand Prix.' By moving the front firewall rearward, the body's front fenders were pushed forward to give more front tire coverage as required by UK law. Short, stubby and ugly, in an attractive sort of way, the buggy featured the same high quality finish that had been a hallmark of the original Meyers design.

Designed for a shortened VW chassis, the GP kit consisted of the glassfiber body and front hood, glassfiber dashboard and steel frame, windshield (in a polished alloy frame), and various fittings to put it all together. Extras included a hardtop plus the requisite buggy accessories such as bumpers, headlights, rollbars, exhaust systems, and wide wheels and tires.

Following a move in 1968, to Hanworth Air Park on the outskirts of London, the GP was well placed to gain maximum publicity from the trendy London scene and fashionable personalities (including pop stars such as Cliff Richard). Major successes in autocross were what secured its future initially, and there was an instant demand from those keen to follow in its off-road footsteps.

Encouraged by appearances in *Motor* magazine in August 1968, and in *Car* in September of that year, the GP epidemic spread like wildfire as car builders rushed to be part of the new craze.

Besides its own production facilities, GP was also using sub-contractors to help keep up with demand during 1969. Kits were also being sold by agents throughout the country, and the buggy often appeared with the agent's own name. Hence, the GP became the Beardalls buggy, the Skyspeed buggy, and the JPC buggy, amongst others. Scotland was covered by agent Geoff Rosenbloom, a keen autocross enthusiast who drove the GP to several championship wins. Northern Ireland was the base for GP's Irish agent, Robbie McBurney & Sons in Ballymena.

GP exhibited at the Birmingham Sports Car Show late in 1969, and at the Specialist Sports Car Show in London in early 1970, in a concentrated effort to stimulate demand.

The alloy windshield-framed Mk I GP Beach Buggy is still avidly sought by buggistas in the UK. Many have been built to show-winning standard by enthusiasts keen to experience the thrills of driving a wind-in-the-hair fun car. (Courtesy *Street Machine*)

Models A-Z

Buggies were modified to the extreme in the 1980s/1990s. This GP Buggy features a flip-up bodyshell and fully-chromed running gear and engine. (Courtesy Mike Key)

Period perfect 'Beachcomber' GP Beach Buggy built in 1972 by Andrew Bennetts and Ian Wishart. (Courtesy Andrew Bennetts)

The early 1970s saw the GP buggy in its element: customers were snapping up the kits so quickly that the company could hardly keep up. Advertisers were using them to promote anything from fashion clothing to pop groups, and die-cast toy manufacturer Corgi also produced its own miniature version.

By now, GP had diversified the range to include the long-wheelbase Super Buggy to encourage exports, whilst the hardtop LDV pickup buggy was introduced in 1972. Despite a successful showing of its buggies at the Geneva Motor Show that year, a fire at GP's main premises left the company floundering until a new, permanent home was found at Isleworth, Middlesex.

Following the departure of Pierre du Plessis, John Jobber took control of the newly re-formed company, now called GP Concessionnaires Ltd, and set about updating the country's favorite buggy. The all-new GP Mk II appeared in 1977, proving that it was possible to survive oil crises, changing laws surrounding the construction of home-built vehicles, and the vagaries of the British weather.

A line-up of GP buggies outside the company workshops at Hanworth Air Park on the outskirts of London in 1969. (Courtesy GP Projects)

The GP Beach Buggy with its classic, simple lines. Fender extensions were added for road legality after a few brushes with the law, but were also a requirement for serious autocross work. (Courtesy Custom Car)

GP BEACH BUGGY MK II

DATA PANEL

Production dates
1977-date

Numbers built
2000 (approx)

Export markets
Switzerland

Wheelbase
78.75in

Identification tips
Moulded-in glassfiber windshield frame, styling ridge to front hood design, wider wings and enclosing rear bodywork to engine bay at rear; side panels between wheels

Having established itself as one of the best-known names on the British buggy scene in the early 1970s, the GP was poised to become one of the longest surviving designs in production. Manufacturer GP Concessionaires needed to ensure the basic buggy design would conform more easily to the stringent vehicle construction regulations of foreign markets, and thus the GP received a face-lift in 1977 to become the GP Beach Buggy Mk II.

Without losing any of the stubby cuteness of the original design, the most noticeable change was the width of the fenders. At the front these became wider, with a narrower return edge, whilst at the back, the rear body section became wider and deeper. The latter offered greater coverage for the exposed engine bay, and the fenders covered wider tyres. The fenders also had a small flare to the wheelarch, thus avoiding interference between the body and the tyre under full suspension load.

There were improvements inside the buggy, too: a redesigned flange, mounting the bodyshell to the shortened VW floorpan, meant a better fit, and the storage well beneath the back seat was changed to prevent the body interfering with the heat exchanger units of the VW engine (a problem on early bodies). A new dashboard was introduced which had a much wider central section to allow greater provision for fitting a larger number of instruments and switches. Being deeper in design, it also overcame the problems of fitting late-model VW speedometers into the shallow dashboard fascia on the Mk I.

A stronger hood was fitted to the front of the buggy, and featured a central styling ridge on which the fuel filler cap sat. This was further improved later in the year to incorporate an all-in-one glassfiber windshield frame moulding, with a return edge around its perimeter. This change was the result of the steadily increasing buy-in

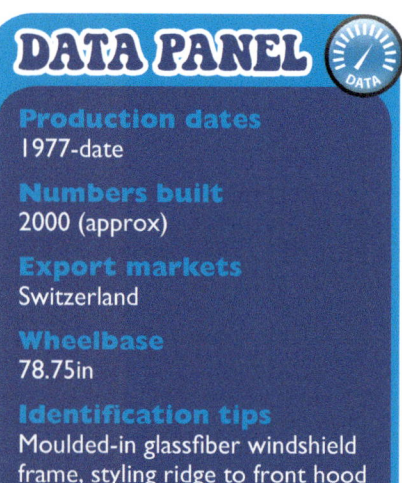

GP Beach Buggy Mk II was tested in Autocar *magazine and proved itself a capable off-roader. (Courtesy Autocar)*

Models A-Z

The Mk II GP buggy differed from the earlier model by having a revised glassfiber windshield surround, stronger front hood and wider wings, with a lower section to the rear fenders for greater legality.

Mk I and Mk II GP buggies on the beach. Big off road tires were essential to get a grip in the soft sand, whilst the roll-cage is protection in the event of the driver inverting the vehicle.

prices of polished alloy windshield frames, and the requirement to have a universal front hood design for the entire range of GP buggies. By having a fixed windshield angle, the frame allowed an exact location for the newly-revised hardtop with gull-wing doors (principally available for the export market). A similar attachment was used for the hardtop sections on the revised, long-wheelbase LDV and Ranchero buggies, which, together with the Super Buggy, were fast becoming the mainstay of GP's buggy production.

The bodyshell section of the GP, below the waistline between the wheels, had looked somewhat bare from day one, and this area was also tidied up. To form proper wheelarches and cover the exposed glassfiber matting, a pair of neat, sculpted side panels were produced. These increased the buggy's legality and kept much of the mud and water thrown up by the front wheels out of the vehicle interior.

A series of features in *Hot Car* magazine in 1981 showed the construction of an off-road-ready GP Mk II, and provided some neat publicity for the buggy at a time when kit-cars began to come to the fore once again in the UK. GP changed its name to GP Projects to reflect a move to production of other kit-built vehicles such as the Porsche Spyder replica and the Madison. The GP Beach Buggy Mk II and Super Buggy projects passed to autocross champion Roy Pierpoint in the early 1990s, and marketed under the name of GP Buggies. Another move, in 1997, saw the two projects taken over by VW enthusiast David Kuschel. The GP project has changed hands several times since 1999, and the quality of the bodyshells has undoubtedly suffered from this. Kits are still available from UK VW specialist Kingfisher Kustoms, though a noticeable number of reproduction GP kits have also surfaced on internet auction sites in recent years.

A pair of Mk II Beach Buggies photographed for a magazine feature when buggies made a welcome return to the kit-car and VW scene in the 1980s. (Courtesy Volksworld)

GP publicity shot with a variety of the company's buggies taking center stage. (Courtesy GP Projects)

GP SUPER BUGGY

DATA PANEL

Production dates
1969-date

Numbers built
1500 (approx)

Export markets
Switzerland, Spain, Germany, Middle East, West Indies, Singapore

Wheelbase
94.5in

Identification tips
Elongated SWB buggy with covered rear end and removable engine hatch. Later versions had a more angular side to accept interchangeable hardtops, and a revised front hood with glassfiber windshield frame

With sales of the short-wheelbase GP buggy going from strength to strength, and export markets beckoning, the buggy was redesigned to fit the full-length VW chassis in autumn 1969. This move meant that the buggy complied with the strict laws of those countries where shortening of the floorpan was outlawed, and paved the way for a new chapter in the success story that was GP.

Looking very much like a stretched version of the short-wheelbase buggy, the Super bolted onto the unmodified floorpan, and thus recommended itself to the novice builder. Better suited to use as a road car, due to lack of effective ground clearance, the buggy also offered seating in comfort for four. The only styling difference was at the rear where the body swept down to cover the exposed engine and offered mudguards for full street legality. Access to the engine was through a removable rear hatch in the bodyshell.

From its debut at the Specialist Sports Car Show in London in late 1970, the Super was an instant hit in foreign markets, and export orders flooded in. Spurred on in Britain by the appearance of a build-up feature in *Cars and Car Conversions* magazine that year, the only change in design was to the front hood, which grew a central styling ridge. The new hood helped strengthen the front end, and was adopted on all future redesigns of GP buggies thereafter.

To promote the car, GP took a stand at the Racing Car Show in early 1971, and followed this up with a display at the Geneva Motor Show in Switzerland the following year. This became the key to the company's future as it looked more and more to export markets, and also provided the catalyst to continually develop the kit.

As GP went on to develop other buggy styles, such as the LDV (Light Delivery Van), it made commercial sense to use a single main tub moulding for all models, which could then accept the different roofs. The Super buggy was updated, therefore, in 1975, with the bodyshell from the LDV, which had wider wings and a redesigned

The 1981 James Bond movie For Your Eyes Only featured three GP Super Buggies. (Courtesy copyright Danjaq, LLC & United Artists Corp)

Models A-Z

The Super Buggy provided seating for four, and simplified construction as chassis shortening was unnecessary. The design was changed so that the interchangeable roof designs of the LDV and Ranchero buggies could also be fitted.

'Heart of Gold' was a modified Super with widened fenders, fitted side panels, and unique custom paintwork by 'Frantic Fred.' The buggy ran a polished Type 3 VW engine, visible through a clear plexiglass engine cover.

rear end. The wing section was elongated further forward along the body tub, and had a flat top edge on which the LDV hardtop normally sat. The fenders were now wider and had a small lip running along the bottom edge for additional strength and styling.

Inside the bodyshell, the rear seat area was also revised, with the previous battery and storage wells dispensed with to lower the seats in the rear of the vehicle. The VW battery now sat in its original home on the floorpan, covered by the rear seat unit. With a hinged and padded backrest that could fold flat, the buggy could carry a large amount of luggage, and was now a more practical and sensible form of transport than ever before.

With over three-quarters of production going abroad (mostly the Middle East) the Super continued to be developed. In 1977, the revised front hood with glassfiber screen frame from the short-wheelbase buggy was added, allowing the bolt-on hardtops to be used. Two years later, further revisions to the shape included wider and reshaped wings, and a change from the previously available sculpted side panels to long, boxier designs.

After a series of owners, the GP Super Buggy has been in a state of flux since the late 1990s, and has largely lost its market to newer designs. Nevertheless, the project is now under the ownership of Kingfisher Kustoms in Birmingham, and the buggy is available to special order.

An early GP Super Buggy fitted with side panels and front hood from the later re-styling of the buggy makes an eye-catching show-winner. (Courtesy Mike Key)

The Super Buggy design was altered to allow parts interchangability between the GP models. The boxy side panels were a late addition to the design. (Courtesy Purestock/Alamy)

85

GP LDV (LIGHT DELIVERY VAN)

DATA PANEL

Production dates
1970-1996

Numbers built
250 (approx)

Export markets
Greece, Germany, Austria, Switzerland, USA, Australia, South Africa

Wheelbase
94.5in

Identification tips
Two-seater, long-wheelbase buggy with reverse-angled hardtop roof and flat pickup bed. Late models had flat windshields and a removable roof section

In late 1970, an interesting extension to the basic buggy range originated from the home of the Beach and Super buggies. During visits to potential export markets such as Greece and Cyprus, GP proprietors Pierre du Plessis and John Jobber had seen ordinary saloon cars converted to utility-type trucks with open backs. Believing they could produce a VW Beetle-based Light Delivery Van to meet the market for such vehicles, du Plessis and Jobber set to work to modify their existing buggy design.

Taking a Super Buggy bodyshell as a starting point, the rear fenders were widened and extended forward to create a mounting point for a glassfiber roof section. This reverse-angle hardtop was moulded in one piece, together with the front hood and glassfiber windshield frame (which accepted an Austin A40 Farina rear window as a windshield). The rear cab window was made of plexiglass, and the pickup bed was made of marine plywood, and provided a floor area of 11sqft and a carrying capacity of 10cwt.

Demonstrating attention to detail, GP offered some nice accessories to finish off its neat little truck. These included the sculpted glassfiber lower side panels that sat below the body waistline, the chromed grab-rails for the sides and rear of the pickup area, and a neat tonneau cover for the rear deck to keep it dry.

Officially launched at the 1971 Racing Car Show in London, the trendy pickup van never really captured the imagination of the home audience.

Interest in the buggy increased, however, following a build-up feature in a series of articles written by Dermot Bambridge for *Hot Car* magazine late in 1972. The LDV also had its first outing at the Geneva Motor Show the same year, which began to generate enquiries for exports (many of the buggies finding their way to countries such as Switzerland, Germany and Austria). Proving that the LDV's appeal wasn't limited to Europe alone, licensed production also began in America, Australia, and South Africa.

The cab section of the LDV was always designed to have some form of weatherproof doors (these were available as vinyl side screens with clear windows, or glassfiber units with sliding windows). The latter were heavy units and caused problems with strain on the supporting hinges. In 1974 they were changed to lighter ABS plastic. At the same time, a redesign of the dashboard allowed proper

The LDV took the GP buggy a stage further with the concept of a pickup truck for small businesses or farmers. Mostly they were built as custom-style vehicles.

Models A-Z

vents to be installed to demist the screen of the closed cab.

Perhaps the most significant change in the LDV history came in 1977 when the entire GP range became rationalised so that the same front hood fitted all vehicles, and the long-wheelbase buggies shared the same basic body moulding.

Revisions to the shape were noticeable in the flat windshield (and removable hardtop section on later vehicles), and wider fenders front and rear. Inside, the body tub featured the same rear seat moulding as on the later Super buggies, which could (if the pickup bed was removed) accommodate a rear seat conversion for two, somewhat exposed, passengers. The side panels were also changed for the boxy items from the modified Super Buggy.

Despite a lack of promotion, the LDV remained in production up until 1996 when the whole GP buggy operation moved from second owner Roy Pierpoint's company, GP Buggies, to David Kuschel.

GP brochure advertising the LDV (Light Delivery Van) buggy shows off the stylish lines of its neat little truck.

Period 1970s LDV cruiser with slot-mag wheels and chrome fittings.

The front windshield was originally a curved item, but was changed to a flat one to rationalise the whole range of GP models. Later LDVs had a separate hardtop, which, once removed, transformed the buggy into a true open-air convertible.

Room for a small one in the back? Neat LDV pickup bed seems the ideal home for this toy VW, painted to match the Outrage VW drag race team colors.

GP RANCHERO

DATA PANEL

Production dates
1974-1996

Numbers built
50 (approx)

Export markets
Sweden, Switzerland, Austria, Germany, Middle East

Wheelbase
94.5in

Identification tips
Estate/stationwagon buggy with opening hatchback rear window, curved windshield, and one-piece front hood/windshield/roof on early models. Removable roof on later versions. Sculpted side panels, or boxy, scooped panels below the body waistline

Following the example set several years earlier by Dean Jeffries with Kyote II, his multi-hardtopped Stateside buggy, UK manufacturer GP decided to widen the appeal of its Super Buggy by adding a proper stationwagon hardtop. Billed as a 'buggy estate car,' the Ranchero was endowed with all the fun-orientated characteristics of GP's regular buggy, but in an extremely practical package. Being a full four-seater stationwagon, with a fixed glassfiber roof, it was completely weatherproof, and a lot easier to insure.

Introduced late in 1974, the Ranchero took the GP LDV theme a stage further, and was based around one of the long-wheelbase Super Buggy bodyshells. The main addition was the all-in-one front hood, windshield frame, and hardtop roof section. With a rear lifting tailgate and a window with hinges and lock taken from the Hillman Imp car, as well as a curved Austin A40 Farina rear window as a front windshield, the Ranchero really did seem a practical proposition.

Doors were offered as an option, and were available as either glassfiber units with sliding plexiglass windows, or steel-framed vinyl side screens, both mounted to the front windshield frame. These added to the practical nature of the buggy and made the interior very comfortable, especially when the original Beetle heating system was in operation. As with all GP kits, the bodyshells were moulded in fire-retardant resin (a requirement for foreign markets), and finished in a range of plain pigmented colors or sparkling metalflake.

True to form, the 1975 Geneva Motor Show proved the springboard from which

British-built 'Thunderbug' started life as a badly-neglected GP Ranchero kit, and became a show-winning buggy with a custom velour interior. (Courtesy Mike Key)

Models A-Z

the Ranchero buggy was launched on an unsuspecting world concerned about the oil crisis and motoring economy. Besides the usual European export markets (Switzerland, Austria and Germany), the Ranchero made inroads into countries as diverse as Sweden and Saudi Arabia, as well as other Middle Eastern destinations.

Like the LDV, the Ranchero had the improved, vacuum-formed ABS doors, and, in 1977, a revised front hood and hardtop section incorporating a flat windshield. The wider fender sections and improved rear seat moulding from the Super Buggy body tub were also used (the bodyshells became fully interchangeable at this time). One final improvement was a modification to the hardtop roof to make it removable, and able to share the new front hood and windshield frame from the short-wheelbase Mk II GP Buggy. The range of GP buggies was now complete and totally adaptable. By starting with an open-top, long-wheelbase Super Buggy, an LDV or Ranchero hardtop section could be added at a later date, if required, to meet changing needs.

The Ranchero could be all things to all people: the nearest equivalent to a proper stationwagon, but still retaining the buggy heritage; a panel van for business use or a mobile advertising wagon for those promoting their services. GP supplied a pair of eye-catching, custom-painted black Rancheros, with gold 'John Player Special' signwriting, for promotional use by that company.

By 1994, the entire range of GP buggies had passed from the hands of GP Projects to a new Ascot-based company called GP Buggies. Run by ex-autocross champion Roy Pierpoint, the Ranchero was kept available, though few were sold. More recently, the GP buggy operation has moved again and the Ranchero and LDV options have been dropped from the range. Those that remain will be examples of a good idea that never quite found the commercial niche of their predecessors.

The show-winning 'Thunderbug' proved that a stationwagon buggy didn't have to be boring. The vehicle had a fully chromed engine and suspension. (Courtesy Mike Key)

The Ranchero again proved the versatility of the GP range of buggies. With a stationwagon-type hardtop, the buggy became a practical form of daily transport. (Courtesy GP Projects)

'Doors,' in the form of vacuum-formed plastic or steel-framed side screens, were available as an optional extra for Rancheros.

With an opening rear tailgate taken from a Hillman Imp car, the Ranchero was as versatile as many modern hatchbacks. (Courtesy GP Projects)

GT BUGGY

DATA PANEL

Production dates
1997-2007

Numbers built
SWB: 5 LWB: 95

Export markets
Egypt, Ireland, Holland, Belgium

Wheelbase
SWB: 82.5 LWB: 94.5in

Identification tips
Long-wheelbase classic-looking buggy, with either an alloy- or glassfiber-framed windshield. Central styling ridge to front hood, and GT badge on the front. Wide rear fenders and squared-off licence plate mount

With a rekindled interest in buggies in the late 1980s and early 1990s, it was, perhaps, inevitable that many older buggy moulds were dusted off and production restarted. New and original designs were thinner on the ground, and it wasn't until 1997 that an all-new British buggy design saw the light of day.

The GT Buggy, styled by Melvyn Hubbard for UK manufacturer GT Mouldings, captured the period look of a classical 1960s–style buggy, but had many fresh ideas of its own. With the increasingly strict construction and registration requirements for kit-built vehicles in the UK, the new buggy was designed from the outset to fit an unmodified Beetle platform chassis, as this avoided the need for cutting and shutting the floorpan, making the kit simplicity itself to build.

To compensate for the look of the longer bodyshell, the rear wheelarches were widened to accommodate extremely large diameter wheels and tyres, thus correcting the visual imbalance. At the rear, the cavernous arches of the buggy swung round to form a pleasing engine cover, with a sculpted central section forming a licence plate mount.

Reminiscent of the EMPI Imp when viewed directly from the back (though substantially wider), the new buggy was an attractive combination of sleek curves and brutal masculinity. The entire rear part of the bodyshell was fully supported underneath with strengthening bars that continued along the length of the buggy sides, and added torsional rigidity to the bodyshell. The top edge of the body had the ubiquitous (and entirely necessary) soft-top rain lip to keep weather out when a top was fitted.

From the front, the buggy captured the cuteness of traditional-looking vehicles with its snub-nose front hood, recessed front licence plate mount, and central styling ridge. A flush-mounted fuel filler sat in the centre of the hood, giving a clean, modern look. The polished alloy windshield frame slid into grooves on each side of the dashboard (which was an integral part of the front hood moulding), and sat low to emphasise the raked-look of the buggy.

For those building on a budget, an all-in-one hood and integral glassfiber windshield frame was also offered, with a separately moulded dashboard. So the buggy couldn't be confused with others, a neat moulded-in 'GT' badge was positioned on the front of the hood.

Inside the body tub, other neat design features prevailed: notably the rear seat area, which allowed the location of the battery in a separate well, and meant that a VW independent rear suspension could be fitted to the VW floorpan. A raised moulding under the rear seat also

Traditionally-styled, this Egyptian-built GT Buggy poses in the desert sun.

Models A-Z

White stripes on this GT Buggy are color-impregnated in the sunshine yellow gelcoat.

A trio of GT Buggies were built by Kingfisher Kustoms for the Coca-Cola 'Enjoy Summer' promotional tour of UK tourist attractions.

allowed for proper clutch release arm clearance (a major fault on many early designs). The inner bodyshell sides featured strengthening ribs moulded into the body tub, whilst the flange that rests on the rear of the floorpan provided proper mounts for location of the rear body bolts.

The GT Buggy immediately made its mark on the scene, with individuals and companies alike enjoying the contemporary design, ease of build, and seating for four. A trio of promotional vehicles were built for an 'Enjoy Summer' Coca-Cola tour of British leisure attractions, which saw the buggies fitted with specially-made ice cooler boxes in the rear seat area. Similar vehicles were also built for a Liptons Iced Tea promotion. The GT Buggy was later developed into a short-wheelbase design, but very few were built before the company ceased all buggy production in 2007 to concentrate on other work.

Hustler-styled rear end of the GT Buggy covers wide wheels and the VW engine in style.

GT Buggy promotional material.

The GT Buggy is a long-wheelbase design, but looks shorter than most due to the visual proportioning of the rear fenders and the sculpted side panels.

DATA PANEL

Production dates
2002 to date

Numbers built
Unknown

Export markets
Spain

Wheelbase
78.5in

Identification tips
Very modern sportscar-like design, with opening front hood and rear panel, inner liners front and rear, curved wheelarches and side scoops; contoured dashboard with central console; twin-hoop roll bars

A synthesis of Ferrari 308, Lotus Elise and Audi TT sportscar concepts combine to make the Hoppa Street Buggy entirely fresh and original. (Courtesy Ultra VW)

With buggy popularity reaching new heights in the UK during the latter part of the 1990s, it was inevitable that someone would try and design a model which brought the buggy concept right up to date. Like many designs, the 'Hoppa son of a Beach' buggy design began life as a rough design on a scrap of paper. By working this way and building up a style integrating a mix of curves with sharp lines, rather than modifying an existing design, the new concept was a fresh, sophisticated buggy, which paid homage to the basic idea rather than slavishly copying it. The idea – penned by John Warner, a design technician at TWR (Tom Walkinshaw Racing) – was to combine a modern street buggy concept with that of a new sports car. With plans to offer only turnkey cars powered by Subaru Impreza engines, John had great ambitions for his new creation. With colleagues Oli Thorndale and Barry Howard, the three set up a new company called Fubar Factory, and enlisted the help of John's father, Barry, a full-size clay model maker for Vauxhall during his working life, to build the basic buck pattern. The body panels were designed using traditional automotive modelling techniques, including foam sheets and clay. Designed for and based on a shortened VW Beetle chassis, but using an integral steel support frame, the Hoppa concept had a modern convertible sports car appeal, and was aimed at a market far beyond that of the traditional buggy buyer.

The bodyshell pulled from the TWR-fabricated moulds had a hint of Lotus Elise about it, with opening front hood and rear hatch, curved Fiat 126 windscreen, side air scoops, rear head restraints, and chromed roll-hoops. The buggy was a world away from the first Meyers Manx, which celebrated its 40th anniversary at the time of the Hoppa launch.

Neat design features of the Hoppa body included removable inner liners that could be lifted out to give superb access to the engine and gearbox at the rear, and the VW suspension at the front. The liner that surrounded the VW fuel tank up front gave builders a really neat, professional finish. The buggy seemed destined for a bright future, but John Warner's move into employment in the British car industry effectively halted the project. Rather than see the design abandoned, however, his father, Barry, took on the whole project, re-named it Hoppa Street Buggy, and moved to Devon where he looked to manufacture it.

Working in partnership with local VW and sportscar restorer Phoenix Coachworks, run by Gary Bastin who took care of all the mechanical work on the buggies, and also manufactured the steel frame and shortened the chassis, Barry Warner took the Hoppa forward. Now offering the buggy as a self-assembly kit, prices became more attractive to buyers, and the kit generated a lot of attention worldwide. The modified

Models A-Z

buggy used ideas sourced from modern car design, such as the dashboard top being covered in Alcantara to prevent reflected glare, and a neat contoured dashboard and central console to house modern instrumentation. Despite the modern styling approach, the Hoppa still had the right number of nostalgic styling cues to connect it to predecessors, such as the separate headlights, exposed engine, and wide wheels under the cavernous arches. With soft-tops and a hardtop in development for the buggy, the Hoppa looks set to provide fun-in-the-sun motoring for a whole new generation of buggy enthusiasts.

Vivid paintwork ensures the Hoppa Street Buggy gets noticed wherever it goes. (Courtesy Barry Warner)

Designed to cruise fashionable city centres rather than dunes, the Hoppa Street Buggy looks like no other. (Courtesy Barry Warner)

Styling of the buggy pays homage to the basic concept of the first Manxes, whilst proving stylish and sophisticated for the modern age. (Courtesy Barry Warner)

Now available in pure kit form, the Hoppa Street Buggy is still VW Beetle-based, but you'd hardly know it. (Courtesy Barry Warner)

HUMBUG & BEAUJANGLE CAN-AM

DATA PANEL

Production dates
Humbug: 1969-1971
Can-Am: 1972-3/1985

Numbers built
US: Unknown, UK: 6

Export markets
UK

Wheelbase
89.5in

Identification tips
Ultra-low Group 7-style road buggy with tilted-back seats. VW headlights on front fenders, rear engine access panel, and large curved side panels

In the US, by mid-1969 the buggy scene was rapidly changing, with two very distinct directions being taken by designers: the first toward pure racing buggies, built as tubular frameworks, with large race-prepared VW or Corvair engines; and the second toward buggies that looked more like sportscars and were strictly for street use.

Sensing the direction in which the market for road buggies was going, American Fiberglass Products of Berkeley, California, introduced the Humbug in April 1969. Styled as a pseudo sportscar, but retaining some of the features of previous dune buggies, the Humbug had been thought through with regard to the chassis. Rather than use the customary 80in wheelbase, shortened VW Beetle floorpan, the design called for shortening the floorpan by 5in between the pedals and front suspension. This method greatly simplified the task by eliminating the need to shorten the shift lever, handbrake cables, and clutch cable. Such surgery resulted in a front-to-rear weight distribution of 35 per cent and 65 per cent, thus giving the Humbug superb handling qualities.

The Humbug body was a compact unit comprising the main bodyshell, and side and rear panels (which had a low, Can-Am-influenced style). Even with a windshield fitted, the car had an overall height of just 36in, and the body's high rear deck area allowed plenty of room for a variety of engines, plus the VW fuel tank. The vented rear panel and side panels also completely enclosed the engine and wheels, thus making the buggy totally legal in all states. The body was designed so that the driver sat in a steeply reclined bucket seat, with a line of vision between the two raised front fenders that conveniently housed the stock VW front headlights.

Other parts from the VW – such as the electrical equipment, speedometer and rear lights – could also be used, though items like the windshield and wheels were aftermarket parts. Extra fuel tanks, for long distance driving, could also be fitted behind the cavernous side panels.

Giving the impression of a Group 7 racing car, the Humbug was one of the first serious attempts to cross the divide between buggy and sportscar, and used an amalgamation of parts sourced from both dune buggy and race car suppliers.

Although the engine on this example looks somewhat naked, the car could be fitted with an all-enclosing rear panel, for legality and weatherproofing.

Models A-Z

In 1972 the buggy caught the attention of British customising company Beaujangle Enterprises in Salford, Manchester. Partners Nik Sandeman-Allen and Phil Smith imported a bodyshell from the original manufacturer, and quietly went into production, renaming the 'new' buggy the Beaujangle Can-Am. Launched in April 1972 to an expectant motoring press at the Mallory Park racing circuit, the American Can-Am series Group 7-styled car generated a lot of favourable comment from journalists more used to seeing sportscars than dune buggies.

The company (renamed Beaujangle Sales Ltd) made a point of advising customers to properly lower the VW front suspension and decamber the back to give the vehicle the sort of handling the swoopy bodywork promised. Optional extras included the alloy-framed windshield, wire-mesh engine access panel and an interior trim kit. Later in the year, Beaujangle introduced a hardtop with gull-wing doors to make the buggy more appropriate for British weather, but this did little to improve sales. By 1973, the receivers had been called in and the firm was liquidated.

Neither the Beaujangle Can-Am nor its original American cousin, the Humbug, survived. In 1985 a UK company called Lemazone attempted to resurrect the design, but it was a short-lived affair and the buggy finally disappeared.

The Humbug/Can-Am was a mere 36in high, even with a windshield fitted, and crossed the divide between buggies and the growing number of VW-based exotic kit-cars. (Courtesy Custom Car)

A period advertisement from the 1970s giving the impression that the Humbug was in the same league as a Group 7 racing car.

The design appeared in the UK under the name of Beaujangle Can-Am, taking its name from the American racing car design heritage. A gull-wing hardtop was also developed for the car. (Courtesy Custom Car)

The Humbug had a Can-Am-styled body with a low windshield or a pair of fly-screens. VW Beetle front headlamps were used on the curved front fenders.

HUSTLER

DATA PANEL

Production dates
1969-1972

Numbers built
350 (approx)

Export markets
Unknown

Wheelbase
SWB: 82.5in LWB: 94.5in

Identification tips
Squared-off licence plate area to rear of bodyshell; rectangular indent near the front of the hood (for maker's name); raised lip around the top edge of the bodyshell. Often fitted with wheelarch extensions as part of moulded side fairings

From small beginnings as an agency for the British GP Beach Buggy in 1969, Essex Proto Conversions, run by brothers Terry and Colin Cordingley, quickly went on to develop its own design – the Hustler. The first model was a long-wheelbase kit which was quickly dropped due to its somewhat ungainly styling, and chassis flexing problems associated with the longer wheelbase.

Instead, a new version was developed for the VW chassis shortened by 12in (a wheelbase similar to the stateside EMPI Imp). This allowed the traditional shortened look, but still gave reasonable legroom for driver and passengers in the 2+2 seating layout.

The Hustler kept the classic design of period buggies, but was produced with the British climate and legal requirements firmly in mind. This resulted in several styling features unique to the buggy, which complemented the extremely well-finished bodyshell. Most noticeable were the side fairings which formed front wheel spats, and the all-enclosing rear wheelarches to prevent spray being thrown up from the tires. This coverage of the rear of the body also offered some engine protection, and went a long way toward ensuring complete street legality. The fairings also gave a more finished look to the complete car, and provided a flat area along the lower part of the buggy's side on which to emblazon the manufacturer's name.

The name 'Hustler' also appeared in the small rectangular indent on the front hood above the licence plate, which was fixed to a flat area on the front hood where it extended down to cover the somewhat exposed VW front suspension. At the rear, the buggy bodyshell had a neat, truncated look, with the rear wings swept round to finish in a flat mounting for the back licence plate. The rear of the bodyshell also featured a stepped design to the lower edge of the wings, adding strength to the whole moulding through the use of compound curves.

Beneath the rear bodyshell, moulded-in stiffeners added to the rigidity of the design (also providing a mounting point for the glassfiber inner arch mouldings that the manufacturer had thoughtfully provided to prevent mud and water being thrown into the exposed VW engine). To keep rainwater on the outside of the vehicle when a soft-top was fitted, a small lip was moulded into the top edge of the bodyshell, though with limited success. The soft-top was a pram-type affair, and fitted over a folding double-hoop frame, regardless of whether or not a rollbar was installed. It gave reasonable headroom at the rear of the car for four people to travel in relative comfort.

Proving the strength of the design, EPC's well-appointed demonstrator takes to the air in a spot of off-roading. (Courtesy Quadrant Picture Library)

Models A-Z

From its original premises of Service Garage at Chelmsford, the firm quickly moved to meet the demand of the buggy boom in the early 1970s, and relocated its offices to Hornchurch, Essex (though retaining workshops in Chelmsford).

A late addition to the accessories available for the Hustler was a leathergrain-look hardtop with optional 'porthole' windows on each side, together with a rear window. Whilst practical in the wet, the hardtop spoilt the otherwise chic lines of the buggy, and few were actually made.

The Hustler proved to be one of the better British buggies in terms of design, quality and finish, but it suffered the same fate as others when the buggy scene faltered in 1972. Despite one final move to nearby Dagenham, the over-traded company ceased operating later that year, and bailiffs arrived to repossess the company's factory and equipment. The Hustler design finally disappeared, but did provide the inspiration for the GT Buggy design which was to follow in the 1990s.

A Hustler buggy rebuilt in the 1990s shows the buggy's lines to perfection, and oozes period charm. (Courtesy Mike Key)

The GP-inspired Hustler buggy was built to be practical, and with the British weather in mind. This 1970s example is fitted with GP buggy side panels.

Period advertisement for Essex Proto Conversions, maker of the Hustler buggy.

The Hustler buggy appeared in promotional advertising of the day – here on a WH Smith gift card from the 1970s.

HUSTLER GT

DATA PANEL

Production dates
1970-1972

Numbers built
50 (approx)

Export markets
Unknown

Wheelbase
82.5in

Identification tips
Faired-in headlights to front hood. Curved front windshield in glassfibre frame (part of front hood moulding). Central console over part of the VW transmission tunnel

The GT version of the Hustler added a different front hood and revised dashboard to the well-conceived buggy. The headlights were standard 7in round units from a Mini.

Essex Proto Conversions decided early in the buggy boom that the ideal way to capture a larger part of the market was to offer a variety of kits, all based on the same chassis. The idea was that when a customer wanted a different vehicle, he or she could change the body rather than the complete car. The 12in shortened VW chassis, used for the Hustler buggy, became the basis for another version, the GT Hustler (as well as a glassfiber sportscar called the Pinza GS).

The GT Hustler was aimed at those who wanted a sportier look and better performance than offered by the original, tried and tested, traditional-looking buggy. The polished, alloy-framed windscreen look was therefore replaced by a new front hood, designed to fit the standard buggy bodyshell, but featuring headlamps faired-into the hood, and a curved windshield in an integral glassfiber frame.

By being moulded as a unitary item, the screen frame had the added advantage of being the same color as the front hood and main bodyshell, and was strengthened at the sides to avoid cracking when the tension of a soft-top was applied to the top edge.

Headlamps were standard 7in British Mini design, and the windshield came from an Italian Fiat 500 or 600 saloon (the sales literature claimed that this design would add another 15mph to the buggy's top speed).

Looks were vastly improved: gone was the stubbiness of the traditional type of buggy hood with stand-up headlamps, in favour of something that approached a contemporary design for the British customer.

Inside the car, the dashboard was changed to accommodate the curvature of the front screen, but it was still a neat, leatherette-look glassfiber design. Unusually for a buggy, this was manufactured in both right- and left-hand drive format, rather than a universal fitting to suit either. Another neat feature was a matching central console, which was made to fit under the dashboard and form a tray over the VW Beetle transmission tunnel, extending back past the emergency brake. This allowed more room for additional instrumentation, giving a more sportscar-like impression. This console was subsequently made available for all Hustler buggies, giving the interior a more professionally-finished look.

EPC wanted its customers to be able to produce well-finished buggies without the need to import expensive American equipment. In line with this desire, EPC produced a large number of extras at very reasonable prices, the most noteworthy of which were the excellent bucket seats which were eagerly purchased by those working to a limited budget when building their buggies.

Models A-Z

A GT Hustler, at a buggy convention in the 1970s.

The optional side panels, with boxy rear arches, helped legalise the buggy by covering the engine and tires. A pram-effect soft-top gave headroom for two rear seat passengers.

Construction of the GT Hustler was slightly more complicated than with the original, and required the windshield wiper armature to be lengthened to ensure a complete sweep of the wiper blades over the larger screen. The petrol tank neck also had to be repositioned to allow a central filler, avoiding the glassfiber headlamp pods. Nevertheless, the GT Hustler looked well finished, especially when topped with a chrome flip-up racing filler cap, and achieved a separate identity from the basic design of the standard buggy.

The GT Hustler shared the same fate as the original Hustler when EPC went into liquidation in 1972 (another casualty of the buggy boom ending). The GT Hustlers that remain are a unique reminder of one of the better 1970s buggy designs.

The GT Hustler, like its GP-inspired brother, was a well-made kit, and often found itself used off-road.

The GT Hustler's good looks were admired by many, including Diana, Princess of Wales, who owned a 1971-registered vehicle.

99

INVADER

DATA PANEL

Production dates
1971–1991

Numbers built
150 (approx)

Export markets
Greece

Wheelbase
80in

Identification tips
Finned rear section to the back of the bodyshell; curved windshield in an alloy frame on Mk I kits, and a GRP frame on Mk IIs; the sleek aerodynamic look of the Mk II bodyshell was deeper, to allow for large tyres, and also had an opening engine hatch

During the early 1970s buggy craze, it came as no surprise to find a buggy appearing at Britain's most prestigious annual car event, the London Motor Show. Built for *The Daily Telegraph Magazine*, by rally driver John Sprinzel at his Paddington workshop, the exercise was intended to show that a fun car could be built by anyone with some mechanical knowledge – or a helpful local garage.

Rather than stick with a homegrown buggy bodyshell, the magazine imported a sleek Scorpion L T body, windshield, lights and seats from leading US manufacturer Desert Fox Sand Buggies of Phoenix, Arizona. Built with a Porsche engine, this eye-catching vehicle made its debut at the show, freshly sprayed in gleaming gunmetal paint, and with huge chromed wheels. After all the attention it received at the show from press and public alike, the buggy was soon heading for a new home, and production at SP Motors of Birmingham (which already produced a classically-styled vehicle called the GB Buggy).

It wasn't long before the buggy reappeared in its new guise. Called the Invader, it featured only a few changes to the basic shape, and had the covered headlights, all-accommodating wide wheelarches and rolled door sills of its predecessor, but the front and rear lights were replaced by more easily accessible British units. The only other change SP Motors proprietor John Cullen made was the production of a specially-made, curved, Triplex windshield and alloy frame.

Launched in 1971, and manufactured by a sub-contractor to meet the steadily increasing demand, the Invader made its mark in a big way. Marketed very much as a complete kit, customers received a very comprehensive package consisting of bodyshell complete with bonded-in fuel tank, front and rear lights, plexiglass headlight shields, curved windshield in

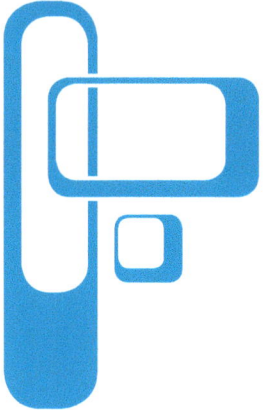

On the beach with the Scorpion L T buggy built by rally driver John Sprinzel for the Daily Telegraph Magazine *for the London Motor Show in 1970.*

Models A-Z

alloy frame, two quilt-effect bucket seats, wrap-around matching rear seat, rollbar, rear twin-bar bumper, fan guard, quick-release chrome filler cap, and the essential nuts, bolts and building instructions (in fact, almost everything the builder needed, bar the VW chassis and running gear). Whilst this approach meant that the Invader was almost twice the price of other UK-made buggy kits, it did ensure that customers' Invaders were built to a very high standard.

A Mk II version of the Invader soon followed, and featured a number of updates on the original kit. The Mk II had a 3in deeper main body tub to allow better tire clearance under the wheelarches. It also featured a glassfiber windshield surround, and had an opening in the rear deck for much easier engine access. A hinged glassfiber engine cover now sat on the rear deck to ensure full weatherproofing.

A serious fire at the factory in 1971, and changes to the proprietor's main business, meant that, by the mid-1970s, production of the Invader was seriously restricted, although the kit did remain available throughout the upheavals. In 1975 one last development was announced – a Model T-type hardtop with porthole windows in the sides. Shortly after this, kit manufacture was taken over by Croy Glassfiber Products, which had been SP Motors' sub-contractor for many years. Small numbers of kits continued to be produced until 1988 when the project moved to southern-based buggy laminator GT Mouldings (though it was subsequently passed on to a buggy enthusiast and has not resurfaced).

Currently no longer available, the Invader remained in production for a full 20 years: a long time for any buggy design.

One of the best Mk I Invaders built in Britain was 'Little Chev,' powered by a chromed and polished 6-cylinder Chevrolet Corvair engine.

The Invader buggy was directly sired from the American Scorpion LT buggy. This neat example sports US-themed paintwork.

The sleek Invader design made the buggy more 'street' than 'sand,' though it could still cut it off-road when required. (Courtesy Quadrant Picture Library)

A regular feature at 1970s buggy conventions, the design is less common now due to the renewed popularity of the classic Manx design.

The Dune Buggy Handbook

The Manx Dune Buggy Club, formed by Bruce Meyers in the 1990s, regularly holds events for 'buggistas' to enjoy with like-minded enthusiasts. (Courtesy Mel Baker)

A prize pair! Streetracer-styled JAS buggy is followed by a customised VW Bay-window Bus. (Courtesy Mike Key)

The Manta Ray II Kyote buggy design was developed by Dean Jeffries specifically for the Monkees' film *Head* before going into production. (Courtesy Dan MacMillan)

Mooneyes 'Dune Runner' dune buggy with retro-diamond vinyl upholstery, gold metalflake paint, chrome, and surfboards. (Courtesy Mooneyes USA Inc)

Gallery

The American Deserter GT buggy was also made in Germany. This one reflects a current European trend; single-color paintwork and high-tech engineering.

John Leso's Manx drag racer is built on a custom tube chassis, uses nitrous oxide for extra power, and Porsche brakes to stop it at the end of the quarter-mile. (Courtesy Mel Baker)

The sleek lines of the Deserter GT were developed from the Bounty Hunter design by Autodynamics in the US.

Bruce Meyers' sophisticated street buggy The Manx SR featured flip-up doors, and removable roof panel. (Courtesy Mel Baker)

Buggies cry out to be customised, and this GP Beach Buggy features frenched rear lights, custom interior and color-coded engine. (Courtesy Mike Key)

The Dune Buggy Handbook

Built by the US LoCash racing team, 'Junkyard Turbo' is an example of a modern take on the traditional Manx-styled dune buggy. (Courtesy Mike Key)

Blue metalflake Prowler buggy is used for what it was built for; powering across the sand and into the dunes. (Photo Tom Wood/Alamy)

American buggies, the Bounty Hunter and Renegade, have also been made in Britain. This pair enjoy a cruise on the beach in England. (Courtesy Mike Key)

Ultra-clean Prowler buggy in eye-popping Kawasaki paintwork is enough to make other road users green with envy. (Courtesy Mike Key)

This British-built Classic Manx appeared in a television advertisement for a telephone company. (Courtesy Mike Key)

Gallery

The Sidewinder buggy was a fresh take on the traditional Manx design, but with wider coverage for tyres, and better engine access. (Courtesy Mike Key)

Rainbow-effect Mirraflake sparkles in the gelcoat of this black Sidewinder buggy, finished with Porsche 'cookie-cutter' wheels and stinger exhaust. (Courtesy Mike Key)

East Coast Manx in the UK still makes the traditional buggy design. This is its demonstrator, with flower-power hardtop, mag wheels and baja exhaust. (Courtesy Mike Key)

The Doon buggy first appeared in the UK in 2001 in SWB form, with a LWB version arriving two years later. The modern design was patterned from scratch. (Courtesy Chad Chadwick)

Long-wheelbase Volksrod buggy is given a street-racer look with a low roll bar and flyscreen. (Courtesy Mike Key)

British Manta Ray buggy is given a unique look with twin front lights faired in to the sweeping front bodyshell.

The Dune Buggy Handbook

The JAS Speedkits buggy was a latecomer to the ranks of British designs, being produced from 1998, and is still manufactured in SWB and LWB designs. (Courtesy JAS Speedkits)

Dirk Tinck from Belgium made the pattern for this one-off buggy from scratch. The design became the Surf Buggy, produced in the UK by GT Mouldings. (Courtesy Mike Key)

Many copies of the Manta Ray buggy have appeared in the UK, including the CTR and the Seaspray. This Seaspray model runs a monster 2.5-litre Type 4 VW engine.

Fuscia metalflake paint on this JAS buggy makes it stand out, and was the de rigeur finish on many buggies during the buggy boom of the 1970s. (Courtesy Mike Key)

Classic shape of the GP Beach Buggy has rarely been bettered. With mag wheels, white interior and plenty of chrome, this example shines on a summers' day. (Courtesy Mike Key)

The Manta Ray helped launch the buggy scene in the UK when a build-up feature on the model appeared in *Custom Car* magazine.

Gallery

Cute early GP Beach Buggy with metallic paint, high-back seats and Sprintstar wheels for a period-perfect feel. (Courtesy Mike Key)

The EMPI Sportster could be bought as a kit of parts, or created from plans using metal sheet, like this British-built car. (Courtesy Mike Key)

BF Meyers promotional shot from the 1960s. Note the Manx hardtop, and pop-out rear window. (Courtesy Ludvigsen Library)

Manx-type buggy with nitrous-injected 2,332cc engine uses wheelie bars out back to stop the lightweight car flipping over on acceleration. (Courtesy Mel Baker)

The Dune Buggy Handbook

BF Meyers & Co built a couple of canary yellow lifeguard Manxes for the LA County Lifeguards. This one, now restored, once worked the Zuma beach area. (Courtesy Mel Hubbard)

'Kick-Out' traditional Manx design at Pomona auto show. The buggy is dubbed 'Mr Manx,' and owned by Bruce Meyers. (Courtesy Stephan Szantai)

The British FF Buggy has its origins in the American Balboa buggy design, but with a revised front hood and neat sculpted side panels for a classic look. (Courtesy Mike Key)

The sleek lines of the Renegade buggy were Corvette-inspired at the front, and perfect for drag racing with its aerodynamic shape.

The Tow'd was Bruce Meyers' second-generation buggy designed purely for off-roading, using a tube frame rather than a shortened VW Beetle floorpan for lightness and strength. (Courtesy Mel Baker)

French-built Hustler buggy at a VW show looks purposeful with a Type 4 VW engine for power.

Gallery

The EMPI Imp was truly an icon of US buggy design, was marketed well, and became a real competitor of the Meyers Manx. (Courtesy Jim Maxwell)

The wedge-shaped Mangosta buggy was developed by Detroit automotive stylist Karl Krumme, and incorporated ideas from passenger cars. (Courtesy Mel Baker)

Bottoms up! The driver gets more than sand in his mouth as this GP Super buggy gets 'on its head' in the 1981 James Bond movie *For your Eyes Only*. (Courtesy copyright Danjaq, LLC & United Artists Corp)

The Australian buggy scene was stifled by onerous construction laws after the first wave of production in the late 1960s/early 1970s. New buggies are few and far between, but some still get built. (Courtesy *VW Trends*)

Dutch-built Hustler buggy fitted with VW Bus suspension for extra ground clearance, and a Type 4 engine for torque in the sand. (Courtesy Henny Jore)

Berrien's Roadster-T buggy was originally produced by a company called Sand Dancer in the US, and closely resembles the Berry Mini-T.

The classic Meyers Manx buggy kit has been made under licence in France since the late 1990s. These two Belgian-built Manxes enjoy fun on the beach. (Courtesy Stephan Szantai)

The EMPI Imp was designed primarily for road use, and the company specialised in supplying matching accessories such as seats, Sprintstar wheels, and engine hop-up parts. (Courtesy Mike Key)

The view most other drivers will see, as this buggy features a high-performance engine. (Courtesy Mike Key)

Gallery

Designed as a LWB buggy from the start, The GT Buggy bodyshell comfortably covered wide wheels and high performance engines. (Courtesy Mike Key)

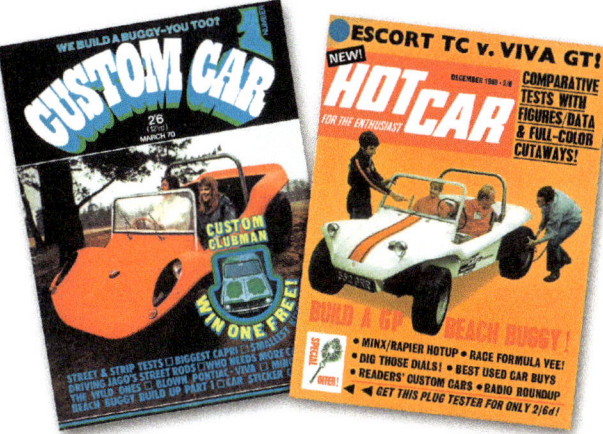

Two leading automotive publications, *Custom Car* and *Hot Car*, promoted buggies in the UK from the late 1960s to early 1970s.

At the height of the British buggy boom, two books were published that gave information on buggy construction, legality, and details of manufacturers.

The British Kombat buggy was a close reproduction of the 1970s Vulture buggy design with rectangular headlights and an opening engine cover. (Courtesy *Volksworld*)

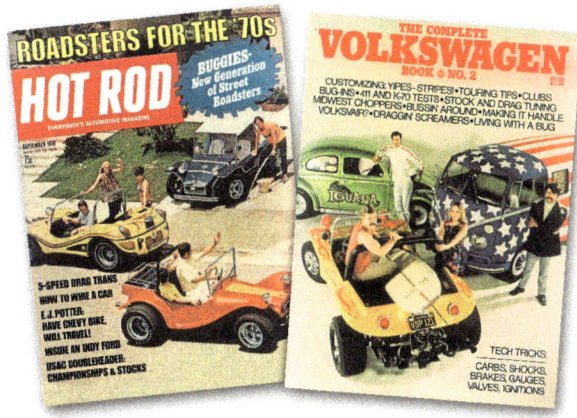

Buggies appeared on the front covers of many US publications, including *Hot Rod* magazine and Petersens Complete Volkswagen Book.

Drag racing buggy is put through its paces by builder Lloyd Mosher, a seasoned VW racer since the 1970s. (Courtesy Stephan Szantai)

John Meade's 2.3-litre buggy can cover the quarter-mile in 10 seconds at 134mph! (Courtesy Stephan Szantai)

Gallery

Fully restored 1968 Meyers Manx buggy is period-perfect, right down to the Gates Commando tyres, and now resides in Canada. (Courtesy Stephan Szantai)

The EMPI Imp has been reproduced in both the US and mainland Europe in recent years. This Imp was built in the UK to resemble the Revell model kit of the buggy.

Left: First of a new breed of buggies in the UK was the GT Buggy. The long-wheelbase design made the kit easier to build on a full length Beetle chassis.
Far left: Cruising in the hot California sun. This Sandwinder buggy shows what it's all about! (Courtesy Mike Key)

The Kyote II, with interchangeable hardtops, was designed as the ultimate multi-functional dune buggy that could also be used open-topped. Back section removed, and the Kyote II turns into a dune buggy pickup. Dean Jeffries' design has featured in many American TV shows and a ZZ Top music video. (Courtesy Custom Car [far left] & Dean Jeffries [left])

The Dune Buggy Handbook

Star-spangled metalflake Mk III Volksrod is superbly detailed with chrome engine and stainless steel roll bar. (Courtesy Mike Key)

The Berry Mini-T was a cross between buggy and retro-rod styling. Whilst many were manufactured, few remain today. This one was on display at a VW show. (Courtesy Jim Maxwell)

This hot-rod looking American Desert Fox buggy features a quilted white interior and period-perfect whitewall tyres. (Courtesy Stephan Szantai)

Metalflake finish on this Rough Terrain-type buggy from Kentucky is complemented by a neat velour interior. (Courtesy Mike Key)

Joe Hogue's Sandwinder 'Spolier' buggy named 'Sweet Brandy' features racing-style split-rim wheels and Mickey Thompson tyres, plus an 'inches deep' candy paint finish. (Courtesy Rob Hallstrom)

Gallery

US buggy manufacturer Berrien Buggy Inc began selling the Citation buggy in 1969 as a dealer for Bremen Speed Equipment in Indiana. (Courtesy Jack Schiffer)

The British Vulture buggy featured in-built Cibie headlamps and plenty of coverage for wide wheels. The design was later reproduced as the Kombat, as seen here.

Italian buggy rebuilt by top British car customiser Andy Saunders to look like a 1970s Corgi toy GP Buggy with mural and Whizzwheels. (Courtesy Mike Key)

Fibre-Tech Engineering buggy features lowered suspension, high-tech engine, and vivid paintwork. (Courtesy Keith Seume)

The American-designed Renegade buggy was made in Britain under licence. This GT Mouldings kit was built into a show-winning car with Candy Red paintwork. (Courtesy Mikle Key)

JACKSON'S KUSTOM BUGGY

DATA PANEL

Production dates
1970-1972

Numbers built
25

Export markets
Cyprus

Wheelbase
82.5in

Identification tips
Hustler buggy bodyshell with additional side fairings and neat wheel spats. The interior is fitted with a leather-grain effect dashboard and central instrument console

A Kustom Buggy named 'Nittybug' was built by John Jackson for Anita Harris, and had plenty of chromed accessories to sparkle in front of the TV cameras. (Courtesy Topham Picturepoint)

With manufacturers rushing to begin production of new buggy designs in the UK in the early 1970s, it came as a refreshing change to find one supplier which specialised in building buggies to order, using other manufacturers' bodyshells. John Jackson, a garage mechanic specialising in Formula Vee work, began his operation under the name of Kustom Buggies in London's Lattimer Road in Shepherds Bush (where classic British TV series *Steptoe & Son* was filmed).

Besides building and finishing all manner of customers' buggies, such as Rats, Bugles and Sharks, Jackson's main trade was the supply of special versions of Essex Proto Conversions' Hustler buggies. Whilst using the same basic bodyshells, the vehicles were also fitted with neat fiberglass side fairings and mud spats to each fender, cushioned with a thin rubber bead to prevent cracking. These spats enabled fitting of the extra wide wheels and ex-racing tyres bought direct from Firestone for the rear, and the wide Jaguar tires bought as seconds (from Henleys Jaguars) for the front.

Often produced in glittering metalflake colous, the Kustom-built Hustler bodyshells were supplied as either kits or complete turnkey cars, though most were destined for an export market in Cyprus. The owner of a large holiday complex there had seen the Mini-Moke used in the cult-TV series *The Prisoner*, and wanted a quantity of buggies for use by holiday guests.

To meet the demand, buggy bodies were readily supplied by Colin Cordingley at EPC, whilst Jackson often travelled to Luxembourg with a transporter to buy virtually new VW Beetle floorpans, and VW and Porsche engines from VW dismantlers. With the mechanicals imported as scrap, it was possible to produce a fully finished vehicle for the low price of £450. However, the subsequent overland export

Models A-Z

of complete buggies, in the days before containerised shipping, presented major problems.

Both Jackson and his Kustom Buggies benefited from the goodwill of parts suppliers such as Graham Hill and his Speedwell operation; VW engine specialists Cartune; Wooller Engineering (which made the first UK VW wheel spacers); and original BMW motorcycle importer Roger Locke (who went on to import Bosch and Hella parts). All of these companies provided parts on loan to the fledgling buggy company.

The traditional-looking Kustom Buggy was described in the sales brochure as a "kooky scout car or Kübelwagen gone haywire," and it certainly was an eye-catching buggy with its neat interior, complete with central console and a choice of no fewer than six designs of racing bucket seat in a Black Mamba finish. To complement the front seats, a rear seat conversion could be ordered, as could padded PVC side panels for added comfort. A folding soft-top, or fiberglass hardtop, kept the whole ensemble dry and weatherproof,; just a couple of examples of the excellent optional extras available from the company's extensive catalogue.

The Kustom Buggy was a darling of both small and big screens, appearing as 'Nittybug' in the TV series *Anita in Jumbleland* with Anita Harris, and on a Top Rank cinema advertising feature filmed at the famous Pinewood studios. These exploits gave useful exposure in the local *Shepherds Bush Courier* magazine, and helped fuel demand for the buggy.

Of good quality, excellent construction and value-for-money prices, the Kustom Buggy would have made a significant impact on the British buggy scene but for one thing: its main supplier, Essex Proto Conversions, became too big too soon, and suffered financial collapse in 1972. This meant that competitively-priced bodyshells were no longer available, which effectively sounded the death knell for the Kustom Buggy.

Classic lines of the built-for-TV 'Nittybug' Kustom Buggy, with its large wheel spats, and pram-style soft-top. (Courtesy John Jackson)

Kustom Buggy advertisement from 1970 showing the low price of a newly-built buggy – possible due to careful purchase of nearly-new VW components abroad.

Jackson's own demonstrator was a metallic red left-hand drive example. The British motoring press was unaccustomed to driving wide-wheeled left hookers, and the buggy was driven into a tree during a review for a British magazine. (Courtesy John Jackson)

Jackson's Kustom Buggy was one of the stars of the British TV series *Anita in Jumbleland*, featuring Anita Harris. The green metalflake buggy had a white interior and plenty of room for childen, dogs and guest celebrities. (Courtesy Ron McFarlane)

JAS

DATA PANEL

Production dates
SWB: 1998-date LWB: 2003-date

Numbers built
Unknown

Export markets
Unknown

Wheelbase
SWB: 82.5in LWB: 94.5in

Identification tips
Noticeably angular front fenders and a generally rounded appearance to the rear with one small raised area for the numberplate lamp. LWB version fits the unmodified VW Beetle chassis, and the more recent LWB model has a more stylised shape to the rear panel above the engine

Buggies are back! The JAS demonstrator poses for a magazine feature in the late 1990s. (Courtesy Total VW)

GP Speed Shop employee John Davies – who had worked on chassis-preparation for the trailblazing British buggy company since 1969 – was one of the original team that designed and developed the archetypal GP Beach Buggy kit in the 60s. Having also done all the chassis work for the famous GP Spyder replica kit, John decided in 1998 to put his experience to work and create his own buggy.

With his wife, Sharon, he set up a new company called JAS Speedkits (the JAS standing for John And Sharon), specialising in VW chassis preparation and sales of buggy kits and related accessories. Noticing that there was a shortage of quality kits in the UK In the late 1990s, he carefully researched and set about redesigning and sculpting his own design from scratch, but with more than a passing nod to the original 60s style of the much-loved Hustler buggy. This ensured the design incorporated the overall strength, legroom and much of the appearance of the former design.

The resulting short-wheelbase design fitted the same 12in shortened VW chassis as the Hustler, to give back seat passengers some space, and also to ensure the buggy had respectable road handling, unlike some other tail-happy designs.

Classic in appearance, the JAS was also contemporary enough to satisfy the requirements of a new audience. At the front, the buggy design had a noticeably angular look to the front fenders, coupled with a front hood that sported a bolt-on alloy windscreen frame that was both tall and upright. At the rear, the JAS buggy bodyshell had a very rounded look, sweeping back from the rear fenders but with few concessions to the type of built-in engine cover sections seen on most other period buggies. The curved back of the bodyshell was designed to accept the stock VW 'tombstone' rear lights, and an aftermarket numberplate lamp sat on the panel's one small raised section.

Contemporary press gave the JAS the thumbs up, and with a local glassfiber laminator producing the bodyshells, a fuscia pink demonstrator was unveiled to the world, bearing the legend 'Buggies are back!' across its front. An appearance at the Volksworld show in 1999 continued to raise the profile of the buggy, and orders rolled in. Perhaps surprisingly, given the tightening of rules on vehicle construction around this time, a long-wheelbase version of the

Models A-Z

buggy only appeared in 2003. Nevertheless, the stretched version of the JAS was duly announced, and made building of the kit much simpler, negating the need for specialist help in chassis shortening. The two designs have continued in tandem since then, but with one further development In late 2010 – a revised version of the long-wheelbase design was patterned to help give a more aesthetically-pleasing style to the rear of the buggy. Looking more Manx-like, with a raised section around the engine access area, the new design was a welcome addition to the range.

Though the vagaries of the kit car world have seen production fluctuate through the years, the high quality of the JAS buggy looks to have assured it a place in buggy history, as it continues to please buggy builders looking for a unique fun car.

Below: Modern and neat, this JAS is a enthusiast's dream vehicle for those long cruises on a sunny summer's day. (Courtesy Mike Key)

Left: This JAS buggy features a neat Interior, plenty of brightwork, and hot-rod style 'tear-drop' rear lights. (Courtesy JAS Speedkits)

Metalflake finish was popular in the 1960s, and is still de rigeur on many buggies today. (Courtesy Mike Key)

The revised version of the long-wheelbase JAS buggy is available for builders who want an easy-to-construct fun car. (Courtesy JAS Speedkits)

KANGO

DATA PANEL

Production dates
1985-1990

Numbers built
12

Export markets
None

Wheelbase
94.5in

Identification tips
Angular bodyshell with fixed central targa bar and in-built roll bar. Multiplicity of hardtop and soft-top options and doors. Moulded-in wiring tubes

South Africa might seem an unlikely place of origin for a new buggy design, but the country has long been a hotbed of buggy activity, right from the earliest days of the Lolette design.

Kango Cars brought the buggy up to date with its novel interchangeable, hard-topped design, the Kango, which was then imported and produced under licence in the UK by Dave Fisher at Midlands-based VW specialist Kingfisher Kustoms.

The Kango was a smart-looking – if somewhat angular – vehicle that was designed for the standard VW Beetle chassis, and gave a modern slant to the versatile US Kyote buggy with its different roof sections. The kit was sold as an assembled body with windows, door catches and side panels already fitted, which made assembly very simple once the donor chassis had been prepared.

The main body had a moulded-in rollbar which was part of the fixed Targa-type roof, and the cab section (which could be a buggy 'T' roof or a saloon full roof) was pre-bonded to the body. A choice of front hood panels could be ordered, so customers could choose between conventional stand-up buggy headlights or in-built lights to make the vehicle more saloon-like. The interior had a dashboard panel with a large instrument binnacle, and a glovebox on the passenger side.

Beneath the body waistline, side panels were pre-bonded onto the bodyshell, and 25mm plastic hoses were bonded into the body to accommodate the wiring harness (a neat touch). The double-panel construction of the bodyshell, and the strengthening box sections in the body, contributed to torsional stiffness and made the Kango a very civilised and versatile kit for on- or off-road use.

A saloon option of the kit had a rear canopy, with hinges, locks, stays and seals, which effectively enclosed the rear of the buggy and was lifted on gas-assisted rams. To make the car weatherproof and fully lockable, lift-off side doors with lock striker plates were provided. These had aluminium frames and sliding windows for a production car feel, which could be completely removed and replaced with soft doors with large zip openings, similar to side screens on a conventional buggy. The hinged doors gave easy entry and exit due to the wide opening and low side sill.

The Kango bodyshell was very modern and angular, and an excellent concept, though commercially never as successful as traditional designs.

Models A-Z

The Kango was a multi-purpose buggy design from South Africa, and continued the concept of the US-built Kyote II buggy with its interchangeable hardtops.

The slanting rear roof section of the Kango had a moulded-in rollbar, and was the fixing point for the opening rear canopy or soft-top.

A second option gave the vehicle a full-window canopy to enclose the rear, shaped as the hardtop option. A pickup-style, steel-braced soft-top could also be ordered. This was fitted with slide and stud fixings, making the buggy totally versatile as well as extremely practical.

Like the Kyote, interior space was vast by buggy standards, and the Kango offered four different loading and seating configurations: three or four seater with luggage space, or a pure two seater with a glassfiber cargo deck at the back, like a small delivery truck. Needless to say, this was another factory option.

The front hood gave access to the fuel tank, spare wheel and a tool kit, which were useful options rarely seen on a buggy. The in-built headlamps and tail lamps had plexiglass covers for a neat, finished appearance, whilst safety features included pick-up points for the seat-belts on the built-in roll bar, and unitary construction of the main bodyshell for maximum strength.

Although the Kango van option for the rear deck never materialised, the overall buggy concept was excellent. However, it never really caught on in the UK and few examples survive.

Front headlights could either be recessed into the front hood, or mounted on pods, as with a conventional dune buggy.

Shown in the catalog like a giant construction kit, the Kango could be put together in a large number of different formats to suit the needs of the customer.

121

KELLISON SANDPIPER

DATA PANEL

Production dates
1968-1971

Numbers built
1000 (approx)

Export markets
None

Wheelbase
80in

Identification tips
SP-I was a traditional buggy with a custom hardtop. XP-I had a unitised and smoother body with a quilted seat interior and neat, twin-tube bumpers. The pickup version had a large flatbed and sloping front hood with twin styling ridges

With an unfortunate number of disreputable businesses setting up to sell buggies in the late 1960s, it came as a refreshing change when Kellison entered the field as a very serious-quality manufacturer. Operating in Lincoln, California, the company emphasised the difference between its quality products and long heritage in the glassfiber business and those of the get-rich-quick bootleggers who disappeared with customers' deposit cheques. In November 1968, Kellison acquired the dune buggy and sportscar division of Lincoln Industries, and entered the world of buggy production.

Leaving Lincoln Industries to continue with its industrial glassfiber division, Kellison took responsibility for completing the outstanding orders for dune buggies. In order to improve the unsatisfactory level of quality and service to Lincoln dealers, Kellison set up an aggressive dealer profit program to create a co-operative distribution network for its buggy kits through all 1200 dealers. Backed up by large stocks of buggy bodyshells, comprehensive sales aids and finance programs, the Kellison buggies inevitably made a significant impact on the buggy world.

Kellison's first buggy, the Sandpiper Roadster SP-I, was very much a traditional vehicle, designed to fit the shortened VW chassis. Apart from a front hood styling ridge, the bodyshell was very Manx-inspired, but did have the option of a cute glassfiber 'C-cab' hardtop. Designed with strengthening ridges built into the roof and an oval rear screen, the hardtop was both practical and aesthetically pleasing. The second buggy, the Sandpiper Roadster XP-I, was a more radical departure from the norm, with a futuristic look about it and a list of accessories that would fill a

Kellison XP-1 buggy owners enjoy some off-road fun in a blue metalflake vehicle with custom quilted interior.

Models A-Z

One of the later Kellison buggy kits was a Super 'T' pickup, which followed the lines of the Berry Mini-T, and was designed for use on a shortened chassis.

Kellison's traditional buggy design, the Sandpiper Roadster SP-I, was soon joined by the more futuristic XP-I and a 'T'-bodied roadster pickup.

parts book. Still based on the 80in VW floorpan, the XP-I had a longer, flowing bodyline, with the hood, dash panel and body all one piece.

With stand-up headlights, twin-tube chromed front bumper bar, and squared-off windshield, the buggy design had an original look, rather than being a copy of ideas that had gone before. To ensure individuality, four different styles of tops, skidpans, chrome wheel rims, quilted effect seats, dual exhaust systems, rollbars and tow bars could be ordered from the extensive catalog.

As with several other manufacturers at the time who began to look toward meeting the demand for utility-type buggies, Kellison's third design was an interesting 'T'-bodied roadster pickup. Designed for either a shortened or standard chassis, the pickup was also a one-piece bodyshell, with the tailgate moulded directly from that of a 'real' Model-T vehicle. The large, open back could house camping gear, the family groceries, or large, bulky items for delivery. The back could be blanketed with a Naugahyde-covered tarpaulin or an optional reinforced glassfiber deck.

The two-seat cockpit of the buggy could be enclosed with a moulded hardtop similar to that used on the SP-I, for all-weather practicality. The pickup appealed not only to buggistas and slalom racers, but the diehard street roadster enthusiast,

Due to the relatively large number of kits sold, quite a few still survive, and this pristine example of a Kellison Roadster pickup appeared at a VW custom show in California.

too, and quickly became Kellison's best-selling kit.

Kellison also manufactured panels for Beetles, Sprites, MGAs and Lotuses, as well as the Grasshopper dune buggy body (an enclosed '27 Model-T bucket-type vehicle originally produced by J W Black's Paradise Motors in Paradise, California). One of the company's last automotive products was a kit-car called the Shark, produced for a VW floorpan shortened by 10 inches. A futuristic sportscar design, destined for 6-cylinder Corvair power, the Shark was never in the same league as the buggies, and quickly faded away.

Professional advertising, well thought out brochures, and large stocks of body kits ensured that Kellison buggies made a huge impact on the US buggy scene.

KYOTE (MANTARAY II KYOTE & KYOTE I)

DATA PANEL

Production dates
Mantaray II Kyote: 1968-1969
Kyote I: 1969-1970

Numbers built
Mantaray II Kyote: 100
Kyote I: 250

Export markets
Unknown

Wheelbase
80in

Identification tips
Recessed front headlights in curved front fenders (Mantaray II Kyote); later in front hood (Kyote I). Sweeping front hood to one-piece body design. In-built fuel tank and optional side tanks behind curved side panels

Dean Jeffries' fame derives from the automotive creations he dreamed up for Hollywood over the last forty years. Jeffries began his career working as a pinstriper on Indianapolis race cars, but soon went on to create his own race car, the Mantaray. Built from a pre-war Maserati Grand Prix racer, the Mantaray won the Tournament of Fame at the Oakland Roadster Show in 1963, and launched Jeffries into showbiz, with Hollywood increasingly keen to use his design and building talents.

An early creation was the futuristic-looking touring car called the Monkeemobile, shown each week in the opening sequence of the Monkees' TV show. The project soon led to another vehicle, this time designed for a Monkees movie called *Head*. As well as the melange of flower power, psychedelia and music, the script called for a dune buggy to cruise across the desert in a bizarre sequence where it is attacked by a giant.

Although the Monkees vehicle was essentially a one-off, built on a floorpan shortened to an 80in wheelbase, it was re-worked for production once filming was over. The Jeffries buggy, called the Mantaray II Kyote, was introduced in August 1968, and set new standards in dune buggy design and construction. The translation of lines on paper to curves in glassfiber

The Mantaray II Kyote was amongst a group of buggies that featured in a special issue of Playboy magazine in 1969. (Courtesy Alexas Urba)

Hollywood customiser Dean Jeffries designed the Kyote originally as a one-off vehicle. Parked in the Hollywood hills, the Kyote glistens in the Californian sunshine.

124

Models A-Z

was carried out with meticulous care, and the Kyote realised Jeffries' dream of a streetable VW sportscar that was rugged enough for off-roading, too.

At the front, the smooth hood swept down in a graceful curve, and the curved fenders housed a pair of recessed headlights which could be covered with protective plexiglass shields. The one-piece body moulding had an in-built dashboard and took a full complement of instruments, whilst, at the rear, the wide fenders could cover 12in wheels and tyres, so the car was legal for street use. The rear deck of the buggy formed another graceful curve, gave good coverage for the engine, and offered a mount for the VW rear lights.

Later additions to the basic bodyshell (now re-named the Kyote I) included re-siting of the headlights into the front hood to prevent tyre-to-body interference, and curved side panels that ran from the body waistline to the floorpan. These housed long-range fuel tanks for extra mileage, or they could be used as additional storage spaces if side pockets were cut into the main bodyshell.

In a bid to improve aerodynamics and cover the VW suspension, a nose section was developed for the area beneath the front hood. An engine cover that attached to the body was also offered, and could be easily removed (merely by releasing the bolts) to ready the car for off-road use.

The Kyote I kit was offered in various stages of completeness: just a body; with all mounting hardware and a windshield; or with all panels for street use. Jeffries also offered franchises on the Kyote kit, and thus other versions of the buggy were made, including the Irwin Sportster produced by the Irwin Boat Company in Weston, Ontario.

Although the buggy sold well for street use, Jeffries wanted to develop a Kyote racer, and so, late in 1968, a very specialised dune buggy rolled out of his styling shop in Hollywood. Undergoing continual change and development following its Mexican 1000 debut at Baja, the Kyote racer proved to be a mobile test-bed for construction details on the street cars, as well as providing a rolling advertisement for Jeffries' handiwork.

Though the Kyote was superseded by the Kyote II, Jeffries still has the production moulds for both models. Recently refurbished, they are now looking for a new home, and might signal the relaunch of one of the best Stateside buggy designs.

The Kyote I had a gracefully curved elevation to the one-piece bodyshell, and a detailed interior.

Contestants in the International Bikini Contest swarm around Dean Jeffries' Kyote buggy. (Courtesy Dean Jeffries)

On location with the Monkees filming one of the psychedelic sequences for their movie Head. Many 1960s and 1970s TV shows featured the Kyote, including the popular Bewitched. (Courtesy Dean Jeffries)

One of the many Kyote copies was the Italian Momo buggy.

KYOTE II

DATA PANEL

Production dates
1970-1972

Numbers built
150

Export markets
UK

Wheelbase
94.5in

Identification tips
Long-wheelbase body with opening doors and tailgate. Multi-purpose hardtop arrangement, and folding rear seat unit giving flat-bed cargo area

Following the launch of the Kyote, its designer, Dean Jeffries, quickly realised that customers wanted different things from their buggies, so he set about designing a machine that would be all things to all customers., and the Kyote II was born. A multi-convertible dune buggy that could be used as a stationwagon or panel truck, or, with rear hardtop removed, a pickup. For those wanting an open-top buggy, the pickup roof could be removed to give a full five-seater touring buggy. A fastback top, complete with spoiler, was also available, designed for those looking for a GT sportscar.

The new buggy was a one-piece moulding which fitted the full-length VW Beetle chassis, and had all the support bracing laminated in. The bracing was important as the design incorporated hinged side doors and an opening tailgate, requiring durability at both the hinge and latching points. The doors – obviously something of a luxury on a dune buggy – allowed easy entry and exit, and the tailgate gave access to the rear luggage area and engine bay beneath the glassfiber deck.

The new buggy was made of hand-laid glassfiber, and strict quality control at the factory ensured a superb fit and color match of all parts, even if ordered individually at later dates. Customers purchasing the complete kit with doors, side panels, engine cover and hardtop roofs enjoyed the added bonus of having the various parts pre-installed on the basic body at no extra charge. Building was thus simplicity itself, aided by the template marking on all body parts showing exactly how the kit and all the accessories went together.

The Kyote II body could accommodate either the Type 1 VW engine or the pancake engines from the Type 3 Squareback or Fastback, as well as Corvair units. With the installation of the upright VW engine, a special fiberglass shield was provided to cover the vertical fan shroud, though this did take up some of the usable cargo space in the flat bed area of the rear deck.

The versatility of the Kyote II design was also apparent in the interior of the bodyshell. A glassfiber rear seat platform sat over the rear of the VW floorpan tunnel, and accommodated the battery beneath it in the stock VW location. The second well could be used for storing tools, for example, whilst behind, the rear floor panel could be flipped over to enable the buggy to carry cargo, or raised to provide seating.

A Kyote II races in the Hollywood hills. This pirate-red example was the very first bodyshell from the new moulds. (Courtesy Dean Jeffries)

Models A-Z

The rear top section, which bolted securely to the main body section, could be removed to give the open bed pickup option. Undoing a couple more bolts meant that the front cab section could be removed for the full, open-top buggy look.

Given the versatility of the buggy – and the widespread availability of VW parts – it was perhaps inevitable that the Kyote II came to be used by various law enforcement agencies. The Los Angeles County Sheriffs' Department immediately realised the buggy's value in helping at beach emergencies: two black and white-painted Kyote IIs, with massive tyres for on and off-road work, were used to patrol the Californian beaches. The buggies sported Sheriff emblems on each side, a large conglomeration of red and amber lights atop the rear mounted roll bar, and even sirens.

Like its shorter brother, the Kyote II has remained a classic design, and one that has survived the test of time. Dean Jeffries would dearly like to see a new owner take on the Stateside project and bring it back to life. The British version, however, is still very much in production.

The Kyote became a natural cover star for various US buggy magazines of the period, and an open-top Kyote II appeared in the ZZ Top pop video for the song 'Legs.'

Dean Jeffries showed how the rear window opened, or could be removed, on the stationwagon hardtop. (Courtesy Dean Jeffries)

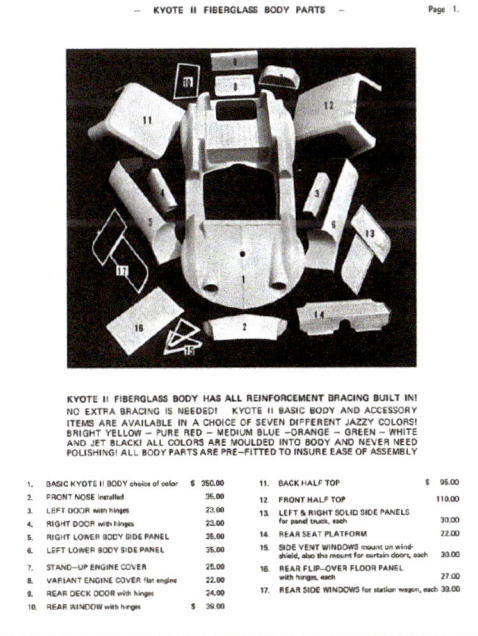

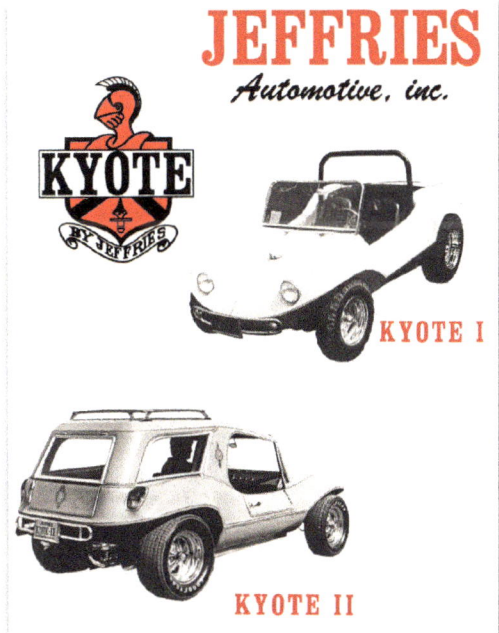

Far left: A photograph in the Kyote brochure shows the many different parts that went into making up the full kit.

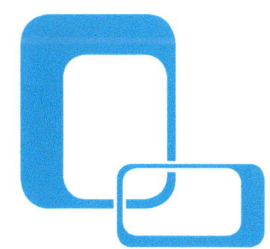

Left: All the parts available for the Kyote II buggy were shown in the comprehensive Jeffries Automotive catalogue.

127

KYOTE II

DATA PANEL

Production dates
1971-1976, 1991-date

Numbers built
75 (approx)

Export markets
Belgium, Oman, Eire, Spain, Middle East

Wheelbase
94.5in

Identification tips
Curvaceous body line with inset headlights. Later examples lack doors and an opening tailgate, but have a front panel for fuel tank access. Cars feature a fixed front valence and curved side panels to lower body tub

American Steve Remp was the Kyote II owner who arrived in England in 1971 hoping to set the UK buggy scene alight. Having obtained from Dean Jeffries the British production rights for the Kyote II, and with US-built examples of the long-wheelbase car and a short-wheelbase Kyote racer in his possession, he soon geared up to make Britain 'Kyote country.'

From premises near London's Vauxhall Bridge, his company, Design Dynamics, opened for business and operated under the grandiose name of The Dune Buggy Centre. Despite Remp's enthusiasm, however, the UK buggy scene was already on the wane by late 1971 and this, combined with a desire to sell complete cars rather than just kits, resulted in slow sales.

The British Kyote II kits replicated their Stateside counterparts, with opening doors and tailgate, and interchangeable hardtops. The bodies were exquisitely moulded, with metal reinforcing for the door striker and latch mechanisms, strengthening at stress points, and, as a safety feature, were laminated in fire-retardant resin. These desirable features pushed kit prices higher than most other buggy offerings, and prevented the Kyote II from achieving its full sales potential.

By 1973, Steve Remp had decided to move on, and left partner Phil Ayres to take control of the Kyote project. Despite a name change to Dune Buggy Constructors, the snail-like production rate of the buggy continued, the only manufacturing difference a small production ID plate moulded into the buggy's front bulkhead.

By 1974 the project had passed from Ayres to GP Concessionaires, having lain untouched at his Berkshire sub-contractor for a year. One of the pioneers of British buggies in the UK, GP seemed to be the saviour of this truly original design which had so influenced the Stateside scene. However, the GP Ranchero buggy kit virtually duplicated the multi-functionality of the Kyote II hardtops, and it was soon

The Kyote II is a timeless and original design which has survived changes in fashion. This neat Metalflake-finished example is a GT Mouldings kit.

Models A–Z

The Kyote design fitted the stock VW Beetle chassis, and used VW rear light units. The front headlights were eventually changed to British 7in Mini units. (Courtesy Kingfisher Kustoms)

Built for the Sultan of Oman by Kingfisher Kustoms, this pair of Kyote IIs were built to have fun in the sand. (Courtesy Kingfisher Kustoms)

pensioned off and the extremely worn moulds eventually broken up.

Although the British buggy bubble burst before the Kyote II had had a real chance to show its paces, by the late 1980s a rekindled interest in all things VW brought fresh hope. Salvation came from an unexpected source when a second set of production moulds came to light and went on the market. Buggy maker GT Mouldings, manufacturer of the Manta-Ray kit, added the Kyote to its range with Dean Jeffries' blessing, and redeveloped the kit for British and export markets.

To keep prices realistic, the opening doors and tailgate were dropped, and the bodyshell manufactured as a more conventional unit. To aid access to the front-mounted fuel tank, an opening panel was added to the front hood, and sat in a neat recess. Noticeable was the fact that the headlight pods were now level, and slightly increased in diameter to take a standard 7in European lamp. The windshield frame was also changed to a glassfiber item so that complete color co-ordination was achieved throughout.

At the rear, the flat deck area was redesigned to take the upright Type I VW engine, a requirement of export markets. To cater for the unreliable British weather, raised soft-top rain rails were also added to the bodyshell sides.

Over 40 years on from its original design, the Kyote II is still in production by UK company KMR Buggies, which took over manufacture in 2003, a testament to the creative skills of Dean Jeffries and the enthusiasm of those who have kept the buggy in production ever since.

Period advert for the Kyote II and the Dune Buggy Centre. Custom Car magazine praised the Kyote as being the best design ever to hit British shores, but its late arrival on the scene, combined with high prices, prevented the buggy achieving real impact

Redesigned Kyote II had no doors or tailgate, but featured sculpted side panels, an opening front hood for access to the fuel tank, and better weatherproofing for the British climate.

LIMITED EDITION CALIFORNIAN

DATA PANEL

Production dates
1983-1987

Numbers built
30 (approx)

Export markets
None

Wheelbase
94.5in

Identification tips
Angular styling: very boxy side panels, low arch to front fenders, rectangular multi-unit rear lights and acutely-angled glassfiber windshield frame

Although the heyday of the British buggy scene occurred in the late 1960s and early 1970s, renewed interest in kit-cars generally, and buggies in particular, in the 1980s saw a few new names and manufacturers arrive on the scene. Limited Edition Sportscars of Warrington, Cheshire was about to prove, with the introduction of the Californian in 1983, that buggies never die.

Limited Edition, run by Terry Walsh, had exclusive regional distribution rights for companies such as GP Specialist Vehicles and Geoff Jago Custom Automotive. The company had also supplied the GP buggy range to customers in the north of England. However, the desire to produce an original buggy was too great, and so GP eventually agreed to design and manufacture a modified version of the long-wheelbase car and re-badge it for this market.

The plan was to take styling ideas straight from the US west coast and bring the buggy right up to date with a macho, off-road look.

The Californian was based on the tried and tested GP body shape, but with black rectangular Cibie headlamps and a Baja-style tail. Other differences included a bronze-tinted front windshield set in a glassfiber frame, which was rectangular and very acutely angled, and a low-gloss, black leathergrain dashboard.

The main bodyshell featured a small flare to each of the fenders, with a particularly noticeable wheelarch enclosure behind the front wheels and tyres. This flowed down into a return edge which, in turn, connected to the wide and boxy side panels mounted below the body waistline. The panels flared out at the rear to form a second wheelarch, before tucking under the widened rear fenders of the main bodyshell.

Combined trailer-type, multi-light units were mounted on rectangular mouldings each side of the central engine cover bulge, which gave a minimal degree of cover to the VW engine beneath. The cover also provided a mount for the licence plate and lamps, as well as an identification badge for the manufacturer.

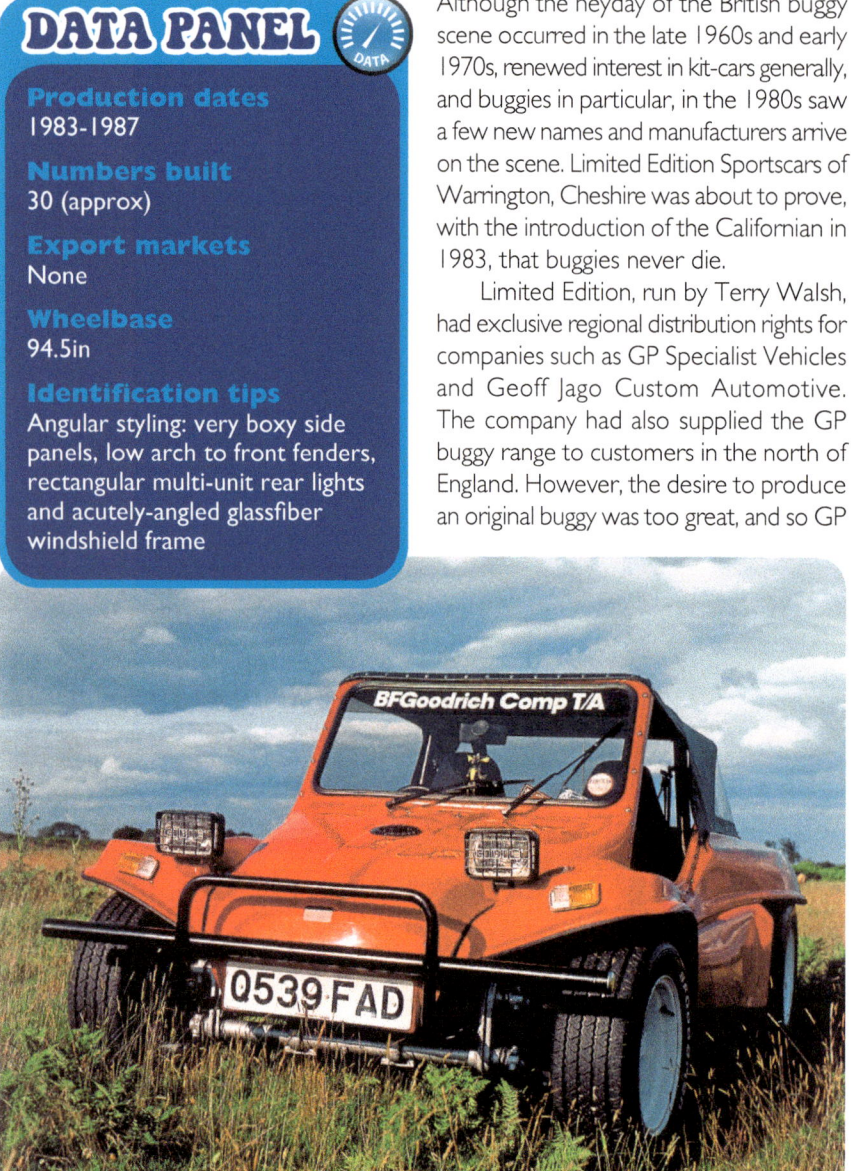

Limited Edition Californian buggy was a modified version of the GP Super Buggy, made for the company by GP Specialist Vehicles.

Models A-Z

With soft-top fitted, the Californian was equally at home in the unreliable British climate.

The Californian had a particularly tall, rectangular windshield fitted in a glassfiber frame, plus noticeably flared fenders and boxy side panels.

Because it was based on a full-length VW Beetle chassis, the Californian was easy to build, since the running gear needed no modification, and provided seating for four, plus a small luggage area behind the rear seat squab. Limited Edition could also supply a fully prepared rolling VW chassis for those who wished to minimise the work involved in building the kit into a complete vehicle. All the customer had to do was bolt down the glassfiber bodyshell, install the steering and wiring, and fit the seats.

Two alternative kits were also available – a starter kit for those working to a budget, and a complete kit which contained everything essential to assemble the Californian that was not found on the base vehicle. All the parts needed to bring the starter kit up to the higher specification later on (such as side panels, roll bar, complete set of lights and a fanbelt guard) could be purchased separately.

With a soft-top and a heater fitted, the Californian was certainly a practical vehicle, ready to tackle the fickle British climate. Promotional literature emphasised that the buggy was "equally at home cruising the street or exploring the back roads," and that the kit represented an excellent way to create a stylish leisure vehicle at reasonable cost. Economical as it was, the buggy proved to have limited appeal and, though kept available for four years, was eventually phased out as the company concentrated its efforts on distributing VW aftermarket parts to the growing Baja Beetle, custom and Cal-look scene. Limited Edition itself was eventually bought out by Kingfisher Kustoms, and its northern branch closed.

Designed to look as if the buggy had come from the US west coast, the Californian had black rectangular Cibie headlamps and a 'Baja-style' rear end to the bodyshell.

Noise levels rise as this Californian buggy prepares to leave the start line at Avon Park drag raceway in Britain.

MANGOSTA

DATA PANEL

Production dates
1969-1971

Numbers built
6 (approx)

Export markets
None

Wheelbase
80in

Identification tips
Low front hood with stand-up headlights; side-mounted fuel tanks with flip-up fillers; optional vinyl or walnut dashboard fascia

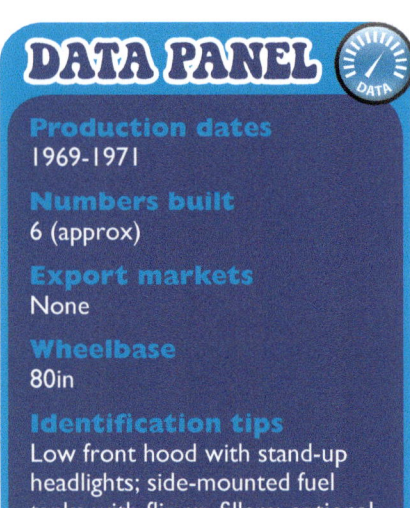

The Mangosta buggy, developed by a Detroit automotive stylist, incorporated many features from passenger cars. (Courtesy Randy Carlson)

In 1969, Karl Krumme of the Design/Development Company, Ventura, California, developed a new buggy design called the Mangosta (Spanish for mongoose). The new bodyshell was a more sophisticated unit than most, and was produced for the shortened VW platform chassis. Experience of restyling cars for Detroit auto manufacturers had given Design/Development a good grounding in automotive design, although the model was late entering the dune buggy industry.

The company's kit – which incorporated ideas from the passenger car field – aimed to make the project of converting a VW Beetle into a buggy as simple as possible. The body was created in several different moulds, the separate pieces of which were then jig-joined to produce the unitised bodyshell. To aid construction, all the mounting points for the stand-up headlights, the windshield, and late model VW tail lights were pre-drilled at the factory. The rear lights were mounted flush on the slanting rear panel to ensure legal conformity in all states.

The wedge-shaped design gave the buggy very modern styling, and made the short-wheelbase vehicle appear longer than it actually was. The low front hood line was possible due to the twin, 6-gallon capacity fuel tanks being mounted in the sides of the vehicle, with the filler caps situated just ahead of the rear fenders. This obviated the annoyance of placing tank brackets in the front end where the tank proved hard to reach on a traditional buggy design. The wide front fenders provided a mount for the early VW indicator units, and a front bumper cleverly followed the shape of the nose section to provide some protection and ensure street legality.

At the rear, the body extended low to cover much of the otherwise exposed engine, and kept the design legal for street licensing, without losing the sleek but rugged looks. Tall tyres were given room for travel during off-roading and did not foul the wide wheelarches, thus avoiding cracking the glassfiber. A fanbelt guard and skidplate were available as optional extras, also made of glassfiber to match body color.

The interior was full of novel ideas for a buggy, and made the Mangosta design stand out from the rest. The driver and passenger seat had a high-back, quilted-effect design, set low in the vehicle to ensure the occupants were well within the sides of the bodyshell for safety. Again, taking ideas from production cars, Krumme offered a choice of dashboard facias, which could be ordered in either a padded vinyl finish or walnut. Both had a central pod which housed the VW speedometer and switchgear. A padded rollbar, and side panels that gave a roll-edge to the bodyshell top, increased the feeling of luxury. Although

Models A-Z

This luxuriously-appointed demonstrator cost over $30,000 to build back in 1970, and was used in company advertisements. (Courtesy Randy Carlson)

primarily a two-seater, a rear seat option with padded top was also available.

Design/Development, selling kits and fully assembled vehicles, produced buggies that were better finished than the competition. The company's workshop facilities were able to handle the construction of any vehicle requested by customers, from street or off-road cars to totally one-off vehicles. Creating cars with complete co-ordination of parts that worked together visually, Design/Development produced a stylish and streetable buggy that could also survive a few trips in the great outdoors.

Had it arrived a few years earlier, the Mangosta, with its new ideas, could have influenced the buggy scene considerably. As it was, it helped pave the way for a generation of VW-based kit-cars that came after the buggy movement.

A 1970s advertisement for the Mangosta showing the soft-top that was available as an optional extra.

The wedge-shaped buggy had a low front hood design as the fuel tank was moved to the rear seat area. Later models used two separate tanks mounted in side panels. (Courtesy Mel Baker)

Rebuilt Corvette-red example was originally featured in *Hot VWs* magazine way back in 1969. (Courtesy Mel Baker)

MANTA RAY MK I-III

DATA PANEL

Production dates
1969-date

Numbers built
Mk I: 35 Mk II: 250 Mk III: 52

Export markets
Belgium, Holland, Malta, Corfu, Canary Isles, Iceland, Far East

Wheelbase
78.5in

Identification tips
Unitised bodyshell with recessed headlamps; neat Kamm-tailed rear. Mk II bodies had headlights set lower down and further forward; Mk IIIs had a rain lip and Manta Ray badge on the hood

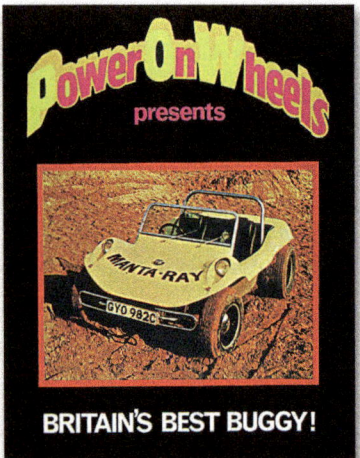

Front cover of the Power on Wheels Manta Ray brochure from the 1970s.

The Buggy Shop of Send in Surrey, was set up in 1969 by Aidan Harrington and Roy King to produce the Sports buggy, a traditional design influenced by the GP and the Manx. Working from the premises of Connaught Cars, where Harrington was the forecourt manager, the Sports buggy began to find a niche in the rapidly growing UK buggy marketplace.

By autumn 1969, the entrepreneurs had developed a more radical design called the Manta Ray, with faired-in headlights and a neat Kamm-type tail. Based on the Mantaray II Kyote design seen in a Stateside magazine, the sleek bodyshell, designed for a shortened VW chassis, was certainly one of the most attractive of the unusual-shaped UK buggies. With backing from Alan Brown, a director of Connaught Cars, a new and aptly-named operation called Power on Wheels was formed to manufacture the buggy.

The Manta Ray was unusual in that, although of one-piece construction which made it simple to build, the design complicated access to the fuel tank, suspension and engine. Bodyshells came with a frame installed under the front hood for the modified VW fuel tank to fit into, whilst another frame behind the dashboard acted as a mount for the steering column and windshield frame. The flat dashboard offered a home for the instruments and switchgear, which could be sited to the individual builder's own design. The large arches of the front and rear fenders ensured wide wheels and tyres could be fitted legally, though the recessed Cibie headlamps were in danger of being knocked out of their pods if the buggy was off-roaded.

Despite some early bodyshells being somewhat thin, the Manta Ray was good value for money, and offered in several packages from a basic kit to fully wired-up and ready for assembly. What secured the Manta Ray's future was the appearance of a dayglo red example on the front of the first issue of trendsetting magazine *Custom Car* in March 1970. This publicity was backed up by a series of build-up features over several months in the same magazine, which created a healthy demand for the new buggy.

Like many buggies of the time, the Manta Ray design was prey to imitation. Two such buggies, the CTR by CTR Enterprises of Carshalton Beeches, Surrey (which had wider fenders and a noticeably lower waistline), and the Seaspray by Seaspray Beach Buggies of Iver Heath, Buckinghamshire (with wider headlamp pods and rectangular or twin-round light units), appeared during the early 1970s, though few of either were made.

By the summer of 1970 a Mk II Manta Ray had appeared. This model could be distinguished by a styling ridge down the centre of the front hood, plus headlight pods that were further forward and noticeably lower. A deep lip ran around its longer nose, and rain deflectors were added. Production quality was vastly improved when Power on Wheels changed sub-contractor to commercial boat builder C+D Automarine Ltd of West Molesey, Surrey, which also made a buggy: the Manx-inspired Cobra (a re-working of the Buggy Shop's Sports buggy).

After Power on Wheels ceased trading in 1971, the last sub-contractor, JB Developments of Aldershot, Hampshire, took over manufacture and re-launched the Manta Ray in 1972. Despite minimal advertising, the buggy continued in

Models A-Z

The Mk II Manta Ray featured a longer nose, with headlights positioned further forward and noticeably lower to comply with construction and usage regulations.

The Manta Ray was built up as a project car for the super-groovy British magazine *Custom Car*. Issue 1 featured this fluorescent red buggy on the front cover.
(Courtesy *Custom Car*)

production before moving to Volkscare & Custom in Sussex in 1986, and thence quickly to long-established buggy manufacturer GT Mouldings. The company updated the design as the Mk III with a proper soft-top rain rail and a moulded-in Manta Ray badge on the front hood, before making new moulds. Supplied with side panels, the buggy is better than ever, and still available from current manufacturer, KMR Buggies in the Midlands.

Neat Manta Ray buggy built on a space frame chassis, with an aluminium-panelled interior for a race-car look. (Courtesy Mike Key)

Manta Ray buggy brought up to date in Gulf Porsche racing colors. (Courtesy Mike Key)

MEYERS MANX (MONOCOQUE)

DATA PANEL

Production dates
1964-1965

Numbers built
12

Export markets
None

Wheelbase
78in

Identification tips
Monocoque design. In-built steel bracing for mounting the VW front and rear suspension, gearbox and engine to the glassfiber tub. Integral rear seat, fuel tank, and a fold-flat windshield over the opening front hood

The word 'Manx' has become synonymous with dune buggies since the very first glassfiber-bodied example was produced by gifted glassfiber craftsman Bruce Meyers. Having seen the agility of the earliest VW-powered buggies at rat races in California, Meyers knew he could design a better looking, lightweight vehicle that would be fun to drive and would take him further into the outback than was possible in his VW Kombi van.

Working in a one stall garage in Newport Beach, California, during 1963, Meyers used his extensive knowledge of sailboat tooling to build a full-scale mock-up of the world's first 'streetable' glassfiber dune buggy, based around VW Beetle mechanicals. The vehicle, developed from a small-scale clay model, was a simple, open-topped design that looked cute and purposeful. The essence of the design was a stressed monocoque bodyshell that, capitalising on Meyers' understanding of boat design, served as a body, high-swept fenders and frame all-in-one.

The shape provided terrific torsional stiffness, with a central tunnel in the driver/passenger well for the gearshift, a moulded-in, 14-gallon fuel tank in the rear, and extensive use of compound curves throughout to prevent panel movement. Steel bearers were moulded into the shell under the main tub, and provided attachment points for the VW front suspension unit, the rear suspension, and the specially machined aluminum castings which allowed VW pedals, emergency brake, and other parts to be fitted.

The first vehicle, moulded in May 1964 and purely for personal use, was dubbed a Meyers Manx due to its stubbiness, and christened 'Old Red' because of its color. Air-lift suspension units at the rear, from a Chevrolet pickup, enabled inflation up to 65psi in order to carry extra loads in the buggy, or they could be deflated to just 15psi to decamber the rear for town driving. This was changed to a stock VW rear torsion bar assembly due to technical and cost limitations, as Meyers built further kits for customers who had seen, and wanted a copy of, his neat little off-roader.

The VW Beetle drivetrain and engine were attached to the framework that was glassed in place at the back of the tub, helping to distribute the load and stresses over a wide part of the entire body/chassis. At the front, the hood opened to provide storage for a spare tyre, the battery and

Classic Eric Rickman photograph of a monocoque Manx in mid-flight for the front cover of the August 1966 Hot Rod magazine. The driver is Bruce Meyers.

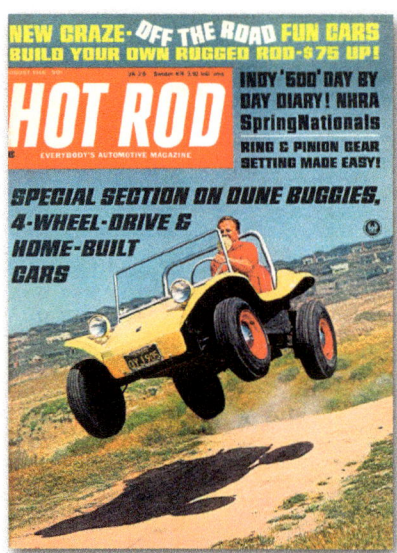

Models A-Z

The world's first glassfiber-bodied dune buggy design was the Meyers Manx. Only 12 of the monocoque buggies were built before being redesigned for the shortened VW Beetle chassis. (Courtesy Melvyn Hubbard)

With the licence plate 'Mr Manx,' Bruce and Winnie Meyers lead the pack at a Manx Dune Buggy Club off-road event. (Courtesy Melvyn Hubbard)

An early Manx promotional brochure showing the Manx cat emblem with stubby tail and battle-scarred sword raised for action.

tools, and gave access to the car's wiring and steering gear. The flat-topped front fenders were designed specifically so that items could be rested on them whilst the buggy was stationary. With a fold-flat windshield, the pod-mounted headlights, and a dashboard shaped to house the standard VW speedometer, switches and grab-handle, the Manx looked just right.

Supplied as a kit with basic hand tools for self-assembly, and finished in a choice of five impregnated colors, the Manx had sufficient room to accommodate four adults in reasonable comfort. The buggy immediately became the cover car darling of motoring journals such as *Hot Rod* and *Car & Driver*.

The off-road Manx proved itself when Meyers and Ted Mangels, a surfing buddy, broke the record of 39 hours for the run between Ensenada and La Paz in 'Old Red.' Knocking over four hours off the time of stunt rider and bike racer Bud Ekins over the difficult terrain, this achievement set the scene for future Manx domination in off-road events, such as the Baja 1000, and the formation of NORRA (National Off-Road Racing Association).

Despite initial success, after producing just 12 kits Meyers was forced to rethink the design to prevent losing money due to the high cost of kit manufacture. The resulting design was a masterstroke, and is covered in the next chapter.

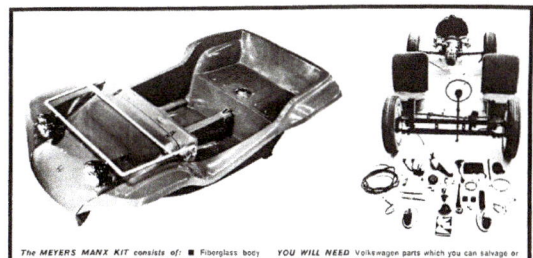

This period brochure clearly shows the component parts needed from the donor VW, which were added to the unitary structure of the monocoque buggy bodyshell.

'Old Red' – the buggy that started the Manx revolution – was built in 1964. (Courtesy Meyers Manx Inc)

MEYERS MANX (VW FLOORPAN)

DATA PANEL

Production dates
Manx/Manx II/Turista/Resorter/Utility: 1965-1971
Kick-Out Traditional Manx 2009-date
Kick-Out SS Manx 2010-date

Numbers built
Manx: 5280
Manx II: 250
Turista/Resorter: 75
Utility: 3
Kick-Out: Not available

Export markets
Worldwide

Wheelbase
Manx/Manx II: 80in
Turista/Resorter: 94.5in
Utility: 80in
Kick-Out: 80in

Identification tips
Manx – Single-piece bodyshell on VW floorpan; separate front hood with Manx emblem; stiffeners under the body except for Manx II kits which also omitted the rear battery and seat wells. Turista/Resorter was a 4-seat vehicle with dropped sides for easy entry/exit; Utility buggy had a covered rear bed for hauling life-saving gear. Kick-Out Manx has wider rear fenders and opening hood. SS version has inset headlights and a curved windshield

Bruce Meyers built the original Manx buggy for the personal satisfaction of fabricating something with his own hands, and then using it himself, rather than establishing a business. However, the first buggies proved the Manx could be a commercial success if the retail price could be reduced to an acceptable level.

Meyers reworked his original design after seeing other dune buggies that were little more than seats attached to a stripped VW sedan chassis, often shortened to improve maneuverability. By changing to a lightweight bodyshell that bolted to a shortened Beetle floorpan, a complete Manx kit could retail at just over $600, making it accessible to a huge market where you only had to find a wrecked VW to build a radically different car, capable of turning heads on the boulevard or winning tough off-road races.

The new Manx was the world's first glassfiber buggy body designed for the modified VW chassis, and the first to be moulded in a single basic piece that bolted to the perimeter of the floorpan. The fender line was identical to Meyers' earlier cars, but the opening front hood was changed to a fixed item with a more rounded shape to accommodate the VW fuel tank beneath. This allowed the bodyshell interior to house a moulded-in battery box and spare tyre well, over which could sit a rear bench seat.

An ABS plastic dashboard, surrounded by a steel frame, sat inside the front hood and provided attachment points for the aluminium windshield frame, which now remained in a fixed position. The headlights were mounted to the inner sides of the front fenders, and, to ensure identification, a Manx sticker was attached to a small raised section on the hood, though this later became a plastic emblem.

The Manx was launched in 1965 as either a Manx 'A' kit with just the bodyshell, front hood and dashboard, or as a more complete 'B' kit that included the windshield, headlights, dashboard frame, rear deck cover, fender beading, spare tyre mounting bracket, and full hardware kit. The Manx was a wildfire success; so popular that kits were built in their thousands to meet demand.

On the beach with a pair of Manxes in an early promotional shot. Grooved Gates Commando tyres were de rigeur on period buggies. (Courtesy Ludvigsen Library)

The clean lines of the Meyers Manx have often been copied, though rarely bettered. The buggies often appeared in promotions for surfing products.

Promotional shot of the Manx as it is about to go 'over the top.' The buggy survived unscathed! (Courtesy Ludvigsen Library)

Classic 'Up the Creek …' period advertisement for the Meyers Manx.

Movie stars – including Dick Smothers and Steve McQueen – drove them, and advertisers used them to promote their wares in magazines and on TV.

To keep up with demand, the BF Meyers & Company operation expanded into larger premises, and was moulding up to 25 kits a day at the height of production (distributed through a network of 200 dealers). The company produced bodyshells to a faultless standard, but almost immediately fell prey to counterfeiters who copied the kit, cut the quality, and dropped the price.

Despite protection by patents, the Manx was an easy shape to duplicate, and the pirates did much to harm the reputation of glassfiber dune buggies and the Meyers operation financially. By 1970, a Manx II kit had been introduced in an attempt to take on the copiers. By making the bodies stackable for easier transportation, omitting the bodyshell stiffeners, battery and tire wells, and using a simplified unitary dashboard and front hood, the price could be reduced. However, the revised buggy lasted only about a year before the IRS moved in and closed the company.

The Manx had appeared in a number of guises, including a long-wheelbase model called the Turista (or Resorter), and a utility model developed for lifeguard duties on LA beaches.

The Meyers Manx was the first and most influential of all glassfiber dune buggies, and has again found favour with a whole new generation of buggistas. Meyers has re-established himself at the forefront of the revitalised US scene with his all-new, long-wheelbase Manxster 2+2 buggy (see separate section), and his new 'Kick-Out' Manx kits in two formats: Traditional (two-seater with opening hood, 2in wider rear fenders, single-hoop rollbar and optional rear deck lid with dual headrests), and SS (Super Sleek, with opening hood and inset headlights, curved windshield, dual-hoop rollbar to match the optional rear deck lid dual headrests).

Kick-Out SS Manx is the latest incarnation of the classic design. The name comes from a surfing term said at the end of the ride. (Courtesy Stephan Szantai)

Classic lines of the Manx are shown off to perfection by this neat example, complete with period hardtop. (Courtesy Stephan Szantai)

MEYERS MANX

DATA PANEL

Production dates
Manx/Manx II: 1999-date

Numbers built
Manx/Manx II: not available

Export markets
Ireland, Holland, Belgium

Wheelbase
Manx/Manx II: 80in

Identification tips
Manx has traditional lines, and a separate front hood; separate reinforcement tubes running from front to rear on each side; front hood and dashboard pre-joined together; flow-coating on underside of the bodyshell. Manx II has no rear seat battery or spare tyre well; bodies more splayed to allow stacking; no reinforcement tubes

Car enthusiast Melvyn Hubbard had been fascinated by the youthful exuberance of dune buggies ever since they first appeared in Britain in the 1970s. Having owned and built a number of custom cars in the 1980s, he progressed to owning a few buggies, including a couple of Hustlers. His further involvement with buggies was confirmed when he styled the long-wheelbase GT Buggy for GT Mouldings. The first of a new wave of UK buggies, the GT was productionised in 1997, and set the bar high for a good-looking and easy-to-build British LWB buggy.

With his glassfiber credentials confirmed, Hubbard made a visit to a VW show in southern France in the 1990s in his orange Hustler buggy, where he met buggy originator Bruce Meyers, who was a guest of the show organisers. In a move to re-establish the Manx name, Meyers had not only set up a Manx owners club in the US, but had also licensed production of his classic Manx buggy design in France. What could be better, Hubbard reasoned, than to make the Manx available in the UK – a situation that had never really happened during the Manx's heyday? Inspired, and with more than a little luck to help him, in November 1999 he found an original Manx II in Southend, Essex, not far from his Gravesend base in Kent. With the agreement of Bruce Meyers he set about cleaning up the body, and made a new set of production moulds. The Manx II was the 'cheaper' version of the Manx kit in the US, with a flat back seat area, a larger badge mount on the front hood, a larger centre console on the dashboard, no tubing reinforcement under the fenders, and the bodies slightly splayed to make them stackable for easier shipment in quantity. The resulting kits made a big impact on the UK buggy scene in the early 'noughties,' as the original Manx had never been seen in Britain before, except for a few private imports.

The Manx sold well, with one of the first bodyshells going on to be built into a show-winning example at the Volksworld show. The enthusiasm for the buggy, and Hubbard's own desire to make a wider range of quality kits, led him to develop the Predator buggy (see separate chapter). However, in 2002, with the Manx scene developing in the US, Hubbard wanted to re-create an original Manx in the UK. Meyers himself had returned to his very first design for the shortened VW Beetle chassis, and reproduced the kit as the 'Classic Manx.' Faithful to the very first bodyshells, the 'Classic Manx' was the most authentic reproduction of the 1960s design yet. A subsequent variant was produced under the name of 'Signature Manx,' complete with authentication tags, badges and fittings, and it was an imported BL (blemished)

Show-winning Manx in the UK was one of the first from the moulds.

A modern take on the Manx theme, with blue-to-red chameleon flip-flop paint and ghosted flames, wild flame wheels and Hoosier tyres. (Courtesy Mike Key)

Classic Manx from East Coast Manx was built by Flatlands Engineering, and used for a phone company TV promotion. (Courtesy Mike Key)

Flower power hardtop sets off this neat bronze metalflake-finished Manx. (Courtesy Mike Key)

product that Hubbard acquired from Bruce Meyers in 2002 from which UK-manufactured bodies were reproduced.

Faithful to the Meyers legacy in every way, the exquisitely-made bodies were often laminated in sparkling metalflake colors to truly replicate the effect of the 1960s/70s. The kit was warmly received by a whole new generation of buggy builders, and for the next couple of years was the best-selling kit for Hubbard's Manx UK operation. However, not one to rest on his laurels, Hubbard diversified into the production of other kits and, by 2004, with the introduction of his Sidewinder design, he passed the project on to Robert Kilham who established a new business called East Coast Manx to make these (and other) buggy kits. The kits remain available currently, and continue the long tradition established by the Meyers design.

Who wouldn't want to go cruising in a buggy like this on a summer's day? The Manx design remains timeless. (Courtesy Mike Key)

Period-style Manx in British Racing Green gelcoat is complemented by a tan interior and hartop for a clean, uncluttered look. (Courtesy Paul Knight)

MEYERS MANX SR

DATA PANEL

Production dates
1970-1971 (BF Meyers)
1974 (Karma Cochworks)
1981 (Heartland Glassworks)
1993 (Manx Motors/Manx Motorsports Inc)

Numbers built
200 by BF Meyers & Co, and approximately 100 by subsequent manufacturers

Export markets
None

Wheelbase
80in

Identification tips
Manx SR has a sports coupé look, with flip-up doors, heavily raked windshield and forward-leaning rear targa top and lift-off roof panel; opening front hood and in-built front headlights; opening rear engine lid; Volvo P1800 rear lights

Top view of the uniquely-styled Manx SR with its sharply-raked windscreen and forward-leaning rear targa top roof.

When Bruce Meyers' Manx started the buggy revolution in the 1960s, other would-be manufacturers also wanted a piece of the action – and new, less reputable copyists sprang up overnight. In an effort to curb the piracy, Meyers went on to design and manufacture other types of kits that weren't so easy to duplicate, such as the all-out off-road Tow'd buggy, and a pure street car called the Manx SR. The SR – short for Street Roadster – was designed as a sports coupé, and was a more upmarket cousin of the Manx buggy. Launched in April 1970 at the Specialty Manufacturers Association Show in the USA (SEMA), its aim was to fill the gap in the ever-growing market for a beautifully-crafted and ageless design that could rival foreign sports cars, but at a fraction of the price.

Styled with the help of automotive designer Stewart Reed, newly qualified from the Art Center College of Design at Pasadena, and George 'Red' Rose, Meyers worked for over a year, using his considerable

skills as a glassfibre boat tooler to create the stunning new buggy design. Knowing the strength and rigidity of the shortened VW Beetle chassis, Meyers based the SR on the same wheelbase as the traditional Manx, giving the buggy overall dimensions of just 142in long, 48in high and 65in wide. To keep the buggy legal in all states, the design had large, all-enclosing fenders for wide wheels and tyres, and a cavernous engine bay able to accommodate physically larger engines such as the Corvair and Porsche. It even had sensible luggage areas under the front hood and behind the seats – and proper weather protection in the form of an interesting forward-leaning and double-skinned rear targa top section, to which could be added a lift-off sunroof panel or soft-top. Here was an all-weather fun buggy that had production car practicalities, yet could be purchased as a kit for a base price of just $895!

The SR's look proclaimed quality in the best Meyers tradition, and the designers made the kit complex, as Meyers wanted to be "damn sure that the new car would not fall into the same trap" with copyists as had befallen the Manx. Thus, the SR used no fewer than 13 separate glassfiber sections (plus the roof), with special brackets, hinges and metal sub-frames to hold it all together. Particularly noticeable were the unique flip-up doors that lifted on special hinges and operated by a cable release, which rose vertically away from the side sill for easy entry and exit. Inside, the interior could be kitted out with high-back vinyl seats and fitted carpets as a factory option. The body itself was formed of a black grained-vinyl-effect inner liner bonded to two colored side body skins, to which the opening front hood, lifting rear trunk lid

Models A-Z

and matt-black dashboard and cowl were all affixed via the clever use of internal metal supporting frames and hardware. Even the two-part doors were bonded together to allow storage inside them, and to give a different inner/outer body color, like a 'real' car. One of the beauties of the styling was the lack of exterior latches or fittings, bolt-heads, fasteners or screws that would otherwise ruin the smooth outer lines of the sleek bodywork.

The design certainly deterred the pirates, but its complexity meant that only about 200 kits and a couple of turn-key cars were made before the BF Meyers & Co operation folded. The moulds were subsequently acquired in turn by Karma Coachworks in California (re-named the Manx SR2), Heartland Glassworks in Oklahoma, and finally, Manx Motors/Manx Motorsports Inc in Maryland.

Manx SR at a custom car show. The design was styled by Stewart Reed and Bruce Meyers, and still looks futuristic today. (Courtesy Stephan Szantai)

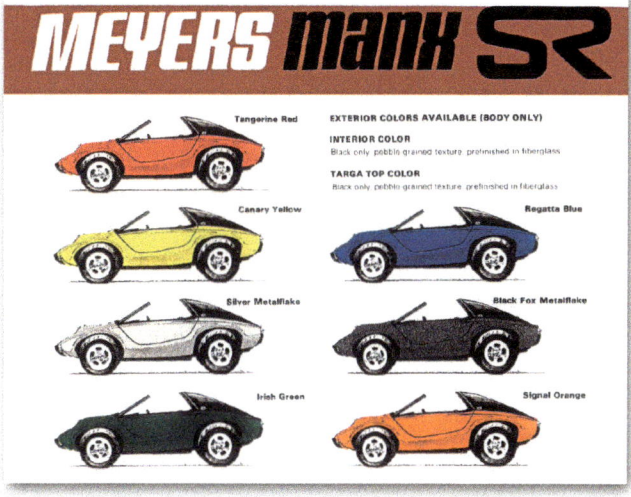

The SR was available in a range of colors from Tangerine Red to Silver Metalflake – and even eye-popping Signal Orange.

Scissor-opening doors are not just for Lamborghinis! The flip-up doors were operated by a cable to release a Beetle front hood catch. (Courtesy Mel Baker)

Tilting front hood gave access to the fuel tank and wiring, and a small amount of luggage space. High-intensity driving lights were set in stylish nascelles.

MEYERS MANXTER 2+2 & MANXTER DUALSPORT

DATA PANEL

Production dates
2002-date

Numbers built
Not available

Export markets
France, England

Wheelbase
Manxter 2+2: 94.5in
Manxter DualSport: 100.5in

Identification tips
Manxter 2+2: long-wheelbase kit built around a sturdy, 8-point steel roll cage with lateral side impact bars; opening front hood; dashboard access panel; lift-off roof panel. DualSport: raised Manxter bodyshell; longer wheelbase and long-travel suspension designed principally for serious off-roading

With the establishment of the Manx Club, and renewed worldwide interest surrounding the Manx in the 1990s, Bruce Meyers was ready to introduce an all-new buggy for a new millennium. In 2002 he announced his new, long-wheelbase buggy, the Manxter 2+2, as an answer to the limitations of the classic-styled Manx. The shape, whilst unmistakably from the Manx heritage, was designed to fit a standard VW Beetle chassis to provide seating for four adults, a much easier build without the need for welding, and real safety through the use of a steel, 8-point rollcage with side intrusion bars, and a rear transmission support to create an all-enclosed safety cage. Modern touches included the body-colored glassfibre windscreen frame as opposed to an extruded aluminium one, an opening front hood for under-hood storage and access to the fuel tank, a dashboard access panel, hard-top and side panels. With 70 parts comprising the full kit, the Manxter 2+2 was a far cry from the basic Manx of the past. Technologically, the buggy could also be endowed with more sophisticated performance parts and engines, such as the water-cooled, fuel-injected and turbocharged Subaru Impreza WRX STI flat four engine. Whilst increasing the price of the finished buggy, the move to these power units took the car a step away from a dune buggy to a more competitive street machine and off-roader. The Manxter began appearing at both Manx Club events and in more serious competition. One Manxter racecar was raced in the gruelling Baja 1000 event, but rolled twice into a ditch at 75mph. As a sign of the quality of the kit, when the buggy was reinstated on its wheels, there was no damage to the cage – although the lights had been wiped out on the car, and the fiberglass needed minor buffing to remove scratches on the fenders.

The Manxter 2+2 could be bought as a 'bare bones' kit for $5595, right up to a more comprehensive kit at $7700. Whilst the buggy was happiest on the street but could

Finished in 'Just Right' yellow, this Manxter 2+2 enjoys the Californian sunshine. (Courtesy Ryan Price)

Promotional shot from Manxter 2+2 color brochure projected the image of the car as a stylish street buggy. (Courtesy Meyers Manx Inc)

go off-road, Meyers' next incarnation of the kit – the Manxster DualSport – was designed with off-roading in mind, though could be driven on the street. The DualSport addressed the need for a stylish and durable off-road machine that remained street-legal, and had a body raised 3in to easily accommodate the heavy-duty, long-travel suspension fitted to the cars. The wheelbase was also extended 6in for better off-road stability. Whilst overall body style was the same as the Manxter 2+2, the car's stance was far more purposeful-looking. To prove the strength of his new buggy, at the age of 76 Meyers entered and raced a DualSport in the Baja 1000 event. Sadly, the engine expired after some 130 miles, but still proved the durability of his latest glassfiber buggy kit.

Other very useful additions to the Manxters have recently included the Meyers Manx proprietary front suspension subframe, which allows the chassis from the later (cheaper and more plentiful) Super Beetles to be used. For off-roading there are also proprietary transmission mounts that allow the transmission to be tipped up for greater departure clearance on the dunes, and a steering assembly that accommodates a 1½ x 1 ratio rack and pinion steering box to improve steering and handling to modern car standards.

With kits available in tempting Californian-themed color choices such as Just Right Yellow, Newport White, Dragon Red, Orange Sherbet and Lime Green, and with Manxter turn-key cars available through agents – including Flatlands Engineering in the UK – it seems the Meyers legend is set to continue for a long while yet.

The Manxter 2+2 and the DualSport have brought the Meyers Manx heritage right up to date for a new generation. (Courtesy Meyers Manx Inc)

The first advertising flyer for the Manxter 2+2 highlighted the heritage of the Manx buggies, and the practicalities of the new four-seater Manxter. (Courtesy Meyers Manx Inc)

View of the Manxter showing the lifting roof panel, and the opening front hood for access to luggage space beneath. (Courtesy Meyers Manx Inc)

MEYERS TOW'D

DATA PANEL

Production dates
1968-1971

Numbers built
850

Export markets
France

Wheelbase
80in

Identification tips
Tube frame chassis with dual rollbar, steering column support and retractable tow bar mount. Glassfiber liner with fixed seat bases and optional front hood section. Tow'dsters add front and rear fenders and an engine cowl

Tow'd in a hole! The lightweight buggy was a very capable off-roader, but had fenders added to make it street legal and re-named the Tow'dster. (Courtesy Melvyn Hubbard)

The US buggy scene of the 1960s had suffered from piracy of better-known designs, and manufacturer inability to meet customer demand for a dual-purpose vehicle that could work well both on the street and off-road. Image-conscious owners had adopted the buggy as a road car, whilst serious race competitors had begun to put down Bruce Meyers' famous Manx as 'too pretty, too nice, to be a good dune buggy.' The growing market for a simple, rugged and cheap buggy led Meyers to design an all-new kit that would meet expectations, yet not be easily imitated.

Listening to suggestions from off-roaders, Meyers rationalised the VW parts needed to build a buggy and produced the Tow'd – a vehicle which didn't have to be driven out to the dunes, but could be towed there by a stationwagon or Winnebago.

In a moment of design genius, Meyers threw out the heavy VW floorpan and substituted a lighter tubular steel frame to produce a buggy that was lightweight, rugged and maneuverable. Incorporating a twin-hooped rollbar for safety, and a steering column support which also provided an instrument pod mount and housing for the retractable tow bar at the front, the frame was difficult to pirate by the average copyist. The frame had pre-drilled mounting plates built in to accept a simple moulded tray that included the seat shapes, and a parcel tray at the back. Initially made of ABS thermoformed plastic, this was quickly changed to stronger glassfiber.

The stock VW front suspension bolted to the frame, as did the rear suspension members and drivetrain components. The fuel tank sat beneath the rear deck within the rollbar structure. Seating was limited to padded cushions in the glassfiber tray, and the spartan interior comprised only the VW steering column, pedal cluster, gear lever cranked back toward the driver, and a pair of steering brake levers. An optional front cowling was produced as a cosmetic extra, though items such as a windshield, lights and horn were omitted as the buggy was not initially road-legal.

Because the buggy was towed to and from its off-road destination, courtesy of the tow bar hook up, with front wheels off the ground, it effectively became a trailer. However, some states required it to be registered as a car as it was a motorised vehicle, and thus needed legalising road equipment. Customers began to demand fenders, engine cowls and a windshield so the Tow'd could also be driven on the street, and to make it more habitable in the dirt when off-roaded. Meyers knew that by covering up his initially stark design he could also reach markets in the east where there were fewer off-road opportunities, and vehicles had to be capable of being driven on the street.

The Tow'd thus became the Tow'dster (Tow'd and street roadster) with the addition of high front and rear fenders, an engine cowl, a windshield and proper lighting equipment. Tyre clearance was good, so that the buggy could still take to the dunes, and an internal bulkhead supplied with the kit doubled as a stiffener between the front fenders and the body, effectively sealing the gap between the glassfiber floor and front hood to keep dirt out.

With the options of a soft-top and front and rear bumpers, the Tow'dster became quite a civilised vehicle, but was always a compromise on the original design, had limited seating adjustments, and more rattles and squeaks than the original Manx buggy. It also became more expensive than the floorpanned Manx, and did little to aid the company's profitability. By 1971 the BF Meyers & Co operation was no more, and Bruce Meyers had departed some time earlier.

The Tow'd was a halfway house toward the pure desert racing buggies used today, and in its short lifetime represented a great leap forward in buggy design.

Go Tow'd advert for B F Meyers & Co promoting the latest addition to the Manx stable.

Meyers Tow'd advertisement showing the component parts of the kit. The buggy was designed to prevent imitations, as had been the case with the Manx.

Bruce Meyers, founding father of the buggy movement, with a superb rebuilt Meyers Tow'd at the Super VW Nationals in France, 1997.

Covering the engine and exposed tires ensured the Tow'dster buggy met the legal requirements of most states, and widened the new kit's market appeal.

Off-road magazines of the period show the Tow'd was, indeed, a very capable off-road machine.

MINIBUG

DATA PANEL

Production dates
1968-1970

Numbers built
200 (approx)

Export markets
None

Wheelbase
80in

Identification tips
Semi-recessed headlights in rounded front hood and tilted-back front windshield. Low sides and long rear deck with standard VW tail lights mounted sideways

It was while attending a sportscar race at Elkhart Lake, Wisconsin, that Avery Greene, general manager of Greene Motors, an authorised VW dealership in Livonia, Michigan, began thinking about the design for a new buggy. This was not just a whim but a realistic way of reusing the many parts from wrecked Beetles traded in at the dealership. With the help of Detroit automotive designers, Greene put together a design for a sports buggy with individual styling that did not copy existing buggy body designs. By early 1968, a clay model had been fashioned, and a glassfiber shop fabricated the new mould for production of the Minibug.

Intended primarily for road use, but strong enough to withstand some off-roading, the Minibug had wide fenders to prevent spray entering the interior, and a sharply raised fender line toward the rear where the deck was extended back far enough to fully protect the otherwise vulnerable VW engine. As a bonus, side-mounted VW tail lights could be fixed to the rear deck, thus utilising standard parts salvaged from the donor VW.

The sweeping sides were also low enough to allow easy entry and exit for the driver and passenger, though the vehicle was low to the ground: a mere 35in from floorpan to the top of the windshield. The separate front hood had a generally rounded appearance, and the stand-up headlights were partly recessed in the body. With raised pod areas behind the lights, the buggy had the look of an English Frog-eye Sprite sportscar.

The windshield had a rounded top edge and a greater degree of tilt to it than most, which helped reduce wind resistance. Proving its use as a street vehicle, the Minibug had the option of either a soft-top with roll-up side curtains, or a full glassfiber, vinyl-effect hardtop. Both attached to a raised lip on the bodyshell top edge for an effective, waterproof fit. Coupled with the standard VW heating and defogging system, with heat piped in through the rear of the bodyshell behind the seats via a VW Bus heat collector pipe, the Minibug really was quite a practical proposition. The rear seat area of the buggy sensibly cleared the standard VW heater boxes without modification of the battery and storage wells, which had been a problem on most early designs.

Styled principally as a road vehicle, the Minibug was nevertheless quite capable as an off-roader. (Courtesy Greene Motors)

Models A-Z

The kit came in either solid or metalflake colors, together with the windshield frame and sealed beam headlights. A floor-mounted support frame which stiffened the inherently weak flat floorpan was available as an optional extra for those wishing to take their vehicle over more demanding terrain. Greene Motors provided a long list of other accessories, including a skidplate, air-lift shock absorbers, and bumpers for off-road use. Tuning parts for the VW engine were also stocked and, for those who wanted to use the buggy seriously off-road, the company developed a modified version of the kit. Sporting rear fenders which were 5in wider than stock, it allowed a VW Transporter reduction gearbox and massive Terra-tires to be fitted.

Being a VW agent meant that Greene had a ready supply of VW parts, and could offer complete damaged cars from which to build the kit, or chassis in stock, or professionally shortened lengths to suit. Designed so as not to replicate a WW II off-road Jeep, it can be fairly claimed that the Minibug succeeded in its aim, although, by 1970, it was past its sell-by date and the VW scene left it behind and moved on.

Minibug advertisement shows the semi-recessed front headlights and general curved lines of the bodyshell.

A modified version of the Minibug kit was developed with 5in wider than stock rear fenders to allow the VW Transporter reduction gearbox and huge off-road tyres to be fitted. (Courtesy Russell Berry)

The Minibug was designed purely as a cost-effective way of using parts from used and crashed Beetles that were collecting in the yard of Greene Motors. (Courtesy Greene Motors)

OCELOT & OCELOT S/S

DATA PANEL

Production dates
1967-1970

Numbers built
450 (approx)

Export markets
None

Wheelbase
80in

Identification tips
One-piece body with large, curved fenders and oval-shaped rear light mount. Ocelot II had a longer front hood and separate dashboard. S/S had an elongated and ridged snout with stand-up headlights, a raised back and proper side panels

For a talented automotive designer to get involved with the dune buggy scene was something of a novelty, but then Roy Dickey was used to producing novel creations. From small beginnings – winning styling competitions in his teens – his post-Art Center School employment was with General Motors, and from there to Chrysler. It was from his own independent design studio, though, that the Ocelot buggy originated.

Getting Dickey's ideas into production in 1967 was the handiwork of Marion Ruggles, owner of Sand Chariots in Anaheim, California, and a former Meyers Manx dealer. From a background building tube-framed buggies and specialising in Corvair engine adaptations, he moved into the buggy business full time. Despite the pair's considerable design and building talent, they chose to modify an existing design, and the Ocelot bodyshell therefore bore more than a passing resemblance to KDM Enterprise's Bushwhacker buggy.

The new kit had shorter front bodywork than the Bushwhacker, and a different headlight arrangement, positioning the lights in the front fenders. Designed as a one-piece kit for the shortened VW floorpan, the bodyshell was long enough to completely cover the extra length of a 6-cylinder Corvair engine. With the greater length, the buggy was better suited to street use, and immediately found public acceptance and orders, through a network of dealers set up across the country. The speed at which the Ocelot kit was launched following the Bushwhacker's debut was so swift that both buggies were introduced to the public through the pages of *Dune Buggies & Hot VWs* magazine in August 1968.

Produced in hand-laid glassfiber, with tubes moulded into the body to strengthen the whole structure, the swoopy body shape was as sleek as its namesake. At the front, standard VW headlights fitted into moulded apertures in the shaped fenders. A twin-tube front bumper protected the hood, whilst the VW fuel tank fitted into a metal cradle beneath, and was filled through a flip-up cap. A flat windshield and frame sat above the dashboard, all part of the unitised design. Various dashboard options were tested, including a teak and leather instrument panel. At the rear, a flat, oval-shaped section to the bodyshell allowed the coverage necessary for longer engines, and gave a mounting area for the tail lights. An insert was subsequently developed to make a removable engine access panel.

By mid-1968, Ruggles had made enough improvements to justify calling a new version the Ocelot II. With a 7in longer hood, the headlights and fenders 2in further forward, and a lower windshield, the buggy was

Design of the Ocelot front allowed fitment of stock VW Beetle headlights in the shaped front fenders.

Models A-Z

visually better proportioned than ever. A new, shapelier dashboard panel was also added, and could be ordered in black or white or body color to match the rest of the kit. With demand for the kits at a steady level, Ruggles and Dickey had other Ocelot-derived designs on the drawing board, including a pickup, camper and stationwagon. Whilst these never saw the light of day, a further Ocelot design – the S/S (Super Sport) – was produced. Similar to the Ocelot II bodyshell, but with a long, shovel-type nose that increased overall length by about 10in, the S/S came close to being a Group 7 car rather than just a buggy. With moulded-in rear seat areas, proper side panels, and a more pronounced engine cover it was, however, an even closer copy of the Bushwhacker, the only visual differences being a slightly modified dashboard and omission of the latter's single light unit at the front of the hood.

Although the company went on to produce another rail-type buggy, the Vaquero, designed to accept the VW front end and Corvair back, it was too little, too late, and the Ocelot disappeared.

Former Meyers Manx distributor-turned-buggy-manufacturer Marion Ruggles produced the Ocelot buggy through his Sand Chariots operation. (Courtesy Petersens)

Customiser George Barris built a pair of Ocelot buggies for the US TV series Groovy, starring host Mike Blodgett. (Courtesy George Barris)

Far left: Ocelot sales were increased not only by a network of dealers across the country, but also by appearances on magazine front covers.

Left: Period advertisement for Sand Chariots' advertisement showing the full range of Ocelot buggies and accessories.

151

PARABUG

DATA PANEL

Production dates
1971-1978

Numbers built
10 (approx)

Export markets
None

Wheelbase
81.5in

Identification tips
Military-styled body with mainly flat panels. Ribbed hood on which a fold-flat windshield is held by small magnets. Removable engine access panel, large wing mirrors and sturdy front and rear crash bars

By 1972, British buggy production had slowed considerably, partly due to the imposition of new purchase taxes on kit-built vehicles in the UK, and also because manufacturers wanted to move on to pastures new.

The launch of the Parabug by North East Fiberglass Ltd in Aberdeen, Scotland was, therefore, somewhat surprising. The launch did coincide, however, with the debut of an equally utilitarian Kübelwagen kit for the VW Beetle chassis by another buggy manufacturer. Billed as a "new order fun car," the design was definitely in a military vein, and bore the hallmarks of a WW II Jeep. Designed by Anderson/Bonar Industrial Design Consultants of Glasgow, the slab-sided body looked more at home in the farming community than with the bright young things of Chelsea, but the quality of the moulding was exceptional.

NEF was a boat-building and industrial glassfiber moulding business, and this experience was put to good use when laminating Parabug bodyshells. Each body had a perfect exterior gelcoat finish to the substantial lay-up of glassfiber, rolled edges for strength and a neat finish, and properly stressed panels with perfect angles for ease of construction. Color choice was unusual, too, described as 'Combat Colors' that included Desert Yellow, Panzer Grey, Marine Blue, Scorched Earth, and Jungle Green.

The Parabug was built on a shortened VW chassis and had excellent engine access

Produced by North East Fibreglass Ltd, the Parabug somewhat lacked the chic appeal of a traditional-looking buggy. (Courtesy North East Fibreglass Ltd)

through a removable rear panel, though this also tended to allow rain water to seep through onto the car's electrics. At the front, the windshield folded flat and was secured to the ribbed front hood section of the vehicle by small magnets, a pair of pins holding it upright when in the vertical position. Front headlights and indicators sat on the flat front nose panel, which was protected from any frontal damage by a robust front crash bar. A similar bar also protected the rear of the vehicle, and doubled as an engine cage.

The high sides and wheelarches emphasised the military look and allowed tall tires to be fitted, which also gave the Parabug outstanding off-road handling. Unlike most buggies with cutaway sides, the Parabug's wide sides offered driver and passenger a great deal of protection from mud and water thrown up by the front wheels. Large rear-view mirrors on each front wheelarch also endorsed the utility look and were extremely functional. Behind the front seats a storage space could be used to house the quick-action soft-top when not in use, or double as a passenger seat. The spartan interior was reinforced by the all-in-one flat dashboard, which was merely an extension of the body tub moulding, and provided a home for the minimalist VW instruments and switches.

The kit was made available in three stages from basic bodyshell and engine cover to a full package, including the folding screen, soft-top and sidescreens, lights, fitted electrics, seats, wheels and crash bars. Each kit provided a steel fuel tank and support bracket which replaced the standard VW item.

Though the kits were available for seven years (a comparatively long time in buggy terms) the company, now renamed

front cover appearance on Hot Car magazine helped publicise the Parabug. The angular body, fold-flat windshield and sturdy crashbars gave the buggy something of a workhorse feel.

Aberglen, ceased production of the Parabug in 1978 with very few kits sold. The buggy's off-road capability was superseded by more specialised vehicles, and the styling never really caught on with the diehard buggy enthusiasts, who favoured the more traditional, classic look.

The production moulds remained with the original manufacturer, but it's doubtful that this curiously-styled buggy will ever be produced again.

Parabug advertising emphasised the fact that the buggy was new and 'front line fashion' for people who wanted action!

Styled by a firm of industrial designers, the Parabug aimed to capitalise on the interest in military vehicles that was in vogue in the early 1970s.

The Dune Buggy Handbook

Advertising & brochures

155

The Dune Buggy Handbook

Advertising & brochures

DATA PANEL

Production dates
1970-1971

Numbers built
150 (approx)

Export markets
Unknown

Wheelbase
SWB: 77.75in LWB: 94.5in

Identification tips
Small rectangular headlights set into a separate front hood. Polished alloy windshield frame, wide rear engine cover, often fitted with a 'scat-pack' chrome engine guard. Gold Powerbug stickers at the front and rear of the bodywork

During the 1970s, companies associated with glassfiber manufacture, or involved in racing and rallying, soon found themselves — perhaps inevitably – becoming caught up in the growing British buggy scene. So it was with Mervyn Aldridge who ran Powerspeed, based in Bromley, Kent. In January 1970, Aldridge decided to produce his own buggy kit called the Powerbug, which was optimistically billed as 'The new dimension in Dune Buggies,' even though the future of the buggy scene as a whole was uncertain.

Available as either a long- or short-wheelbase design, the Powerbug kits were unusual in that the bodyshells were laminated at the company's own glassfiber works, rather than produced by sub-contractors. Although they were manufactured with marine ply inserts for extra rigidity, some of the bodyshells were poorly made, and attracted unfavourable press reports during the rigours of off-road testing.

The aggressive styling afforded by the rectangular headlights built in to the front hood compensated somewhat for the quality of the kit. With the headlights so close together, however, the completed buggy required auxiliary front fender-mounted sidelights to make it road legal. Powerspeed also offered a wide variety of colors, including the option of having the bodyshell and front hood moulded in different colors, if desired.

The bodyshell was very much a traditional design, though the rear licence plate mounting-cum-engine cover was noticeably wider than on most other British buggies. At the front of the hood, and situated between the headlights, a large, gold-colored Powerbug sticker was fixed to ensure easy identification. It also worked as an advertising message, to direct

One of the very few Powerbugs that have survived to the present day. The side panels are from a GP buggy and would not have been part of the original kit.

Models A-Z

prospective customers to the company's door in what was quickly becoming an overcrowded market. A similar sticker appeared on the rear of the bodyshell.

Powerspeed also offered its buggy-building customers a number of additional services, including VW generator rewiring from 6 to 12 volt, and the supply of wheel adaptors so that VW hubs could accept Ford, BMC or Rootes wheels. These adaptors were useful since British-made custom wheels were not available at the time. They also allowed 13in wheels to be used at the front of the buggy to give the vehicle the requisite 'nose-down' stance.

Through its associations with the racing and rallying world, Powerspeed also offered specialised engines – including V8s, Porsches and American Corvair units, together with associated tuning parts – to buggy builders. To prove its expertise, Powerspeed raced a Powerbug in stadium racing during the 1971 season with some success. Familiarity with strenuous competition driving also led the company to develop a kit of parts for strengthening the VW chassis. This kit was welded into the side chassis members and prevented the chassis from flexing, something normally associated with the flat floorpan. This also helped prevent stress cracks forming on the otherwise unsupported body.

Most customers, however, were more interested in the glittering look of the optional metalflake finishes, very much a part of the buggy scene in the 1970s, and which said a lot about the owners who were more conscious of creating the right image in London's Kings Road than any pretentions of off-roading their buggies.

Unsurprisingly, production of the Powerbug was a short-lived affair and the buggy disappeared as quickly as it had appeared. Although a very respectable number were built during its short life, few have survived to the present day, and those that have are often mistaken for other marques. The design retains a 1970s period look, however, and distinctive features that ensure its individuality.

The engine cover panel of the Powerbug was wider than on most contemporary UK buggies, and was sometimes hinged to increase access.

1970s Powerbug advertisement with full details of the wide range of buggy accessories available from manufacturer Powerspeed.

Aggressive styling was a feature of the Powerbug, which used rectangular front headlights built into the separate front hood. (Courtesy Powerspeed)

PREDATOR

DATA PANEL

Production dates
2001-2002 (Manx UK)
2002-2004 (BuzzBugs Buggies)

Numbers built
Not available

Export markets
Unknown

Wheelbase
78.75in

Identification tips
Manx-type styling, but designed for chassis shortened by 15.75in, with wider fenders all round and greater engine access through wider rear bodywork moulding. Dashboard has noticeable downward curves at each end

Having produced the Meyers Manx buggy in the UK since 1999, Melvyn Hubbard had found that customers at his Manx UK operation provided useful feedback on the pros and cons of the US design when built in the UK. Despite the kit being exquisitely laminated, it was designed for an 80in wheelbase, whereas most UK-designed buggies were built for the 78.75in wheelbase. For a builder wishing to re-use the previously shortened chassis from a 1970s buggy, and fit it with new bodyshell, clearly the Manx kit, as it stood, was not going to be the answer. The Manx kit was also designed with sunnier climes in mind, and the narrow wheelarches did not prevent water on the road being sprayed into the car from the wider tyres that modern builders were using. The kit also created some interference problems with tall carburettors and air filters on the larger engines being used nearly forty years on since the design was originated. If a kit could be made to address these problems, it would increase the market for the Manx UK buggies, and make the kits easier for customers to build.

The solution was to build a buggy that had the timeless lines of the original, but which was designed for more practical applications in the UK market. A similar thing had been done by GP in the late 1960s: taking a Manx original and modifying the front bulkhead to fit a slightly shorter wheelbase, thus pulling the front fenders over the front tyres for greater legality. With wider rear fenders and more coverage for the engine at the rear, GP had created its own unique marque which led the way for the British buggy explosion. Bearing this in mind, and starting with a pre-shortened chassis of the correct length, Hubbard modified the front internal bulkhead and chassis flanges of a Manx to get it to seat comfortably in place on the floorpan. With wide wheels and tyres fitted to the pattern vehicle, the bodyshell's fenders were split and widened to adequately cover them front and rear. The rear deck above the engine was also extended backward to give more engine room underneath, and the cut-out on the rear panel was considerably widened to allow better access, and easier engine changing. One final and very noticeable change was to the dashboard, produced as an integral part of the front hood moulding. The Manx original had a central binnacle to house the VW speedometer and switchgear. This had already been increased in size on the Manx II kits to accommodate later speedometers, which required more space between the electrical connections and the return ledge of the dashboard. For the Predator – the new buggy – the dashboard panel was kept flat but had a noticeable curved drop down to the level of the bodyshell at each side.

With moulds prepared, the Predator was launched in 2001, with many kits being built into show-winning examples. However,

Up, up and away! With a 205bhp, 2276cc motor fitted out back, it's hardly surprising that this Predator is capable of huge wheelstands whenever it hits the road. (Courtesy Mike Key)

Models A-Z

Predator buggy built with full tube space frame; aircraft-quality aluminium plate for the floor, and aftermarket pedal cluster are all neat touches. (Courtesy Mike Key)

Presenter Mike Brewer and mechanic Edd China turned a rusty VW Beetle into a Predator buggy for the TV show *Wheeler Dealers* in 2004, in just one week. (Courtesy Discovery Communications)

Street racer-style Predator buggy is a perfect example of a well-detailed and thoroughly modern buggy.

with Hubbard diversifying his interests and already working on other projects, the Predator received little in the way of publicity before the moulds were passed on, in 2002, to David Waspe at fledgling company BuzzBugs Buggies, where they remained virtually unused. The only real exposure for the buggy came in 2004 via the TV show *Wheeler Dealers* hosted by Mike Brewer, in which an ageing Beetle was converted by mechanic Edd China into a Predator buggy in one week, and on a budget of just £2000. Since then, the Predator has disappeared, though it is known that a pirated set of moulds have recently surfaced.

Following Manx lines, the Predator had wider wings and greater engine access than the classic original.

161

PROWLER

DATA PANEL

Production dates
2002-2004 (Manx UK)
2004-date (East Coast Manx)

Numbers built
Not available

Export markets
Unknown

Wheelbase
78.75in

Identification tips
Classic Manx-type shape, but with a flatter back, largely cut away at the centre for easy engine access; flat back seat area; wide rear fenders, and a choice of front hood: either a conventional Manx style taking an upright, flat alloy-framed windscreen, or a smoother hood with curved Renault Dauphine windscreen secured by two alloy posts

Established as a buggy manufacturer under the Manx UK name, Melvyn Hubbard had already introduced the Meyers Manx in Britain, and gone on to develop the similarly-styled Predator buggy. Never one to rest on his laurels, Hubbard then began work on a new buggy in 2002 at the request of an Irish customer. The potential buyer had seen Hubbard's own off-road styled GP Buggy at his workshop, and liked the way the back end of the bodyshell had been widened to cover large off-road tyres, and was largely cut away at the centre of the back panel for easier engine access. Realising the potential in patterning a new buggy, Hubbard agreed to style a new kit that would eventually be called the Prowler.

The starting point was a Classic Manx body, modified to fit a Beetle chassis shortened to a wheelbase of 78.5in – considered the 'standard' length in the UK. Taking measurements from the back of his off-road-prepared GP Buggy, Hubbard then re-created the widened fender look (1.5in wider at the front, and 2in wider at the rear) that the customer was seeking.

The extra width allowed the fitting of wider wheels and tyres, or lowering of the buggy without any tyre-to-fender interference. A neat swage line on the lower edge of the rounded rear fenders followed through to the back panel where the panel abruptly terminated, leaving a large section without enclosure but superb access to the engine. This minimalistic rear did, however, allow lights to be fitted to the small glassfiber sections each side of the opening. To make the new buggy appeal to the widest range of customer, two separate front hood designs were developed. The first was a conventional Manx-style that took a flat, alloy-framed windscreen, and featured a traditional badge mount at the lower front edge. The other was altogether a more inspired idea: having imported a Bounty Hunter buggy bodyshell from the US, what would be better, reasoned Hubbard, than making a front hood for the Prowler accept the Bounty Hunter's curved Renault Dauphine windscreen for a more aerodynamic look? The Dauphine screen was attached to the Bounty Hunter body by two separate cast alloy posts, and both these, and the screen, had to be re-tooled for use on the Prowler. By re-working a traditional buggy front hood to match the contours of the curved screen, and removing the badge mount, the new front hood had a style all its own. Many customers still preferred the traditional style, but there was now a choice.

Adding a pair of traditionally-styled side panels completed the design of the buggy, and it was finally launched in late 2002. Interestingly, the customer who had first sparked Hubbard's imagination for developing the kit didn't buy one! Proving his expertise in glassfiber work, Hubbard

What the buggy was designed for! Blue Metalflake Prowler is put through its paces in the dunes. (Courtesy Tom Wood/Alamy)

Models A-Z

laminated most of the new Prowler buggies in glittering Metalflake finishes, and a queue of customers snapped them up. All seemed to be going well, and Prowler buggies regularly appeared in the pages of VW-oriented magazines. However, a change of direction meant that Hubbard was expanding his range of commercial glassfiber products such as canoes, and the buggies were beginning to take a back seat. To ensure the Manx UK buggies were not sidelined, in 2004 Hubbard sold his complete range of buggy projects to Robert Kilham at new venture East Coast Manx. The company now sells the Manx, Manx II, Prowler, Bounty Hunter and a child-size Mini-Manx from its premises in Rutland. Still finished in metalflake colors, the buggies continue the legacy in the UK.

Above: Kawasaki green Prowler buggy was built to a design that would snap necks rather than just turn heads. (Courtesy Mike Key)

Below: 'Silver Bullet' Prowler easily accommodates the large V8 engine, thanks to the extra-wide access at the back of the bodyshell.

Seen at a Southern Dune Buggy Club event in 2005, this Prowler shines in the summer sun.

Neat lines of the Prowler make it a refreshing take on the traditional lines of a classic Manx buggy. (Courtesy Mike Key)

RAT

DATA PANEL

Production dates
1970-1992 (UK)

Numbers built
400 (approx)

Export markets
Canary Isles, Spain, Middle East, Germany, Rhodesia, Mozambique, Denmark, Israel, South Africa, USA

Wheelbase
SWB: 78.75in LWB: 94.5in

Identification tips
Dummy oval-shaped air intake in the hood of early models. Headlamps inset into low front fenders, wider than average rears. Later LWB cars featured rounded side panels and a squared-off look to the hood

When three friends – Robert Taylor, Anthony Hill and Trevor Pym – decided to start manufacturing buggy bodyshells, the hardest part was choosing a name for their new creation. Using the initials of their forenames they arrived at 'Rat,' and the buggy, derived from another well-known bodyshell of the day, took on a totally new look and became a stalwart of the British buggy scene.

Produced by Fibre-Fab of Crowthorne, Berkshire (owned by Taylor, Hill and Pym), the short-wheelbase bodyshell had a novel front end, with a single, large, oval nostril (strictly non-functional). The front hood sat between fenders, which were very low, and accepted the in-built front headlight units. These could be rectangular, round or, occasionally, twin-round units from an NSU. A separate dashboard, mounted to a steel frame, provided support for the windshield in its alloy frame.

To ensure that wide wheels and tyres could be fitted legally, the rear end of the buggy had noticeable flares to the fenders. This was a distinct bonus for the home builder who would have to add arch extensions to most buggy bodyshells to achieve street legality.

The economically-priced kit, with optional accessories such as candy-striped vinyl hood, sold well following introduction in late 1970. The bodyshells were available in no fewer than 80 different colors to meet individual customer taste, and, in 1974, the Rat was developed into a long-wheelbase buggy to complement its shorter brother. Despite Robert Taylor's and Trevor Pym's departure from Fibre-Fab at around this time, coupled with a change of address, the company survived the collapse of the home market by turning to exports and diversifying into the manufacture of glassfiber panels for VW Beetles and industrial mouldings.

By the late 1970s, the market for buggies was beginning to pick up, and the Rat once again became an option for customers considering an economical kit-car project. The short-wheelbase variant was withdrawn from production in 1979 when it was discovered that the moulds

These Rat demonstrators, in both short- and long-wheelbase form, were parked at the company's works in 1970. (Courtesy Robin Wager)

Models A-Z

were severely warped. A Swedish customer bought them in a last-ditch attempt to mould one last body for himself. The long-wheelbase buggy continued in production but underwent a dramatic face-lift in the early 1980s, with the addition of wide, curved side panels. These sat below the body waistline and formed neat front and rear wheelarches.

The front hood was also changed, to a moulding derived from the American Balboa kit, with a squared-off look and central styling ridge, into which the fuel filler cover sat. The dashboard changed, too, becoming an attractive, full-width unit that accepted right or left-hand drive.

The booming kit-car market in the 1980s once again saw the Rat at the forefront of the British buggy scene. The new-look Rat bodyshell, often produced in glittering metalflake, found many new customers, and fired the imagination of a new generation of buggistas. The eventual departure of Anthony Hill from Fibre-Fab, and change of ownership to Tim and Sue Cooksey, gave fresh vigour to the company, which was re-named FF Kit Cars & Conversions Ltd. However, introduction of its new FF buggy meant the Rat was pensioned off.

Although the final nail in the Rat's coffin was another change of ownership and company name (to Stephen Wilson and Country Volks respectively), a single, oval-nosed Rat bodyshell that had emigrated to Australia with former owner Anthony Hil, spawned a whole new generation of Rats 'down under,' and continues in production today.

Period advertising of the Rat buggy showing the incredibly cheap introductory price for kits in no fewer than 80 different colors.

Below: Promotional leaflet for the later incarnation of the Rat buggy, which changed the front hood to one borrowed from the US Lido buggy design.

Short-wheelbase Rat buggy with a difference – a Renault 2.7-litre V8 engine sits mid-mounted on a shortened VW chassis with reversed gearbox. (Courtesy Mike Key)

The oval air intake to the front of the hood was a novel idea, though strictly non-functional. The side panels on this example are from a GP buggy.

165

RENEGADE

DATA PANEL

Production dates
1969-1970

Numbers built
30 (approx)

Export markets
England

Wheelbase
80in

Identification tips
Curved windshield, low inset headlights in Corvette-shaped front. Swooping bodyline, unitised hood and dashboard moulding. Identification plate under rear seat.

With many dune buggy producers happy to slavishly copy other designs on the market, it came as a refreshing change when Glassco Fiberglass Fabrication of Van Nuys, California, introduced the Renegade. By having its own fiberglass design and production facilities, though principally for making Catalina boats, the company was able to carefully style and shape its own design when it decided to enter the already overcrowded buggy market in 1969.

Having acted as subcontractors for production of the first five Bounty Hunter bodyshells for partners Mel Keys and Brian Dries, company bosses Glynn Samuels and Howard March used one of the kits as the starting point for their own design. The resulting product was one of the sharpest-looking American buggies. It had hints of the Chevrolet Corvette about it, but managed to retain a look all its own. The top part of the front hood, dashboard, windshield and frame are visibly derived from the Bounty Hunter, though the rest was extensively re-worked, rounded and smoothed to give a flowing sports car shape.

Based on the shortened VW Beetle chassis, the buggy was designed to take VW Squareback, Corvair flat engines, or Porsche powerplants. Anything else would have left it underpowered, and would have been incongruous with its sporting looks. The low, swooping rear end precluded tall engines with off-road filters, but looked purposeful and brutal, as well as providing an area on which to mount the individual rear light units and licence plate.

At the front, the sharply-pointed nose and lower panel covering the front suspension provided better aerodynamics than most, and the curved windshield, attached to an aluminium post at each side, also gave less wind resistance. Beneath the hood, in which sat a racing fuel filler, a modified VW Beetle fuel tank rested in the glassfibre cradle of the main bodyshell moulding. Small, round headlamps completed the stunning looks of this most individual of US buggies.

The Renegade bodyshell was so well proportioned, with its curved rear and sweeping sides raking forwards to the stylish front, that it seemed to be moving, even when still. Viewed from any angle, the effect was a pleasing change from the traditional dune buggy norm, and ensured the Renegade found favour with automotive

The sharply-pointed nose of the well-proportioned and Corvette-inspired bodyshell gave the buggy the illusion of movement even when stationary. (Courtesy Sport Buggies)

Models A-Z

journalists and a press more attuned to the styles of production sportscars of the day.

Due to its expertise in commercial fibreglass work, Glassco was able to offer the kits in a wide range of solid colours or glittering Metalflake. The latter endowed the kits with an eye-catching sparkle that enhanced the already flamboyant design. The superbly crafted Renegade kits also had a moulded-in identification plate on the rear seat area which gave the name of the kit and the manufacturer's details.

Wishing to capitalise on its innovative buggy design, Glassco quickly set up a network of dealers and distributors across the country, and marketed the Renegade kit as a dual purpose buggy for street and off-road use. But the auspicious start was not to last for very long. Arriving late in the US buggy boom, the Renegade missed the peak sales opportunity of the mid-1960s, and interest rapidly evaporated as customer attention turned to different automotive trends.

Despite a short lifespan in its native America, salvation for the Renegade came from another country – Britain – when an original set of moulds was exported for licensed production there (see Renegade UK). Although the US Renegade story ended abruptly, the design has lived on, continuing to delight a new audience of buggy builders in the years since.

Period advertising from Glassco highlighting the exciting features of the design, including a curved windshield for greater aerodynamics.

Glassco Fiberglass Fabrication designed and produced the Renegade in its own tooling shop, and marketed the buggy as a low-dollar sportscar. (Courtesy Road Test/Dune Buggy)

A Porsche engine and wide mag-type wheels with racing tires were features of the Glassco company demonstrator. (Courtesy Sport Buggies)

RENEGADE

DATA PANEL

Production dates
1970-1976, 1995-date

Numbers built
310 (approx)

Export markets
America, Belgium, France, Germany, Spain, Greece, Sweden, Malta, Iceland, Canary Isles, Saudi Arabia, Australia, Singapore, the West Indies

Wheelbase
80in

Identification tips
Ford Anglia windshield in either alloy or glassfiber frame, Renegade identification plate under rear seat, Corvette-inspired look to pointed front with headlights inset into neat nacelles

From US beginnings, the Renegade made its debut in the UK in 1970, courtesy of the strangely-named Pell Abrahams Broadcasting Corporation Ltd, run by London-based Phillip Pell. Starting with a set of imported Californian Glassco moulds, the aim was to produce the Renegade in Britain under licence – quite a novel idea at the time.

Using the same 80in wheelbase as its American cousin, the bodyshell was moulded with a metallic finish called Fireflake, in a range of vivid colors with names such as Randy Red and Bilious Blue! The main differences to the Stateside original were the windshield and the rollbar; the former coming from a British car called the Ford Anglia and mounted in a polished alloy frame, and the latter made by UK rally-safety expert John Alley Racing. Of double bar construction, angled together at the top and mounted to the strongest point of the chassis and the rear suspension, then covered in matt PVC to give it a targa look, it was probably the strongest buggy rollbar produced.

Acknowledged by the UK motoring press as one of the most desirable models available during the buggy heyday, the demonstrators built by Eresbug Co PABC (to give the company its abbreviated title) were usually of poor grade, however, and did little to enhance a quality image for the kit. Seeing an opportunity, motor accessory dealer Bob Ridgard acted as agent for the kits, selling them through his business, Little Big End. With his subsidiary operation, The Four Seasons Buggy Company, building beautifully finished Renegades for customers, the buggy's future began to look brighter.

This rosier outlook was further enhanced when The Four Seasons Buggy Company took over full production of the kits and moved to modern premises in Suffolk, where the company began selling cars to local US servicemen at the many airbases in the area. Whilst most manufacturers and their buggies had disappeared by 1972, the Renegade continued through to 1974 before lack of sales forced it out of production. By then the buggy had acquired a pair of sculpted side panels which enhanced the sweeping lines of the body.

Before its final demise, the company also swapped a Renegade bodyshell for a Belgian Au-Ki bodyshell produced by Apal. The Renegade was restyled in Belgium, into a new buggy called the Jet, and the Au-Ki became the Renegade T in Britain (see separate section).

Though the moulds passed to British buggy builder GP Concessionaires in 1975, there was little demand for new kits. Following a long gap in production, a resurgence of interest in buggies in the mid-1990s saw the Renegade resurrected in 1995 by GT Mouldings, and manufactured from all-new production moulds. Faithfully replicating the curvaceous lines of the

The sleek lines of the Renegade buggy were Corvette-inspired at the front, and had a dramatic sweeping curve at the rear. This car is a successful drag-racer. (Courtesy Mark Gredzinski)

Models A-Z

original shape, the only major difference concerned the windshield frame, which was produced in strengthened glassfiber to accept the original Ford Anglia screen.

The chrome rims of the low, inset front headlights used on 1970s Renegade kits were also changed to glassfiber, color-matched trim-rings for the UK specification aftermarket lamps that were available in the 1990s.

From its Stateside origins in 1969 to the present day, the Renegade has proved itself a true survivor, and is a testament to good design in a world full of buggy lookalikes. It has also re-established itself as a firm favourite with those involved in the growing VW drag racing scene. The Renegade is currently manufactured by Midlands-based KMR Buggies.

Designed in the US, the Renegade was made under licence in the UK by PABC, and used the curved windshield from the Ford Anglia 105E. (Courtesy Custom Car)

Period advertising brochure for the Renegade.

GT Mouldings' relaunched version of the Renegade used a strengthened glassfiber windshield frame and headlight trim-rings, but otherwise was an exact reproduction of the original. (Courtesy Mike Key)

Few buggy designs have ever bettered the looks of the Renegade. The timeless styling has appealed to generations of builders in a production history spanning more than 40 years. (Courtesy Mike Key)

RENEGADE 'T'

DATA PANEL

Production dates
1973-1974 (UK)

Numbers built
10 (approx)

Export markets
US

Wheelbase
94.5in

Identification tips
Unusual 'sit-up and beg' rod-styled buggy. Fenders form pseudo running boards on double-skinned bodyshell. Opening engine hatch. Standard VW Beetle indicators and rear light units

Given the growing presence of the hot rod movement in Britain at around the same time as the buggy boom, it was, perhaps, inevitable that those dune buggy manufacturers influenced by the hot rodding world would tend to continue with production.

In 1972 Bob Ridgard's company, The Four Seasons Buggy Company at Brandon, Suffolk, did a straight swap of a Renegade buggy bodyshell for an Au-Ki rod-styled buggy, produced by Belgian manufacturer Apal. This was a derivative of the original US Berry Mini-T IV that had been reworked for the European market. The Au-Ki was a proper four-seater, designed for the full-length VW Beetle floorpan.

With new production moulds made, the renamed Renegade 'T' buggy became available on the British market. The bodyshell was superbly made and sported some innovative design features. Strong and rigid, thanks to the unique double-skinned construction of the glassfiber bodyshell, the design even featured a proper hinged engine cover that allowed full access to the VW powerplant beneath.

The overall look was a real departure from traditional dune buggy styling, with sit-up-and-beg screen and high-riser soft-top. The body had a very squared-off front, with the lower panel doubling as a mounting for the licence plate or mock radiator shell, and featured stand-up buggy headlamps mounted on pods each side of the smooth front hood. The front fenders flowed down behind the wheels and tyres to form pseudo running boards, before becoming wide rear fenders at the back of the vehicle. Standard Beetle front indicators and rear light units were fitted to the fenders, and looked perfectly in keeping with the overall retro-styling.

The body waistline rose noticeably at the rear, where it enclosed the rear seat and parcel shelf area; the interior was particularly spartan. One neat touch, though, was the curved dashboard, which swept back from the windshield mounting and provided a home for the VW speedometer and electrical switchgear. The windshield was fitted in a polished alloy frame, and had a vintage look with its 'wider-at-the-top' stance and curved bottom edge.

Many extras were available for the kit, including the full-length vinyl soft-top, chromed front and rear bumpers shaped to the body, and an upholstery pack and seats for the interior.

The buggy was given public exposure on the Four Seasons stand at the Racing Car show in London in January 1973. At the same time, a neat detachable glassfiber

The rising back of the bodyshell enclosed a rear seat and parcel shelf area, thus making it a family-type buggy for four. Engine access was superb, due to the large removable cover. (Courtesy Custom Car)

hardtop was made available for the kit. Proper doors and a hardtop began to make the Renegade T an all-weather machine, more appropriate for the British climate. However, with the company owner's business interests elsewhere, the Renegade 'T' never really got the kind of push it needed to help it make an impression with the British public.

One of the very few bodyshells that was built into a complete buggy eventually found its way to the US with its American serviceman owner, and started a new chapter in the design's ongoing production. With minor modifications to the engine hatch in order to incorporate a spare wheel well, the buggy was once again renamed, this time as the Tuff-Tub, and put into production. Manufactured by Perfect Plastics of Philadelphia, the buggy survived into the mid-1980s and carved quite a niche for itself in the marketplace.

Fun motoring in an Au-Ki. (Courtesy Auto Archive)

The Renegade 'T' began life as the Au-Ki from Apal in Belgium, seen here at the 1973 International Racing Car Show at London's Olympia. (Courtesy Peter Noad)

The Renegade 'T' design eventually returned to the US, and was re-launched as the Tuff-Tub, achieving excellent sales in the post-buggy boom years.

The Renegade 'T' was an oddball vehicle that capitalised on the changing needs of the public. It did manage to find a place in a market that had diversified considerably, though, once the initial wave of interest in classic-style buggies had dried up.

Shaped and chromed front and rear bumpers were a neat touch, but styling was ultimately at odds with the tastes of UK buyers. The buggy is now a very rare sight in Britain. (Courtesy Custom Car)

SANDPIPER

DATA PANEL

Production dates
1989-1992

Numbers built
5 (approx)

Export markets
None

Wheelbase
78.5in

Identification tips
Smooth front hood with lights mounted on front crash bar. 2+2 seating. Side panels with moulded scoops and fuel tanks mounted behind. Squared-off back with frenched in rear lights and opening engine hatch

In the late 1970s, with the dune buggy scene at something of a low point in the UK, and few manufacturers producing new kits, many older buggies changed hands and were subsequently rebuilt to the tastes of new owners. One such example was a British Bugle buggy, bought in 1978 by enthusiast John Bishop as a project in need of major remedial work.

After overhauling the VW mechanicals and adding a larger engine, the Bugle bodyshell was refitted to the VW floorpan in very much original guise, complete with large, tinted, plexiglass rear window in its glassfiber surround. The new buggy, christened 'Citybug,' and finished in a vivid gold metalflake finish, had something of a tough, off-road look about it and an aggressive stance. However, a second rebuild altered the looks of the car dramatically, and paved the way for production of a set of new glassfiber moulds.

By removing the original Bugle headlight pods from the front hood and filling over the panel, a much smoother look was achieved. Illumination was now courtesy of Cibie Oscar lights mounted on a front crash bar, extending forward of and below the front bodyline. This bank of lights at the front, coupled with the turn signal units, gave the buggy a very distinctive look, as well as excellent illumination at night.

At the rear of the bodyshell, the wheelarches were shaped to the curvature of the massive rear wheels and tyres. Rear lights, from a British Rover SDI, fitted into special recesses in the panels at the back of each of the fenders, and gave a squarer look to the bodyshell. The engine hatch, into which the licence plate was frenched, allowed superb access to the VW engine within.

The traditional glassfiber rollbar surround, with its plexiglass screen, was replaced by a much more substantial roll-cage, and the rear-mounted fuel tank gave way to two separate units mounted behind the sculpted side panels on each side of the buggy. With the new-look complete, the buggy was used on a daily basis, as well as taking part in many VW shows of the time.

Not content with a pure one-off design, however, its owner decided to make further modifications before fabricating a production mould and offering the new buggy design for sale. The main difference was to the buggy's interior, which now had a small rear seat area, rather than the small trunk which had been a hallmark of the pure two-seat design of the original Bugle buggy. The new buggy, now named the Sandpiper, was therefore a more sensible arrangement, suitable even for everyday use.

The other very visible change was alteration of the side panels, which went from the previously sculpted type to more boxy-looking units featuring in-built ducts which could house engine oil coolers if required. These also still covered the twin custom-made fuel tanks, which sat behind them on each side of the vehicle below the bodyshell waistline.

Though more practical than ever before, few Sandpipers have ever seen the light of day. The buggy moulds were

By repositioning the headlights and smoothing out the front hood, the Sandpiper buggy took on an entirely different appearance to the Bugle kit.

Models A-Z

last used by Midlands-based company Bears VW Supply, but have since gone to a new owner. It will be interesting to see if the Sandpiper has a second coming with the new wave of interest in all things VW.

The production version of the Sandpiper had fuel tanks positioned on each side of the bodyshell, and was covered by small and rather boxy side panels.

The rear arches of the Sandpiper bodyshell were shaped to accept huge off-road tires, whilst the engine cover panel became an opening hatch to improve access.

No problems here with seeing in the dark! The Sandpiper used a bank of Cibie lights mounted to the front crashbar, ahead of the glassfiber bodywork.

Sandpiper at a Southern Dune Buggy Club gathering in Britain.

173

SCORPION LT

DATA PANEL

Production dates
1968-1971

Numbers built
Unknown

Export markets
UK

Wheelbase
80in (VW)
79.5in (with Corvair engine)

Identification tips
Aerodynamic bodyshell moulded in one piece. In-built metal fuel tank. Front headlamps mounted behind plexiglass covers. Curved windshield in polished alloy frame. Curved dashboard with floor-mounted central console

Desert Fox Sand Buggys designed the Scorpion LT to be used with either VW or Corvair power. Side panels were a later option for the kit. (Courtesy Auto archive)

Built to operate off-road or on the street, Desert Fox Sand Buggys' Scorpion LT began life as an SCCA road racing vehicle, with a body designed to fully cover all four wheels. From 'club racing' to award winner at the NCCCA Winter National Custom Car Show in Los Angeles, the Scorpion LT was a welcome departure from the buggy norm.

Conceived in late 1968 by designers Russ Leford and Bernie Truter, the first production bodyshell was pulled from the moulds in early 1969. Unlike previous company offerings – The Fox and the Desert Fox – which were more conventionally-styled, the Scorpion LT's one-piece, glassfiber bodyshell – with its long, sleek front hood, and flush-mounted rectangular headlamps from a Honda Dream motorcycle fitted behind plexiglass covers – clearly had an emphasis on aerodynamics. The custom-made, high-capacity, metal fuel tank was sited beneath the hood, fiberglassed in place and braced with metal supports to the VW front suspension.

The bodyshell was sleek from any angle, raking back from the main tub to finish with pointed fins at the rear. Tail lights were American (from a 1968 Rambler) and complemented the overall design when fitted flush into the flat rear bodywork covering the engine. The sloping rear deck also extended outward to form the wheelarches, comfortably accommodating the wide custom wheels and tyres which were part of the overall look of the buggy.

Interior-wise, the Scorpion LT had the same futuristic styling as the overall bodyshell. The windshield was curved and set into a polished alloy frame sitting atop the dashboard. This was all part of the unitised body and curved round in front of the occupants. A central console, which bolted to the VW floorpan tunnel, provided a mounting in direct view of the driver for all the gauges and switches.

Seating for the Scorpion LT buggy was also unique: a pair of front bucket seats, finished in an attractive quilted and deep-buttoned vinyl, with a matching wrap-around seat for the rear passenger area. A chromed buggy rollbar was floor-mounted and situated above the heads of the front seat occupants. Whilst a soft-top option and gull-wing hardtop were available as additional accessories, the design looked better without them, and they were rarely used.

To complement the overall bodyshell design, a pair of equally aerodynamic side panels for the lower body tub were made available late in the Scorpion's production life, and looked very attractive. These fitted below the already noticeably low waistline of the body sides.

Unusually attentive to detail, the designers had also thought about the different engine choices available to builders. For a stock VW engine, the VW floorpan required shortening to a standard 80in length, and for a Corvair engine mounted to the floorpan with VW transaxle, the

Models A-Z

floorpan was shortened to 79.5in. This extra half-inch difference allowed enough clearance for the Corvair's generator, and was achieved by re-positioning the forward front bulkhead during lamination of the main bodyshell.

Original and innovative, the Scorpion LT was a breath of fresh air in buggy design, but, coming late as it did in the scheme of things, missed the opportunity to achieve the volume sales that early runners capitalised on. Although well made and well received, it suffered the same fate as most other glassfiber buggies as customers moved to lightweight dune rails in the early 1970s. By 1971 it was all over, though the design survived in Britain, where it became known as the Invader.

Scorpion brochure shows off the dramatic new buggy design.

The sleek Scorpion LT was a departure from the traditional dune buggy shape, and was conceived as an SCCA road racing vehicle. (Courtesy Wes Grant)

Seating in the buggy was courtesy of attractive quilted and deep-buttoned vinyl units, with a matching wrap-around seat for the rear passenger area. (Courtesy Sport Buggies)

Sleek and aerodynamic, the Scorpion was an attractive marriage of buggy and sports car styling. (Courtesy Road Test/Dune Buggy)

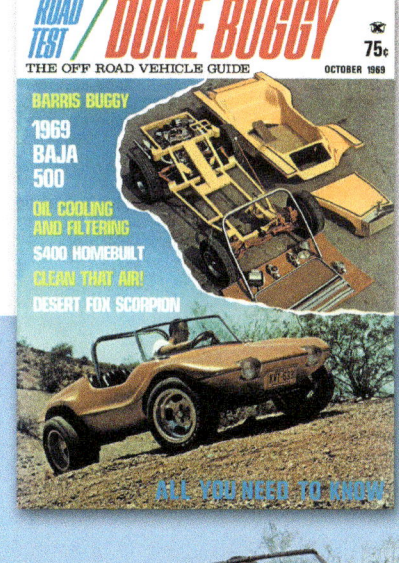

Publicity for the Scorpion buggy was helped by front cover promotion on period magazines. (Courtesy Road Test/Dune Buggy)

SHARK

DATA PANEL

Production dates
1971-1972

Numbers built
300 (approx)

Export markets
None

Wheelbase
98.75in

Identification tips
Pointed nose with rectangular inbuilt headlamps faired into the front wings under plexiglass covers. Chopped-off look to the rear bodywork, with a Kamm-type tail

At the height of the British buggy boom in 1971 it seemed implausible that more buggy manufacturers could enter the already overcrowded market. However, Treacy Ltd, run by Derry Treacy, was to prove everyone wrong with the Shark buggy. With its sleek, pointed nose and chopped-off look to the tail, this distinctive buggy was a case of Shark by name, shark-like by nature.

Introduced early in 1971, the Shark buggy had Ford Escort GT headlights, faired-in to the angular front wings and encased by neat plexiglass covers. The bodyshell also allowed for wheels up to 10in wide at the back whilst remaining street-legal; something of a first at the time. A less desirable feature of the Shark, however, was the fact that poor fabrication work during construction of the original buggy pattern meant that the shape and width of the rear wheelarches differed noticeably from one side to the other. The abruptly chopped-off back, with its Kamm tail kick-up and flat rear panel, allowed a variety of light units, as well as the licence plate, to be fitted. The rear bodywork provided minimal engine coverage, but was a definite bonus for the mechanic who wanted full access to suspension, gearbox and engine.

The body had a conventional separate front hood, with the dashboard also part of the unitised panel. As with the rest of the vehicle's front, the hood was raked forward, and finished abruptly in a point. The VW fuel tank fitted into a recess in the main body moulding, between the front fenders, and a flat windshield in a polished alloy frame was bolted to the side flanges of the hood/dashboard unit, behind the raised windshield wiper mounts on the hood.

The wing sections acquired a rather useful, body-length 'running-board' look, which provided the driver with everything from an arm rest to a flat area on which to stand items whilst the vehicle was stationary.

Sharp Shark at the 1977 National Buggy Convention in Britain. This buggy was named 'Kaleidoscope' to reflect its coloring.

Models A-Z

Their width also prevented the spray thrown up from the front wheels from entering the vehicle interior, further aided by the addition of a full-length soft-top rain lip to the top edge of the bodyshell, which kept water out of the buggy's interior when the top and sidescreens were fitted.

With advertising creating demand for the very economically-priced kit, the operation expanded into a north west London shop called, appropriately enough, The Shark Buggy Shop. With the punchy headline: "This is not just another buggy, but something really new in style," the advertisements ensured a regular queue of customers at the shop, eager to become overnight car builders. The bodies were laminated by a London glassfiber contractor named Shift, and came in a range of bright, solid gelcoat colors.

Based on the VW Beetle floorpan shortened to a wheelbase of 78.75in, the long nose section of the buggy made the overall length of the finished car similar to that of a more conventionally-styled buggy in long-wheelbase format. Despite the visual imbalance, the Shark was an interesting departure from the classical buggy shape, and this, combined with its low price, resulted in very healthy sales figures during the short time it remained in production. However, changes to the business interests of the owner, and in the fun car market (when most were poorly constructed and anything but fun in the fickle British climate), sealed the fate of the Shark buggy. Nevertheless, some of these buggies still survive today, testament to the creative output of the great buggy boom of over 30 years ago.

Mechanical access was superb, with the bodyshell providing minimal cover for the VW engine, and accommodating a variety of light clusters, such as those from an Alfasud Veloce Sprint.

The Shark was well named, and original amongst the myriad of lookalike buggy designs. The low price was certainly attractive to customers.

Despite the large number of Shark kits sold, few are seen at conventions and VW shows now. This rare example is one of the few still in regular use.

Period sales literature shows off the Shark's distinctive shape with its sharply-pointed nose and wide running-board-style wing sections.

177

SIDEWINDER

DATA PANEL

Production dates
2004-date

Numbers built
150 (approx)

Export markets
Unknown

Wheelbase
78.75in

Identification tips
Classic buggy shape with wide engine access at the rear of the bodyshell. Noticeably pointed profile to shape of side sill behind the front wheelarch; smooth front hood; wide central binnacle to dashboard

Having passed on all his buggy production moulds to East Coast Manx, Melvyn Hubbard of Manx Buggies UK continued to laminate other non-automotive glassfiber products. However, it wasn't long before first one, then another enthusiastic potential customer approached him to make them buggy kits. In late 2004, Hubbard was finally bitten by the bug again, and agreed to develop an all-new kit. Knowing that one of the niggles with previous buggy kits had been the unsatisfactory fit between body and the VW chassis, he was determined to get this right with the new design. Starting with a VW Beetle chassis shortened to a wheelbase of 78.75in, he worked to re-shape an older kit to get it seated perfectly to the chassis. This was achieved by actually fiberglassing the body to the chassis so it could not move whilst the rest of the body was shaped.

Once the inner tub was perfected, the rest of the body received his considerable pattern-working skills. The front fenders were extended to accommodate the wide wheels and tyres beloved by modern buggistas, and the side sill was shaped so that it had a very noticeable downward point before rising again into the fender itself. The rear of the buggy continued the wide rear engine access shape that had been originally developed for the Predator buggy. The rear fenders were also wide, whilst retaining the cute indentations to the top edge that not only were a neat styling detail, but endowed the kit with a lot of strength through the use of compound curves. At the front, the hood design was kept smooth and uncluttered with no badge mounts or styling ridges in sight. To ensure that more instrumentation could be added to the dashboard, a wide central binnacle was designed that looked neat and functional.

Launched in late 2004, the new design – dubbed the Sidewinder – was promoted at various VW shows, and instantly became one of the best-selling kits of Hubbard's buggy career. Often laminated with a metalflake gelcoat, the Sidewinder was an attractive kit that allowed the fitting of wide buggy rubber under its wheelarches and, with a lowered front VW suspension, gave an aggressive 'pavement-hungry' look. Completed buggies soon began regularly appearing in VW-oriented magazines, which further boosted sales. Proving the strength of the design, the kit looked equally 'right' fitted with a traditional single-hoop buggy rollbar or a more modern, full 6-point rollcage and side-impact bars. Around 150 sales were notched up between the launch and late 2009, and there was even talk of a long-wheelbase version being developed to capitalise on the market for easy-to-build kits that would not be affected by construction and use legislation. Despite

Tangerine dream! This Sidewinder gives a fresh, modern take on the buggy theme, with seating for four, and a full safety roll-cage. (Courtesy Mike Key)

Models A-Z

Metalflake finishes have remained popular for modern buggies, and this Sidewinder has a period look with many vintage parts and stock VW Beetle seats.

With black and polished Porsche cookie-cutter wheels, neat diamond-stitched upholstery, and a glittering Mirraflaked finish, this buggy looks mean and moody. (Courtesy Mike Key)

this future vision for the kit, Hubbard finally decided to call time on both the Sidewinder and Manx Buggies UK. The company name and buggy production moulds were sold to VW enthusiast Ben Lythgoe of Cambridge, where only a handful of kits were subsequently made before production ground to a halt again.

Proving that you can't keep a good buggy down, in 2011 the operation moved again, this time to East Coast Manx where, along with Hubbard's earlier buggies, the Sidewinder has re-entered production under the watchful eye of Robert Kilham. The kit is still available at the time of writing, and seems destined for a long and bright future.

Manx Buggies and the Sidewinder are now in the hands of East Coast Manx, which makes a wide range of kits, including the Manx and Manx II in the UK. (Courtesy Manx Buggies)

STRIPPER

DATA PANEL

Production dates
1980-1984

Numbers built
150 (approx)

Export markets
None

Wheelbase
94.5in

Identification tips
Twin use vehicle, with rail-type steel frame and VW suspension and drivetrain. Lift-off glassfiber buggy bodyshell, louvred rear hatch and opening glassfiber targa top

As dune buggies developed in the US, the trend moved away from glassfiber bodyshells on shortened VW floorpans to lightweight tubular steel vehicles (rails) with little or no body panels. However, demand for closed-cab vehicles still existed and, in 1980, Corsair Cars of Ontario, California, designed a buggy intended to combine the safety and comfort of a closed-cab with the nimbleness of a dune rail. Its Stripper buggy had both street and off-road ability, and was effectively two cars in one.

Designed by Chuck Beck, the basis of the buggy was a fully triangulated steel tube frame for strength and safety, and came ready-fitted with a VW rear torsion assembly and body mounts welded in place. The design was similar to those found in two-seat, off-road racers, but it also had a smooth glassfiber body which transformed it into a neat road car, equally at home on the freeway. The buggy bodyshell could be lifted off by two people in a few minutes by undoing the retaining clips and one electrical connection.

The bodyshell was a hand-laminated unit, often produced in metalflake colors, and the underside was also painted to give protection and a neat finish. The front section of the body was tucked around the VW front suspension, which bolted to the tube chassis, and featured sit-up-and-beg clamshell fenders that flowed down behind the front tyres. Neat and functional, the fenders extended back to a running-board which, in turn, flipped up to form the rounded back fenders at the very rear of the vehicle.

A conventional, polished alloy windshield frame sat on the bodyshell, but had a hinged glassfiber targa top conveniently mounted to its top edge. This could be tilted up to allow access to the interior, and latched down, once inside. An integral glassfiber targa bar extended up from the main body and covered twin metal roll-over bars, which were part of the metal chassis frame. These provided total occupant safety off-road.

The rear of the vehicle allowed full access to the VW powerplant and suspension, and a custom-made fuel tank was seated in the frame above the engine for additional weight over the driven wheels. A louvred hatchback deck lid opened wide to accommodate items stored in the rear luggage compartment, which also mounted into the tube frame behind the main cockpit liner. The main liner was a sturdy glassfiber item that sat inside the framework and remained in place, regardless of whether the buggy was off-road or on the street. To this were bolted the European-style quilted bucket seats and central instrument console, which also covered the mountings for the gearshift lever, pedal brackets and cable housings. The standard VW steering column located to a bracket on the chassis frame.

Stock dune buggy headlamps were bracketed to a sturdy front bumper, which remained in place even with the body removed, so that the vehicle could

The rear of the buggy gave easy access to the VW suspension and engine, whilst the rear-mounted fuel tank sat in the tubular frame above the engine. (Courtesy Petersens)

be used for night-time dune running. Optional accessories included a rear bumper for street use, and side curtains for the closed cab section of the body. Nimble and responsive, strong and light, the Stripper was a true all-rounder, crossing the boundary between traditional dune buggy and slick sand rail.

Despite the advantages of the buggy, it was dropped from Corsair Cars' range as the owner, Chuck Beck, went on to develop products such as the Imsa-style 914 Porsche body kit, and then a faithful replica of the vintage 550 Porsche (James Dean) Spyder under the new company name of Beck Development.

A glassfiber liner slipped into the triangulated steel frame to provide a mount for the seats and the instrument console. Mounts for the steering column, gearshift lever, pedals and cable housings attached to the metal frame.

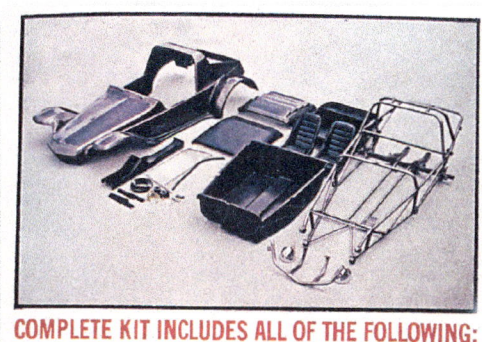

Top left: This detailed brochure shows the component parts of the Stripper buggy. Most bodyshells were produced in a Metalflake finish, and looked good fitted with the targa roof and louvred hatchback deck lid.

The Stripper was effectively two cars in one, as Corsair Cars' brochure shows. By removing the outer bodyshell, a tough, tubular-framed dune rail was left, which carried the suspension, engine and drivetrain.

SURF BUGGY

DATA PANEL

Production dates
1993-2007

Numbers built
3

Export markets
Ireland

Wheelbase
82.5in

Identification tips
One-piece bodyshell, with laminated-in front firewall; unique two-part hardtop arrangement, with lift-off rear deck and built-in head restraints; small side panels giving forward-tilting body appearance

When Belgian buggy enthusiast Dirk Tinck wanted to build a Meyers Manx in the early 1990s, the kits were not readily available in Europe. Deciding that the next best thing would be to design his own buggy following a similar design, he set about the painstaking process of building a wooden pattern from scratch. The design was created by building up a series of wooden ribs and formers to make a shape that would comfortably sit on a VW Beetle chassis shortened to a wheelbase of 82.5in. Final shaping was done in filler over the skeletal shape, before the whole pattern was sealed, and a glassfiber mould made.

From this was taken a one-off bodyshell designed as a single piece incorporating the front hood, and into which a separate front firewall was laminated to make the final structure. The un-named buggy was not just designed to look good, but to be practical, too, as Tinck intended to use the final car to travel to VW shows throughout Europe. With this in mind, patterns were also created for a special rear deck incorporating head restraints to cover the rear seating area. To this could then be added a forward-leaning rear hardtop, which accepted a neat roof panel that attached to the metal windscreen frame. Inside the buggy, a handmade dashboard was patterned from a left-hand drive Ford Fiesta. The left-hand binnacle housed the speedometer and tachometer, whilst a central binnacle accommodated a variety of instruments, switches, and a radio. To the right of the dashboard was a useful small shelf area. Completing the look of the buggy's exterior were a pair of small side panels that gave a macho, downward-leaning appearance to the whole vehicle. Once completed and sprayed in vivid Belgium Touring Security yellow with red metallic flames on the front hood, the buggy was fitted with a 1914cc Type I engine complete with cooling from a Porsche 911 fan sitting in a glassfiber housing. Tinck's buggy became a regular show-goer in mainland Europe, and also crossed the Channel to Britain for an appearance at a VW Action show in the early 1990s, where it won 'best buggy' in the category sponsored by buggy-maker GP Projects.

Neat design uses a two-part hardtop, and a covered rear deck to make an incredibly practical everyday buggy that can still play on the beach. (Courtesy Mike Key)

Models A-Z

Good as the buggy was, what Tinck really wanted was a Manx. By the late 1990s, Manx production had been licensed in both France and Britain, and he finally had the chance to obtain a kit. The one-off buggy was subsequently sold, but the original moulds were still sat in his garage until one fateful day when a chance meeting with the proprietor of GT Mouldings at a buggy convention in Belgium created an opportunity for both parties. The moulds were bought by GT and shipped to the UK by VW parts specialist BBT, which made regular trips to Britain. The moulds were cleaned and a demonstration bodyshell made for exhibition at the Southern Dune Buggy Club event in early 2000, where the buggy was christened 'The Surf Buggy.' Although offered for sale along with the company's other GT Buggies, the very one-off nature of the original kit meant that the moulds were not capable of series production, and only the demonstration model, one kit destined for Ireland, and the original Tinck-built car exist today. The moulds remain with GT Mouldings, and it's conceivable that, one day, production of one of the neatest and most practical of buggy kits will resume.

Original one-off buggy was designed and made in Belgium, before the moulds were brought to Britain by GT Mouldings. (Courtesy Mike Key)

The buggy was painted in Belgium Touring Security yellow, with red metallic flames on the front hood. (Courtesy Mike Key)

Below, left: Designer/builder Dirk Tinck wins 'best buggy' award at British show VW Action in the 1990s. (Courtesy Dirk Tinck)

Below: Surf Buggy's rear shows off the 1914cc Type 1 engine with Porsche cooling fan. (Courtesy Mike Key)

TRAMP

DATA PANEL

Production dates
1970-1971

Numbers built
75 (approx)

Export markets
US

Wheelbase
94.5in

Identification tips
Stand-up headlights, rear-mounted fuel tank in heavily raked bodyshell; moulded rear seats covering spare wheel well. Triangular rollbar and small double-skinned glassfiber windshield frame

With buggy names at something of a premium in the early 1970s, the somewhat unlikely moniker of Tramp was chosen for Richard Oakes' first car design. Later to become one of the UK's leading car stylists, with designs that included the Nova/Sterling, Oakes' sole ambition in 1970 was to build a one-off roadster-cum-buggy for his old Beetle chassis.

Working for Western Laminates, an industrial glassfiber manufacturer based in Brixham, Devon, the original buggy design that emerged, with forward-leaning body styling, was a little unusual. Being a long-wheelbase model, no chassis shortening was required, and the built-in box sections – which also carried heater ducting – made for a very rigid structure. Other noteworthy features included the extremely thick lay-up of the bodyshell, and the way the moulding attached to the chassis (not only by the usual floorpan bolts, but also onto front and rear VW suspension mounts).

The Tramp was one of the first UK buggies to use a glassfiber windshield frame, being integral to the front hood arrangement, and this was double-skinned on the driver's side for extra support. The instrument mounting was a central glassfiber unit extending down to rest on the VW

Photographed for a Custom Car magazine special in 1971, this Tramp buggy enjoys the limelight on the beach at Climping Sands, Littlehampton, England. (Courtesy Custom Car)

central tunnel. The somewhat basic interior was reinforced by the provision of shaped glassfiber front seats, and a removable rear seat unit, also in glassfiber. This latter item provided seating for two, and fitted into place at the back of the body tub, thus covering the moulded-in spare wheel recess and battery box panel beneath.

Whilst the interesting forward-sloping body style was extreme, even in buggy terms, it allowed a rear-mounted fuel tank to be fitted behind the rear bulkhead, forward of the engine. This was a safety consideration in the event of a front-end collision, but did little for weight distribution of the rear-engined vehicle. The rear body styling also had distinctive recessed air louvres each side of the central, squared-off licence plate mounting. On each side of the louvres, shaped mouldings accepted VW 'chapel' rear light units turned on their sides. Visibility of the turn indicators and lights, from the rear and side of the buggy, was therefore improved.

Tramp builders could also purchase a triangulated rollbar which mounted to the strongest points of the chassis, and to the rear of the bodywork between the rear seat binnacles. Besides its function in the event of a roll-over, the bar also acted as a soft-top frame. When fitted, the soft-top clipped to studs mounted on a raised rain lip running around the top edge of the body moulding. Unusually for a buggy, the addition of a soft-top enhanced the overall look of the car, though reduced driver visibility somewhat.

With standard round or rectangular stand-up buggy headlights, the Tramp certainly achieved an identity all its own, and entered full production in mid-1970, with many bodyshells being sold through London-based agent The Bespoke Buggy Company of Wimbledon. This exposure was necessary to ensure the Tramp was available to the fashionable London set; undeniably the sort of customer every manufacturer wanted to attract.

This Tramp buggy appeared at a British buggy convention at Redcar Sands, Cleveland, England, in the mid-1970s, and was well away on the beach.

Western Laminates was an industrial glassfiber manufacturer, so the quality of the Richard Oakes-designed Tramp buggy kit was exceptional.

The Tramp Roadster buggy had an interesting, forward-leaning body style to accommodate the rear-mounted fuel tank.

The euphoria was short-lived, however. With the designer having left the company to begin the Nova/Sterling project, Western Laminates continued production of the buggy but ceased trading in late 1971, at the same time as the British buggy movement ran out of steam. Although far from a one-off, the Tramp has remained one of the few truly original British buggy designs built from the ground up, though limited numbers were made during its short life.

Early 1970s Western Laminates brochure promoting the Tramp buggy.

VOLKSROD MK I

DATA PANEL

Production dates
1968-1970

Numbers built
20 (approx)

Export markets
France

Wheelbase
81.5in

Identification tips
Rugged off-road looks with high fenders and little tyre coverage. Stand-up headlights and a bulbous front hood. Rear wing indents and very exposed engine

Volksrod pioneered the buggy in Britain, developing the Mk I design from scratch, based on photographs seen in US magazines. (Courtesy Volksrod)

As the UK's pioneering dune buggy design, introduced in January 1967, the first Volksrod Mk I was patterned from scratch by designer Warren Monks after he saw photographs of buggies in imported American journals. Monks, long-time associate of the car trade and glassfiber business, subsequently founded the Volksrod company to produce the buggy design on the premises of his main business, Window Change, at Doncaster in Yorkshire.

The prototype was a fairly uncivilised affair, although when first produced the legal aspects of buggy building had not been fully anticipated in terms of meeting Construction and Use regulations. Shown at the nearby St Ledger Race Meeting in September 1967, the prototype caused quite a stir. With slight modification, a production version – the Mk I Volksrod – was offered for sale in 1968, and promoted as: "Simple, stark and designed principally for off-road use, on the beach, autocross, hill climbing, or in the bush." Aided by his secretary, Edna Gardom, Monk's company, Volksrod Ltd, began to take orders for the first few buggy kits.

The buggy consisted of a basic bodyshell moulded in strong, high-impact glassfiber, and a somewhat bulbous front hood moulding and utilitarian-looking dashboard. Other essential parts, such as windshield, rollbar, bumpers, seats and extractor exhaust system, were available as extras. Volksrod also supplied other quality items for its buggies, including chromed headlamps, indicators, and a rear light set, a very useful skidplate for off-roading, and a whole host of wide wheels and large racing tyres to match.

The bodyshell more or less followed the basic principles of its Stateside brethren, with high fenders and a very cutaway look to the body for maximum tyre clearance. The rear fenders had indents to increase strength, whilst the bodyshell back made few concessions to legality. The bodyline rose high above the standard VW air filter, and did little to cover the very exposed mechanicals. At the front, the hood had a flat area at its lower edge on which to mount the licence plate, and a small enamelled badge sat above it on the curve of the hood. The stock VW fuel tank sat beneath the hood, with the tank neck filler exiting near the leading edge of the windshield. Lighting equipment and turn indicators were mounted on the front fenders.

The buggy was certainly a unique vehicle, and caught the public's imagination with its wide wheels, outrageous looks, and superb off-road ability. Volksrod began to nurture the British buggy scene by importing *Dune Buggies* magazine – the journal which had fired Monks' enthusiasm for the project in the first place, and began to reap the rewards as interest in buggies grew.

Models A-Z

A VW chassis is prepared to accept a Volksrod buggy bodyshell. (Courtesy Quadrant Picture Library)

Mind your head! Mk I Volksrod in full flight – the buggy was incredibly agile off-road, and could easily cover the most difficult terrain. (Courtesy Quadrant Picture Library)

By mid 1968, several kits and cars had been sold, though none of the glassfiber hardtops featured in the catalogue were ever supplied. The Volksrod, designed for the VW Beetle chassis shortened by 13.5in, was obviously a pure off-road machine, and Monks quickly realised that the buggy could never be successful in the UK for the reasons it was in the States. If it was to sell really well it had to be a fun town car, capable of long-distance motoring as well as being at home off the road. It also had to be waterproof and generally weatherproof, whilst remaining quickly convertible to its original sportster form when weather allowed.

With new legislation pending, Monks began to redesign the buggy and hence the Volksrod Mk II was born, one of the longest surviving designs in the history of UK buggy production. The original Mk I design was phased out in 1970 as the new design began to achieve significant sales in the rapidly expanding buggy market.

Entry and exit from the buggy was an acquired art, not made any easier by using stock VW seats, as here. (Courtesy Quadrant Picture Library)

The chromed roll-bar was fitted as a safety item, but would probably have been of little use in a roll. Modern buggies tend to use full 6-point roll-cages and side-impact bars – a sign of the times, when safety has become a big issue. (Courtesy Quadrant Picture Library)

VOLKSROD MK II-IV

DATA PANEL

Production dates
1970-1991

Numbers built
Mk II: 250 (many LWB),
Mk III: 100, Mk IV: 50

Export markets
France, Belgium

Wheelbase
Mk II: 81.0in, Mk II FL: 94.5in,
Mk III: 80.5in, Mk IV: 94.5in

Identification tips
Mk II: wing-mounted in-built headlights, folded over and boxed-in side panels and hinged engine cover. 'FL' version fits standard chassis. Mk III: revised front hood with styling ridges, deeper side panels and a rolled edge to the body. Mk IV: long-wheelbase model with larger headlight nacelles

With the limitations of the Volksrod Mk I buggy apparent, and to keep ahead of the restrictive Construction and Use Regulations, Warren Monks and Edna Gardom announced an all-new Volksrod buggy in autumn 1969.

The bodyshell was more sophisticated, designed for road legality, and claimed to be legal in ways that other manufacturers hadn't even thought of. The Volksrod Mk II combined good looks with terrific torsional stiffness, due to large, folded-over box sections which also helped keep mud and water out of the car. The hollow side panel units could be used to take special fuel tanks for 1000 mile cruising, or modified for extra storage capacity.

The rear of the body also gave far more coverage of the engine and wheels and, to compensate for the increased mechanical coverage, a lift-up panel was incorporated which gave excellent access to the engine. At the front, the small, round Fiat 500 headlights were now positioned in the fenders, and the front hood had a smoother appearance than did the earlier design.

The top edge of the bodyshell also sported a proper rain lip to ensure that once the well-fitting top and side screens were in position, the elements were kept out. The Mk II also incorporated the normal VW heater units to keep occupants warm. If a soft-top wasn't enough, Volksrod also supplied a grained, leather-finish hardtop with detachable roof panels to ensure customers could build an all-weather vehicle.

Announced in late 1969 at the Brussels Racing Car Show in Belgium, Monks tied up a deal for the sale and distribution of the buggies throughout Belgium via VW dealers. In Britain, the short-wheelbase Volksrod Mk II appeared at the London Specialist Sports Car Show in January 1970, and at the Northern Racing Car Show in Manchester. It was soon joined by a long-wheelbase variant, the Mk II FL.

The bodies were produced by a Manchester sub-contractor to keep pace with demand, though complete cars were still assembled by Volksrod. In 1970, Monks sold the whole business to Hartsdale Services, run by managing director David Taylor. Secretary Edna Gardom stayed on, and soon witnessed another change as the Volksrod was developed into a Mk III version during 1970, and publicly launched at the DIY exhibition at London's Olympia.

Easily distinguished by a new front hood with two styling ridges, the Mk III also featured deeper box section sides with a proper rolled edge for an enhanced finish and greater strength. An enlarged engine cover and improved

The Volksrod Mk III had distinctive styling ridges on the front hood, and a proper rolled edge to the folded-over box-section side panels. (Courtesy Quadrant Picture Library)

dashboard also appeared on the new model, now produced by expert glassfiber sub-contractor Specialised Moldings.

The new Mk III was in such demand that the company closed its original window business and moved to a larger unit at Askern, North Yorkshire. A licensed French version also appeared at this time called the 'Monks,' produced by Marland in Les Mureaux and, in mid-1971, a stretched Mk IV version with larger 7in headlights appeared in Britain.

As the buggy boom waned in the mid-1970s, David Taylor left the company and it was renamed Volksrod Concessionaires (UK) Ltd in 1972. Under the still-enthusiastic Edna Gardom's control, and aided by her son, Trevor, the Volksrod continued in sparodic production, adding a hardtop with doors to the list of accessories in 1976. Trevor Gardom kept Mk III production going until the 1980s when, in 1984, another change of ownership occurred. Volksrod was sold to John Whitworth and Andrew Leach, trading under the name of Whitlee Engineering in Leicestershire, with glassfiber specialist R&W Moldings now laminating the bodyshells. Another name change to Whitworth Engineering (Volksrod) Ltd. happened with the departure of Andrew Leach, and the increasing involvement of Jeff Copson, who would soon write the next chapter in the Volksrod story.

Star-spangled Metalflake Mk III Volksrod buggy is superbly detailed, and has a fully-chromed engine and suspension. (Courtesy Mike Key)

Neat Mk III Volksrod buggy at a VW show. This model had headlights further forward than the Mk II. (Courtesy picturesbyrob/Alamy)

Mk IV Volksrod buggy was a long-wheelbase model with larger headlights. Low, street racer look suits the buggy very well. (Courtesy Mike Key)

Period Volksrod advertising. Volksrod was not only one of the first UK buggy companies, but also the first importer of US magazine *Dune Buggies* to the UK.

VOLKSROD MK V-VIII

DATA PANEL

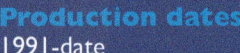

Production dates
1991-date

Numbers built
Mk V: 20 (approx), Mk VI: 2, Mk VII: Unknown, Mk VIII: Unknown

Export markets
Unknown

Wheelbase
Mk V-VII: 80.5, Mk VIII: 94.5in

Identification tips
Mk V: identical to the Mk III apart from removal of the in-built front fender-mounted Fiat 500 headlights, replaced by traditional 'stand-up' buggy units. Mk VI: similar to the Mk III with in-built Fiat headlights, but the bodyshell features a stepped rear shelf to create a rear seating area. Mk VII: similar to the previous model, but now using standard UK 5¾ in. built-in front fender-mounted headlights. Mk VIII: a long-wheelbase version of the same model

Volksrod had proved a real survivor in the UK buggy scene, but the early 1990s saw a further challenge when the supply of Fiat 500 headlight units that fitted the front fender-mounted nascelles all but dried up. Jeff Copson's work at the company soon involved developing the buggy to get round this problem. The solution was to completely remove the mouldings on the front fenders, and revert to the more traditional 'stand-up' type of lights normally used on buggies.

The new Mk V buggy was launched in 1991, but was otherwise an identical model to the earlier Mk III. Around this time, Stuart Hopewell – later to take over the helm of the Volksrod operation – also joined the company. One of the best known examples of the Mk V Volksrod design was Copson's own drag racer 'Midnight Star' that was a regular on the UK drag strips, and which took many trophies in the VWDRC modified class.

Orders for the buggy were slow but steady; then came an overseas order for 10 turn-key short-wheelbase buggies from the owner of many Portugese rental villas. However, the stipulation was for the kits to have the headlights set into the wings rather than separate, as on the earlier models. A misunderstanding with a local motor factor meant that a stock of the Fiat 500 lights were bought, rather than the more commonly available 5¾ in UK-sized lamps. The resultant Mk VI bodyshell therefore featured the smaller lamps, with all of the associated problems that brought. The bodyshell did, however, incorporate a neat rear shelf to create a rear seating area, which was something of a rarity in a short-wheelbase buggy. Only two of the cars (one LHD) were ever built when the order evaporated, and they were sold off.

The volatility of the buggy market, and a general downturn in business, saw further change for Volksrod. Stuart Hopewell left in 1995, and fabrication of the buggy bodies was transferred to Premier Moldings. Jeff Copson also departed in the late 1990s leaving John Whitworth to move premises and re-name the business John Whitworth Motor Services. The snail-like pace of production of the Volksrod buggy was then threatened by the financial collapse of Premier Moldings, but Whitworth and recently-returned part-time staff member Stuart Hopewell managed to save the buggy moulds from the company before the receivers moved in. Without a

Custom-painted Volksrod Mk VIII is a long-wheelbase model, identifiable by the 5¾in headlights that replaced smaller Fiat 500 units. (Courtesy Volksrod)

Models A-Z

laminator in place, production ground to a virtual halt with only a few panels and one spare LWB bodyshell sold.

The new millennium saw a fresh dawn for the beleaguered Volksrod buggy. Hopewell's newly-established VW service and restoration company, working in close co-operation with John Whitworth, began to offer kits for sale from 2005 on. Past Volksrod laminator Mick Reynolds (of R&W Moldings) provided help and advice as the old moulds were cleaned and refurbished so that kits could finally be offered for sale again. Further development also took place, and in 2009 an all-new pair of Volksrod buggies, the SWB Mk VII, and the LWB Mk VIII, both with integral 5¾in headlights faired in to the front fenders, finally appeared. Show appearances soon followed at the Volkswagen Festival in Malvern, and the Volksworld Show in March 2010. It seems the Volksrod, as well as being one of the first buggies in Britain, is determined to continue for a long time yet.

The Mk VII is the current short-wheelbase version of the Volksrod buggy, with the classic shape of the marque, but fitted with easily-obtainable headlights. (Courtesy Volksrod)

Rear view of the Mk VII shows the neat opening engine access hatch. Buggy rear also takes the stock VW Beetle rear lights and numberplate light. (Courtesy Volksrod)

The Mk VI design featured a return to the Mk II-style headlights and a stepped rear seat area inside the bodyshell. (Courtesy Volksrod)

Volksrod Mk V was the same as the Mk III, but had traditional 'stand up' buggy headlights, rather than the previously built-in units. (Courtesy Volksrod)

VULTURE

DATA PANEL

Production dates
Vulture: 1970-1972
Kombat: 1984-1991

Numbers built
175 (approx)

Export markets
Portugal, Sweden

Wheelbase
78.5in

Identification tips
Opening square hatch; one-piece body with inset headlights; functional rear rain lip to top edge of body; flared fenders; Cibie rectangular headlights with chrome rims (glassfiber on the Kombat)

The Vulture buggy began life in Britain in 1970, initially to meet the needs of one man, Malcolm Cracker, an autocross enthusiast. Together with his brother, Cracker had raced at numerous events with cars prepared by their family-owned garage business, Homesdale Motor Traders of Bromley, Kent. Inevitably, having driven other buggies, Cracker's own design, developed from a British GP buggy bodyshell, soon followed.

The design combined the rugged cutaway look of the traditional buggy with a smooth front end and bulbous back that also allowed excellent engine access, courtesy of a lift-up rear panel. Based on a shortened VW Beetle floorpan, the buggy was torsionally stronger than most due to a special chassis strengthening subframe, which could be fitted as an optional extra.

The styling of the Vulture was distinctive, with an all-in-one bodyshell (without a separate front hood), and featured faired-in rectangular Cibie headlamps. The unitised bodyshell necessitated the use of a specially-made petrol tank, slim enough to fit under the buggy's front. Other design features included widened lips to each of the fenders, which easily allowed fitting of the wide wheels and chunky tires which were de rigeur for the traditional buggy look.

The interior of the Vulture sported a dashboard that extended to the floor in a neat central binnacle. This put the mounting for the VW speedometer and all the switchgear in a more visible place within easy reach of the driver. At the rear, the bodyshell also featured a – very necessary – soft-top rain lip along the top edge, which extended forward and stopped halfway along the side sill, making entry and exit for driver and passenger much easier.

Also at the rear, the extra-wide fenders flowed round and ended in a rectangular engine hatch opening, over which sat the squared-off-looking engine panel. This was hinged to the body and sat in a recessed lip on the bodyshell moulding. It was secured by either over-centre clips or straps at each side, and allowed superb access to the VW engine. To ensure complete engine legality, Homesdale Motors also made its own glassfiber fan pulley guard, with the word 'Vulture' moulded in.

The well-made bodyshells were soon bought by customers eager for a slice of the action. The best known example was undoubtedly Malcolm Cracker's own autocross car, which was used very successfully in competition. The first set of production moulds were quickly remade to cater for increasing demand, and to cure early problems of a less-than-perfect finish to the gelcoat on some of the first bodies.

The Vulture was updated and became the Kombat in the 1980s. The new buggy featured side panels, glassfiber headlight rims, and a wider engine access cover. (Courtesy Volksworld)

Models A-Z

The Kombat buggy design kept the Vulture legend alive in the UK throughout the 1980s.

The manufacturer also created some memorable advertising to promote the buggy. With a picture of a menacing vulture leering down, the message was: "Get your claws on one," and customers duly did so. However, the demise of the British buggy scene in late 1971 sounded the death knell for the Vulture. There was one last attempt to restart production when the Vulture moulds moved to another company called Vulrod Motors, run by Michael Jeffs. Unfortunately, only a few more bodies were made, and the project ground to a halt in 1972.

Those enthusiasts who didn't wish to see the Vulture disappear altogether had their prayers answered in the 1980s when a modern day derivative – the Kombat – came into being. Produced by Kingfisher Kustoms of Birmingham, the only differences were the addition of a pair of side panels, glassfiber headlight rims, a slightly wider engine hatch, and a revised dashboard that was of a flatter design but with integral glovebox.

Who wouldn't want to get their claws on one of these? Homesdale Motor Traders' advertising certainly created a demand for the buggies throughout the early 1970s.

Period sales brochure for the Vulture.

Vulture buggy in its true environment – on the beach. (Courtesy Pete Barr)

Originally developed purely for autocross racing, the Vulture buggy could also be built into a show-winner like 'the Guv,' with custom paintwork, a clear vinyl soft-top, and custom-made bumpers.

193

The Dune Buggy Handbook

Darrell Vittone with German actress Lotta Getta in an EMPI Sportster demonstrator. (Courtesy Glenn Miller)

Bruce Meyers loans the world's first glassfibre buggy 'Old Red' to Briggs Cunningham at his famous auto museum in Costa Mesa, California.

John Wayne appeared in the 1968 American war film *The Green Berets*, which included a Manx buggy but is pictured here in a more mundane buggy on set. (Courtesy Auto Archive)

Left & above: Bruce Meyers is regarded as the founding father of the glassfibre dune buggy movement, and has achieved worldwide recognition for his innovative designs.

Celebrity gallery

Racing driver Graham Hill poses with an EMPI Sportster. Hill was Chairman of Speedwell Performance Conversions in the UK.

Steve McQueen takes Faye Dunaway for a hell-for-leather ride in the Corvair-powered Manx buggy in the 1968 United Artists movie *The Thomas Crown Affair*.

Steve McQueen was a seasoned off-roader, and was as happy tuning the powerful engine in the Thomas Crown buggy as acting in front of the camera.

Faye Dunaway was petrified of jumping the dunes when the sequences for the film were shot on the sand at Cape Cod, the flyweight buggy reaching speeds of up to 80mph with McQueen at the wheel.

The Dune Buggy Handbook

Chuck Connors drove a Manx buggy in 1960s primetime US TV show, *Cowboy in Africa*.

Cesar Romero plays a crooked businessman (A J Arno) in the 1969 movie *The Computer Wore Tennis Shoes*, chasing Kurt Russell (Dexter Reilly) in a blue Manx. (Courtesy Michael Ochs Archives)

A paint-splattered Manx buggy meets the long arm of the law in *The Computer Wore Tennis Shoes*. (Courtesy Michael Ochs Archives)

Kurt Russell (Dexter Reilly) and fellow students from Medfield College in a buggy in the film *Now You See Him, Now You Don't* released in 1972. (Courtesy Getty Images)

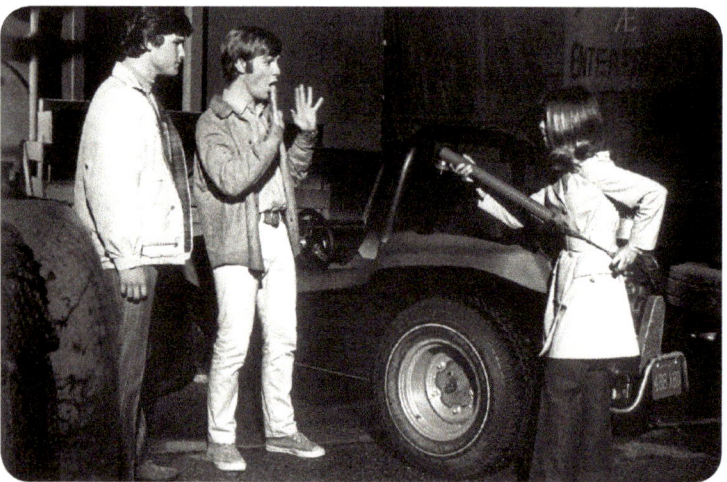

Richard Schuyler (Michael McGreevey) about to be sprayed with an invisibility liquid by Debbie Dawson (Joyce Menges) in *Now You See Him, Now You Don't*. (Courtesy Auto Archive)

Celebrity gallery

Guitar legend Jimi Hendrix played a free concert on the island of Maui in 1970 (included in the 1972 *Rainbow Bridge* film directed by Chuck Wein). Whilst in Hawaii on his 'Cry of Love' tour, Hendrix took time out to drive a Bushwhacker buggy rented from the Hilton Hotel. (Courtesy Ron Rafaelli/Michael Ochs Archive)

Jimi Hendrix tests the strength of the rollbar. Hilton Hotels in Hawaii, Miami, Puerto Rico and Jamaica were customers of manufacturer KDM Enterprises. (Courtesy Michael Ochs Archive)

Elvis Presley (as Greg Nolan) in the Manx buggy used in the opening sequence of the 1968 MGM movie *Live a Little, Love a Little*, co-starring Michele Carey (as Bernice) and a large dog called Albert.

Ken Harrelson (nicknamed 'The Hawk') of the Boston Red Sox baseball team had a special Mini-Volks buggy built by Howard Dunbar in 1970, with wild floral naugahyde top and Fire Flake blue paint job.

The Dune Buggy Handbook

On location with pop group, the Monkees, filming for their psychedelic movie *Head*. The film's prototype Mantaray II Kyote buggy was to become the pattern for production models. (Courtesy Dean Jeffries)

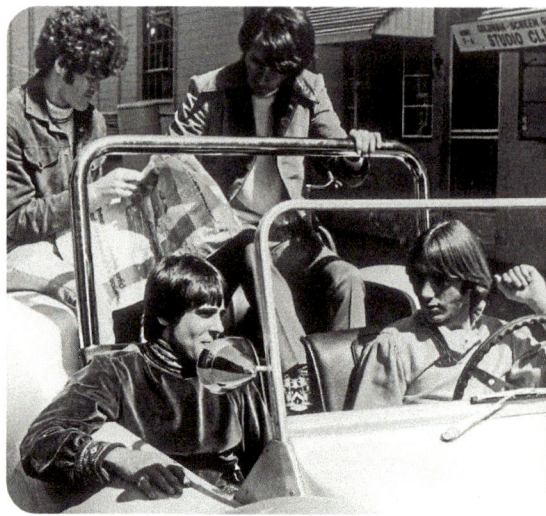

The Mantaray II Kyote buggy was built for the Monkees by legendary Hollywood car customiser Dean Jeffries. (Courtesy British Film Institute)

Miracle Films' British X-rated *Wife by Night* was filmed in Italy, and featured a Puma buggy. (Courtesy Ronald Grant Archive)

Above & right: The Warner Bros/Seven Arts film *Once You Kiss A Stranger* from 1969 included a beach scene with murderer Diana (Carol Lynley) trying to run down Lee (Marthar Hyer) with her buggy. (Courtesy Auto Archive)

Celebrity gallery

Customiser George Barris built a couple of Ocelot buggies for the 1960s Los Angeles beach music show *Groovy*, hosted by Mike Blodgett. (Courtesy George Barris)

Movie poster for Martin Films' *Ready, Willing & Able*. (Courtesy Auto Archive)

Left: Ingrid Steeger, Christine Schubert and Monica Rohde star in a light-hearted adult film from 1977 *Ready, Willing & Able*, which also featured a neat EMPI Imp buggy. (Courtesy Auto Archive).

Below: Anneka Rice poses with one of the two identical long-wheelbase FF buggies used in her primetime TV series *Challenge Anneka*. (Courtesy Auto Archive)

Anneka Rice being filmed by a TV crew for her 1980s series *Challenge Anneka*, driving a long-wheelbase FF buggy. (Courtesy Volksworld)

The Dune Buggy Handbook

Anita Harris poses on the front of 'Nittybug' – her colorful ride in the 1971 TV series Anita in Jumbleland. (Courtesy Topham Picturepoint)

Diana, Princess of Wales, had two elder sisters and a brother, Charles, who all enjoyed car ownership whilst in their teens. Charles' ride was a 1971-registered GT Hustler buggy. (Courtesy Getty Images)

Tiff Needell, Jason Plato, Tom Ford and Vicki Butler-Henderson from TV show *Fifth Gear* pose for publicity photos in a silver metalflake Prowler buggy.

Roger Moore as James Bond 007 is held at gunpoint by Claus, one of hitman Locque's gunmen in the 1981 movie *For Your Eyes Only*. Three GP Super Buggies were used for the beach sequence. (Courtesy Danjaq, LLC & United Artists Corp)

Judy Loe appears as assistant Lulli driving a GP Buggy in the TV series *Ace of Wands*, starring Michael Mackenzie as crime-fighting magician Tarot. (Courtesy Anthony McKay)

Anita Harris was film-tested for the series *Anita in Jumbleland* in a Mk II Manta Ray buggy with co-stars Andrew and Joanna, but it was to be a Kustom buggy that finally appeared in the series. (Courtesy Derry Brabbs)

British TV show *Top Gear* featured several buggies in 1997. Here, presenter Steve Berry gets to grips with a long-wheelbase GP buggy during filming.

APPENDIX

Clubs & forums for owners of glassfibre-bodied dune buggies

Algemene Buggy Club (Holland)
www.algemenebuggyclub.eu

Beach Buggy Club (International)
www.beachbuggyclub.com

Beach Buggy Club SA (South Africa)
www.beachbuggyclub.co.za

Belgian Kit Car Club (Belgium)
www.belgian-kitcar.be

Buggies in Nederland (Holland)
www.buggyvrienden.nl

Buggy Boys (Belgium)
www.buggyboys.be

Buggy Club Schweiz (International)
www.buggy-club-schweiz.ch

Buggy Club UK
www.buggyclub.org.uk
www.beachbuggy.org.uk

Club del Buggy (Argentina)
www.clubdelbuggy.com.ar

Dune Buggy Archives (USA)
www.dunebuggyarchives.com

Manx Buggy Club (USA)
www.manxclub.com

Manx Dune Buggy Club (Australia)
www.manxclub.org

Russian Buggy Club (Russia)
www.buggy-club.narod.ru

Southern Dune Buggy Club (UK)
www.sdbc.co.uk

South West Buggy Club (UK)
www.buggista.com

Dune buggy manufacturers

Berrien Buggy (USA)
Maker of the Nostalgia, Citation, Lancer & Roadster T Buggies
www.berrienbuggy.com

RTS Enterprises (USA)
Maker of the short and long-wheelbase Fiber-Tech Buggy
www.funbodies.com

Manx Club (USA)
Maker of the Meyers Manx, Kick-Out Manx & Manxster 2+2 Buggies
www.manxclub.com

Texas Buggies (USA)
Maker of Manx-style buggies
www.texasbuggys.com

Vegas Buggies (USA)
Viper and Manx-style buggies
www.vegasbuggies.com

BBM-Buggy (Brazil)
Maker of the Tarifa and St. Tropez buggies
www.bbm-buggy.com

Doon Buggies (UK)
Maker of short and long-wheelbase Doon Buggy
www.doon.co.uk

East Coast Manx (UK)
Maker of Manx & Manx II Buggy, Mini-Manx, Prowler, Bounty Hunter & Sidewinder Buggies
www.eastcoastbuggies.co.uk
www.manxbuggies.co.uk

Hoppa Street Buggy (UK)
Maker of the Hoppa
www.hoppastreetbuggy.com

JAS Speedkits (UK)
Maker of the short and long-wheelbase JAS Buggy
www.beachbuggies.co.uk

Kingfisher Kustoms (UK)
Maker of the short and long-wheelbase GP Buggy, Kombat & Kango Buggies
www.kingfisherkustoms.co.uk

KMR Beach Buggies (UK)
Maker of Kyote II, Manta-Ray & Renegade Buggies
http://scorpio.lunarpages.com/~beachb4/

Volksrod (UK)
Maker of Volksrod Buggy
www.volksrod.co.uk

Hot Rod Doesburg (Holland)
Maker of the Hot Rod Sportscar Buggy
www.hotrod.nl

Beach Buggy Australia (Australia)
Maker of the short and long-wheelbase Max FX Buggy
www.beachbuggy.com.au

Sharpbuilt Buggy (Australia)
Maker of the Sharpbuilt buggy
www.sharpbuilt.com.au

Also from Veloce Publishing –

By the 1970s, Dune Buggies were a worldwide phenomenon. This follow up to the very successful first book documents the development of the Buggy into the '80s. Includes reproductions of product advertising, promotional material & Buggy ephemera: a must-have for enthusiasts.

ISBN: 978-1-904788-66-9 • Hardback • 19x20.5cm
• 96 pages

A step-by-step guide to building a Buggy, containing details of equipment and techniques, as well as guidance on the choice of donor car and new components. Build any VW-based Dune Buggy avoiding common pitfalls and expensive mistakes, ending up with a superb, roadworthy multi-purpose vehicle.

ISBN: 978-1-904788-73-7 • Paperback • 27x20.7cm
• 144 pages • 280 pictures

How to get the best handling and braking from your Volkswagen Beetle. Covers front and rear suspension, 'chassis' integrity, suspension geometry, ride height, camber, castor, kpi, springs, shock absorbers, testing and adjustment. (Not 1302 & 1303 models.)

ISBN: 978-1-903706-99-2 • Paperback • 25x20.7cm
• 128 pages

For more info on Veloce titles, visit our website at
www.veloce.co.uk • email: info@veloce.co.uk
• Tel: +44(0)1305 260068
* prices subject to change, p&p extra

New edition of the complete guide to modifying Bus suspension, brakes and chassis for maximum performance. Essential info on aftermarket and interchangeable parts. Now covers all T1 to T5 buses, vans, campers and pick-ups 1950-2010.

ISBN: 978-1-845842-62-8 • Paperback • 25x20.7cm • 144 pages • 460 pictures

The Essential Buyer's Guide

Having these books in your pocket is just like having a real marque expert by your side. Benefit from the author's years of real ownership experience, learn how to spot a bad car quickly, and how to assess a promising car like a true professional. Get the right car at the right price!

Paperback • 64 pages

ISBN: 978-1-904788-72-0

ISBN: 978-1-845840-22-8

Dune Engines LLC

New Dune Imps are ready for delivery. The Dune Imp comes with the body, hood/dash and optional side pods. This dune buggy features clam shell fenders, a hood scoop with a built in tach pod on the hood, molded in rear seats and low sides. It fits on a Type I frame that has been shortened 12". Side pods and hood/dash are also available separately.

New blue metal flake side pod with white inset fresh at the factory.

A rainbow flake hood with gauge pod just out of the spray booth.

Winfield, Illinois
Silver Lake Sand Dunes in Mears, Michigan
http://www.DuneEngines.com
+1-630-492-0809
@duneengines

Community
Expertise
Forums
Events
Photos
Articles
Classifieds

BeachBuggyClub.com

INDEX

Aberglen 153
Ace of Wands 23
Afron Canyon 10
AHS Imp 21, 59
Aidan Harrington 134
Alan Brown 134
Alan Warren 32
Albar 'S' & 'ES' 28, 29
Albert T Queurkletule 116
Alex Dearbom 52, 53
Alex March 40
Alois Barmettler 28
American Fiberglass Products 94
American Racing Equipment 67
Anderson/Bonar Industrial Design Consultants 152
Andrew Bennetts 81
Andrew Leach 189
Angel Unchained 194
Anita Harris 116, 117
Anita in Jumbleland 23, 117
Anneke Rice 62
Anthony Hill 164
Apal 21, 30, 31, 168
Art Center College of Design 142
ATL Explorer 22
Audy Marine 32
Au-Ki 168, 170
Austin A40 Farina 86
Austin Healy 67
Autocar 22, 82
Auto Express 62
AutoCraft 42
Autodynamics Inc 52
Autohaus Kuhn 53
Avenger 57
Avery Greene 148
Avon Park 130
Aztec Avenger GT-12 66
Azteca 66

BAC Woestijarat 21
Baja 100 100, 137, 144
Baja GT 32, 33
Balboa 62, 70, 165
Balboa Park Automotive Museum 25
Barris C-Cab 35
Barris Manufacturing Company 34-35
Barris Sports Centres 34
Barris 'T' 34, 35
Barry Howard 92
Barry Warner 92
BBT 183
Beach Buggy Bonanza 54
Beachcomber 81

Beachcomber Buggy 68
Beardalls buggy 80
Bears VW Supply 173
Beaujangle Can-Am 24, 26, 94, 95
Beaujangle Enterprises 95
Beaujangle Sales Ltd 95
Beck Development 181
Ben Lythgoe 179
Bernie Truter 174
Berrien Buggy 37
Berry Mini-T 19, 36, 37, 75, 170
Berry Mini-T IV 37
Berry Plasti-Glass 36
Bespoke Buggy Company 185
Bewitched 125
Bill Chisholm 12
Bill Harkey 12, 78
Birmingham Sports Car Show 80
BMC 159
BMW 117
Bob Ridgard 168, 170
Bosch 117
Boss Bug 38, 39
Bounty Hunter 40, 41, 53, 163
Brands Hatch 24
Brian Dries 40, 41, 53
BRM wheels 71
Bruce Meyers/B.F.Meyers 4, 13, 18, 25, 27, 48, 74, 136-139, 142, 144, 146,
Brussels Racing Car Show 188
Bud Etkins 137
Budges Buggies 33
Bud Goodwin 66
Bugetta 42, 43, 45
Buggy-LS-Hardtop 28
Buggy-Off 23
Bug-In 71
Bugle Bug 2 22, 23, 43-45, 116, 172
Bugle Automotive Traction and Manufacturing Company of London Ltd 44
Bugle Marketing and Development 44
Bugle Plus 2 45
Build your VW-based dune buggy 20
Burro 12, 60
Bushmaster 46, 47, 150
Bushmaster Company 46, 47
Bushwhacker 48, 49
Buttercup Valley 10
BuzzBugs Buggies 161

C&D Automarine Ltd 134
Camero 67
Can-Am 94, 95
Car 23, 80

Car & Driver 137
Carol Brown 23, 25
Caroll Shelby 46
Car & Car Conversions 84
Cartune 30, 117
Challenge Anneke 62
Chevrolet Vega 73
Chimp 50
Chris Watson 45
Chrysler 150
Chuck Beck 180
Chuck Connors 18
Cibie 134, 192
Cibie Oscar 172
Citation 19
Citybug 172
Claimjumper 50, 51
Classic Manx 140
Cliff Richard 80
Cliff Richard Show 23
Clodhopper 66, 67
Cobra (UK) 134
Cobra (US) 68, 69
Coca-Cola 90
Colin Cordingly 96, 116
Concept One 57
Conestoga 75
Connaught Cars 134
Con-Ferr 18, 42
Con-vair 32, 42
Corgi 81
Corsair Cars 180
Corvair 11, 19, 42, 43, 50, 61, 66, 78, 94, 126, 142, 150, 166, 174
Corvette 78, 166
Country Volks 31, 63, 165
Cowboy in Africa 18
Crown Manufacturing Company 12, 18
Croy Glassfibre Products 101
CTR Enterprises 134
Custoca Amigo 22
Custom Car 22, 26, 134
CW Autos 45

Daily Telegraph Magazine 24, 100
Dave Fisher 120
David Kuschel 83, 87
David Piper 80
David Taylor 188
David Waspe 161
Dean Jeffries 19, 88, 124-128
Dearbom Automobile Co. 52
Dermot Bambridge 86
Derry Treacy 176
Desert Fox 174

Desert Fox Sand Buggys 25, 100, 174
Deserter Series 1, GS & GT 21, 41, 52, 53
Design Dynamics 128
Design/Development Company 132
De VW 21
Diana, Princess of Wales 99
Dick Berry 36, 37
Dick Dean 26
Dick Smothers 139
Dirk Tinck 182, 183
DIY exhibition 188
Dodge 53
Don Amett 50
Don Epperson 20
Don Guth 79
Don Haskin 48
Don Wilcox 19
Doon 54, 55
Dune Buggies & Hot VWs 26, 39, 49, 150, 186
Dune Buggy Constructors 128
Dune Buggy Enterprises 56
Dune Runner 56, 57

East Coast Manx 141, 164, 178, 179
Eckley Tur 18
Economotors 60
Edd China 161
Edna Gardom 186, 188
Eisert Racing Enterprises 42
El Lobo 70
Elvis Presley 18
EMPI (Engineered Motor Products Inc.) 13, 58, 59
EMPI Imp 19, 21, 58, 59, 90, 96, 70
EMPI Sportster 13, 58, 60, 61
Enos '500' 70, 71
Eresbug Co. PABC 168
Essex Proto Conversions 96-99, 116

Faye Dunaway 18
Fennec 55
Ferrari 48, 80
FF Buggy 62, 63, 70
FF Kit Cars & Conversions Ltd 62, 165
Fiat 500/600 98, 190
Fiat 500 Jolly 15
Fiberfab 66, 67
Fiberfab Clodhopper 66, 67
Fiberfab Vagabond 66, 67
Fiber Jet 68-73
Fiber Jet Cobra 68-70
Fiber Jet Enos 70, 71
Fiber Jet Indy '500' 70, 71

205

The Dune Buggy Handbook

Fiber Jet Rough Terrain 72, 73
Fiber Jet Sand Hopper 68, 69
Fiber-Tech 74, 75
Fiber-Tech Manx 74, 75
Fibre-Fab 62, 164
Fifth Gear 200
Fireflake 168
Firestone Tyres 116
Flinstone Scramblers 11
Flathead Ford 9
Flatlands Engineering 141, 145
Ford Anglia 168
Ford Escort 176
Ford Fiesta 182
Ford GT 40 66
Ford Mustang 70
Formula Vee 116
For your eyes only 84
Four Seasons Buggy Company 168, 170
Four Wheeler 9
Fox 174
Frankfurt Motor Show 59
Frantic Fred 85
Fred Jackson 52
Fubar Factory 92
Fun Buggy 35
Fun Hugger 76, 77

Gary Bastin 92
GB Buggy 100
George 'Red' Rose 142
Gene Booth 39
General Motors 150
Geneva Motor Show 28, 81, 84, 86, 88
Geoff Jago 32
Geoff Jago Custom Automotive 32, 130
Geoff Rosenbloom 80
George Barris 34, 35
Georgetown Run 12
Glamis Hill Climb 10
Glass Enterprises 41
Glassco Fiberglass Fabrication 25, 166, 168
Glitterbug 78, 79
Glitterbug Inc. 78, 79
Glynn Samuels 166
GP Beach Buggy Mk I 22, 80, 81, 96, 118, 192
GP Beach Buggy Mk II 81-83
GP Buggies 80-83, 89
GP Concessionaires Ltd 81, 82, 128, 168
GP LDV (Light Delivery Van) 81, 82, 84, 86-88
GP Projects 83, 182
GP Ranchero 82, 88, 89, 128
GP Specialist Vehicles 130
GP Speed Shop 22, 80, 118
GP Spyder 118
GP Super Buggy 23, 81, 84, 85, 88
Graham Hill 117, 194
Grasshopper Buggy 123

Greene Motors 148, 149
Groovy 151
Group 7 94
GT Buggy 79, 90, 91, 97, 140
GT Mouldings 31, 33, 45, 90, 91, 101, 128, 135, 140, 168, 169, 183

Hanworth Air Park 80, 81
Hartsdale Services 188
Hazard 53
Head 124
Heart of Gold 85
Heartland Glassworks 142
Hella 117
Hemet Run 10, 12
Henleys Jaguars 116
Hilder T Thompson 12, 60
Hillman Imp 88
Hilton Hotel 49
Homesdale Motor Traders 192
Honda Dream Bike 174
Hoppa 92, 93
Hot Car 83, 86
Hot Rod 137
Hot Rod Sports Car Buggy 21
Howard March 166
Humbug 26, 94, 95
Hustler (UK) 96, 97, 118, 140
Hustler (US) 51
Hustler GT 98, 99

Ian Wishart 81
Imsa-style 914 Porsche 181
Indianapolis 70, 124
Indio Run 12
Intac Inc. 48
Invader 24, 25, 100, 101, 174
Invader Mk II 101
Irwin Sportster 125

Jackson's Kustom Buggy 116, 117
Jaguar 116
James Bond 84
James Dean 181
JAS Buggy 118, 119
JAS Speedkits 118, 119
JB Developments 134
Jeff Copson 189, 190
Jensen Marine 16
Jerry Eisert 42
Jet 168
Jim Dutchers Speed Shop 71
Jimi Hendrix 49
Jim Taylor 56
Joe Vittone 13, 58, 60
John Aley Racing 30, 168
John Bishop 172
John Cullen 100
John & Sharon Davies 118
John Jackson 116
John Jobber 22, 80, 86
John Player Special 89
John Spratt 54
John Sprinzel 100
John Warner 92

John Whitworth 189
John Whitworth Motor Services 190
JPC Buggy 80
JW Black's Paradise Motors 123

Kango 120, 121
Kango Cars 120
Karl Krumme 132
Karma Coachworks 142
Karmann 59
Karmann GF 21
KDM Enterprises 48, 150
Kellison Inc. 122
Kellison Roadster SP-1 122
Kellison Sandpiper 122, 123
Kellison Super 'T' 69, 122
Kellison XP-1 122
Kick-Out Manx 26, 139
Kingdom 55
Kingfisher Kustoms 83, 85, 131, 193
Kings Road 22, 159
Kit Car 62
Kit Cars & Specials 62
KMR Buggies 129, 135, 169
Kobus Contraine 59
Kombat 193
Kübelwagen 12, 13, 15, 16, 117
Kurt Russell 24
Kustom Buggy 116, 117
Kyalami Nine Hour race 80
Kyote (Manta-Ray Kyote & Kyote I) (US) 19, 21, 124, 125
Kyote II (US) 88, 120, 126, 127
Kyote II (UK) 22, 128, 129

La Tigre 70
Lattimer Road 116
Lee Southerton 55
Leigh Taylor-Young 41
Lemazone 95
Leo Lyons 76
Les Prestwood 13, 60
Lido 70
Light Delivery Van 86, 87
Lightspeed Panels 31
Lime Rock 52
Limited Edition Californian 130, 131
Limited Edition Sportscars 130, 131
Lincoln Industries 122
Liptons Iced Tea 90
Little Big End 168
Little Red Riding Bus 13
Live a Little, Love a Little 18
Lola 80
Lolette 21, 80, 120
London Motor Show 24, 100
London Specialist Sports Car Show 188
Los Angels Art Center School 14
Los Angeles County Sheriff's Department 127
Lotus Elise 92
Lotusmere 45
Lyons Equipment Co. 76

Madison 83
Malcom Cracker 192, 193
Mallory Park 95
Mangosta 132, 133
Mantaray 124
Mantaray II Kyote 124
Manta Ray Mk I 22, 23, 128, 134
Manta Ray Mk II 134, 135
Manta Ray Mk III 135
Manx Dune Buggy Club 25
Manx II 17
Manx Motors 142
Manx Buggies UK 160-163, 178
Manx-Vair 42
Marion Ruggles 150
Marland 189
Max Becker 48
Melvyn Hubbard 90, 140, 160-163, 178
Mervyn Aldridge 158
Metalflake 162, 163
Mexican 1000 18, 125
Meyers Manx (Monocoque) 14-16, 136, 137
Meyers Manx (VW Floorpan) 17-21, 24, 25, 52, 74, 92, 138, 139, 150, 183
Meyers Manx UK 140, 141, 161
Meyers SR 142, 143
Meyers Manxter 2+2 & DualSport 26, 139, 144, 145
Meyers Tow'd/Tow'dster 21, 69, 142, 146, 147
MGA 67
Michael Jeffs 193
Mick Reynolds 191
Midnight Star 190
Mike Blodgett 151
Mike Brewer 161
Mini 98
Minibug 148, 149
Mini-Mercedes 56
Mini-Manx 164
Mini-Moke 22, 116
Mini-T 69
Model T 72
Monkeemobile 124
Monkees 124
Monks 189
Motor 22, 23, 45, 80
Mr Manx 137

NORRA (National Off-Road Racing Association) 137
NCCCA Custom Car Show 174
Newport Beach 15
North East Fibreglass Ltd 152, 153
Nik Sandeman-Allen 95
Nittybug 117
Northern Racing Car Show 188
Nova 184
Now you see him, now you don't 196
NSU 164

Index

Oakland Roadster Show 124
Ocelot/Ocelot II 48, 49, 150, 151
Ocelot S/S 48, 49, 150, 151
Old Red 16, 25, 136, 137
Oli Thorndale 92
Once you kiss a stranger 198
One Six Two Engineering 29
Otto Kross 42

Pacer Wheels 67
Panel truck 35
Parabug 152, 153
Patrick Sumner 32
Paul Newman 18
Pell Abrahams Broadcasting
 Corporation Ltd (PABC) 25, 168
Peppertree Automotive 13
Perfect Plastics Industries 38, 39, 171
Pete Condos 18
Phil Ayers 128
Phil Smith 95
Phillip Pell 168
Phoenix Automotive 48
Phoenix Coachworks 92
Pierre du Plessis 22, 80, 86
Pikes Peak 18, 19
Pinewood Studios 117
Pinza GS 98
Pismo Beach 10, 13
Playboy 21
Polo 62
Porsche 15, 142
Porsche 911/912 71
Porsche Spyder 83
Porsche 550 Spyder 181
Poty Enterprises 72
Power on Wheels 134
Powerbug 158, 159
Powerspeed 158
Predator 140, 160, 161, 178
Premier Moldings 190
President Johnson 48
Prowler 162, 163
Puma 198

R&W Moldings 189, 191
Racing Car Show 84, 86, 170
Rainbow Bridge 49
Rambler 174
Rat 62, 116, 164, 165
Ray Caldwell 52
Ready, Willing & Able 199
Renault 165
Renault Dauphine 40
Renegade (UK) 22, 25, 168, 169
Renegade (US) 166, 167
Renegade 'T' 37, 168, 170, 171
Resorter 139

Richard Crees 54
Richard Oakes 184, 185
Richard Park 32
Rivets 14
Road Runner 56
Road Test Dune Buggy 51
Robbie McBurney 80
Rob Robertson 46
Robert Kilham 141, 164, 179
Robert Taylor 164
Rocket Wheel Industries 45
Rodding Scene 32
Roger Locke 117
Roger Moore 200
Roger Penfold 32
Roger Smith 13
Roland Sharman 44, 45
Rootes 159
Rough Terrain 72, 73
Rover SDI 172
Roy Dickey 150
Roy King 134
Roy Pierpoint 83, 87, 89
RTS Enterprises 75
Russ Leford 174
Ryan O'Neal 41

Sahara 32, 33
Sand Chariots 48, 150, 151
Sand Hopper 69
Sandpiper (UK) 172, 173
Sand Rover 72
Sand Shark 42
Sandmaster 21
Sandmaster Company 50
SCCA (Sports Car Club of
 America) 52, 174, 175
Schwimmwagen 14-16
Scorpion LT 24, 25, 100, 174, 175
Scott McKenzie 11, 51, 61
Sears Roebuck & Co 20
Seaspray Beach Buggies 134
Service Garage 97
Shalako 24, 26
Shark 116, 176, 177
Shark Buggy Shop 176
Shark kit-car (US) 123
Sharman Drag Co. 44
Shelby Cobra 19
Shelbyette GT 57
Shepherd's Bush Courier 117
Shift 176
Shrike 48
Sidewinder 141, 178, 179
Signature Manx 140
Simon 'Chad' Chadwick 54, 55
Skyspeed Buggy 80
Southern Dune Buggy Club 163, 183

Specialised Moldings 189
Specialty Manufacturers Association
 Show 142
SP Motors 100
Special Car Consultants 32
Specialist Sports Car Show 80, 84
Speed Buggies of Chichester 32
Speedwell 117
Splinters 14
Sports Buggies 150
Sports buggy 134
Sportsman Pickup 78
Sportster 58, 60, 61
Sprintstar Wheels 59
Stardust 7-11 50
Stephen Fry 55
Stephen Wilson 165
Steptoe & Son 116
Sterling 184
Steve Berry 200
Steve McQueen 18, 139, 195
Steve Rieman 14
Steve Remp 128
Stevespeed 62
Stewart Reed 142
Stripper 180, 181
Stuart Hopewell 190
Suburu Impreza 144
Super/Mountaineer Pickup 72
Surf Buggy 182, 183

'T'-Bird 57
Ted Kellerman 29
Ted Mangels 13, 14, 18, 137
Ted Trevor 18, 19
Terry Cordingly 96
Terry Walsh 130
The Big Bounce 41
The Bug House 48
The Buggy Shop 134
The Computer Wore Tennis Shoes 24, 196
The Daily Telegraph Magazine 24, 100
The Dune Buggy Centre 128
The Prisoner 116
The Thomas Crown Affair 18, 24, 195
Thunderbug 88
Tijuana to La Paz run 18
Tim Cooksey 62, 165
Tim Figuhr 68, 72
Tom Stout 75
Tom Walkinshaw Racing 92
Tony & Rob Armstrong 45
Top Gear 200
Top Rank 117
Touring Body 75
Tournament of Fame 124

Treacy ltd 176
Tramp 184, 185
Trans-Am 53
Trevor Pym 164
Triplex 100
Triumph TR 3-4 67
Tuff-Tub 171
Turista 139
TÜV 28

Unique Supply 59
United Artists 200
USAC 19
Utility Manx 139

Vagabond Sportster 66
Vaquero 151
Velocidad Inc. 66
Vic Wilson 18
Vogels Birds Buggy 21
Volkscare & Custom 135
Volksmagic 55
Volksrod Concessionaires (UK)
 Ltd 189
Volksrod Ltd 22, 186
Volksrod Mk I 21, 22, 186, 187
Volksrod Mk II-IV 22-24, 188, 189
Volksrod Mk V-VIII 190, 191
Volksvair 19
Volkswagen festival 191
Volksworld 54, 118, 191
Volvo 142
Vulrod Motors 193
Vulture 192, 193
VW Action 182
VW Beetle 11, 13
VWDRC 190
VW Kombi 13, 136
VW Squareback 78, 126, 166

Walt Disney 24
Warner Bros 41
Warren Monks 22, 186, 188
Western Laminates 184
Wheeler Dealers 161
Whitlee Engineering 189
Whitworth Engineering 189
Wife by Night 198
Window Change 186
Winnebago 146
Winning 18
Wooller Engineering 117

Yakima Ridge Runners 10

ZZ Top 127

Volksrod Beach Buggies

The UK's first and still the best!!

Mark 7 SWB & Mark 8 LWB fibreglass bodies designed to fit classic VW Beetle running gear

Kits include: Body shell, bonnet, windscreen, dashboard, engine lid, number plate lamp and head light rims.

We also have a selection of accessories available.
We also service, repair & rebuild ALL makes of VW buggy!!

www.volksrod.co.uk

When the tarmac beckons... Adventure begins

The purest adrenaline drive on the road,

And the most fun you can have in the mud!

Handbuilt to spec, lightweight and immensely strong. Fast road, off road, expedition, the choice is yours

No IVA!

Single donor

Fast easy build

Basic kits just £ 795!!!

On the road base model £ 4995

0845 257 8818   07788 293198

www.Xbugs.co.uk